Kazantzakis

To my wife Cynthia, my sons
Christopher and Joshua,
and to
my teacher, Cecil L. Eubanks

Kazantzakis: The Politics of Salvation

JAMES F. LEA

WITH A FOREWORD BY
Helen Kazantzakis

The University of Alabama Press
University, Alabama

Library of Congress Cataloging in Publication Data

Lea, James F
  Kazantzakis : the politics of salvation.

  Bibliography: p.
  Includes index.
    1.   Kazantzakis, Nikos, 1883–1957—Political and
social views.
PA5610.K39Z775   889′.8′3209   78-8644
ISBN 0-8173-7002-1

Contents

We [are] being deprived of our most precious possession: our spiritual life. In the East, it is destroyed by the dealings and machinations of the ruling party. In the West, commercial interests tend to suffocate it. This is the real crisis. The split in the world is less terrible than the similarity of the disease plaguing its main areas.

Aleksandr Solzhenitsyn
(from his 1978 Harvard Commencement Address)

Foreword

Dear Mr. Lea,

You are quite right in saying that N.K. had an undeserved reputation for being apolitical. If, by the term politics we mean the closed field where today's politicians nearly all over the world fight among themselves by often using the meanest tricks to save their basest interests, then of course N.K. had abolutely nothing to do with politics.

On the other hand, if by the term politics we mean realizing the needs of the historic times we live in, engaging our responsibility in the march of our times and, thereby, giving our life a meaning and a value that transcend us, then N.K. was certainly a writer with political concerns.

Leafing through old faded pages, I came upon what he wrote in *The Symposium* in 1922, at the time he dreamed of learning some manual trade, or as some other Don Quixote, of going to the Soviet Union to proclaim . . . his "post-communist" credo. (*Spiritual Exercises*)

In a dream, he tells in the *Symposium,* his father sees him arriving at home dressed as a monk:

> How have you come home like this, without blood and strength? . . . Rise up! You seek God? There He is: Action, replete with mistakes, fumblings, persistence, agony. God is not the power that has found eternal equilibrium, but the power that is forever breaking every equilibrium, forever searching for a higher one. Whosoever struggles and makes progress by the same method in his own narrow sphere finds God and works with Him. Rise up and go out among human beings. (page 63)

Let us not mention the few cases when he took active part in the politics of his country. As much as he wished, he had no better weapon in hand than his pen to fight against injustice and to stand undaunted before final chaos.

From his talks with Pierre Sipriot of the French radio in 1955, I note:

> A genuine novelist can live only in his own time and by living this reality he acquires consciousness of his own responsibility and

assumes the duty of helping his fellowmen to envisage and solve, as far as possible, the crucial problems of his era. If he acquires consciousness of his mission, the novelist endeavors to compel the reality that is flowing formlessly, to take on the form he regards as most worthy of man.

In another interview with the French writer Pierre Descargues (1955), who asked him about his work, N.K. states:

> The books I write are at their worst disquieting and at their best terrifying because it is necessary to shout the warning to human beings that they are headed for catastrophe, that our world is on the brink of the great void that swallows it up.

Ten years earlier, again in a quixotic attempt, he had made an appeal through the B.B.C. (July 18, 1946) to all the intellectual world leaders to unite in a struggle to save imperiled mankind from the unworthy, cynical, over-ambitious profiteers:

> As in all creative periods, the poet is again becoming identified with the prophet. Let us have confidence in the spirit. At the most difficult hours, when the fate of the world is at stake, it is the spirit that assumes responsibility.

Yes, N.K., the "nihilist," believed in man up to his ultimate hour, man was his only hope of salvation; the man with spiritual values, who struggles endlessly to transcend his own self.

All this and much more can be gleaned from the life and works of N.K. But let me now express my warmest thanks for your essay, which you wrote with so much knowledge and affection.

Voula—Athens   HELEN KAZANTZAKIS
September 1977

Introduction

Nikos Kazantzakis is certainly one of the most intriguing and controversial figures of the twentieth century. His social and political ideas embrace some of the most unique and provocative concepts to be found in modern thought. These concepts and an exploration of Kazantzakis's general philosophy is the subject matter of this essay. In this exploration, the following approach is taken: (1) a brief examination of Kazantzakis in the context of his age and culture, with particular attention to the influence of the dominant ideas current in his lifetime, and of his basic existential vantage-point, the "Cretan glance"; (2) a general explication of the evolution of Kazantzakis' social and political thought, including an analysis of the interrelation of his desire for both social activism and literary accomplishment and his view of means and ends; (3) an exploration of Kazantzakis' approach to history, his diagnosis of the contemporary human predicament, and his theory of the relation of art to politics in history; (4) an inquiry into the empirical import of his prescription for improving the human condition, which includes his "new decalogue" and his "tragic optimism" and is based on classical Greek and Judaeo-Christian insights; (5) an evaluation of the validity and meaningfulness of his views for our time, with special emphasis on his concept of freedom and his view of the importance of hope and despair to political philosophy.

A most difficult part of the endeavor will be the attempt to place Kazantzakis in correct relation to the more important philosophies and systems that shaped his thought. These are the "decisive steps" of which he spoke—Christianity, Buddhism, Mohammedanism, Nietzsche, Bergson, Yorghos Zorba, and Marxism-Leninism. However such an undertaking is essential if one is to understand Kazantzakis' thought. Also, at the outset, the main issues and conflicts of Crete (Kazantzakis' birthplace) and Greece—which to a large extent gave rise to his "Cretan glance"—are discussed. This discussion inevitably tends to be rather superficial because of the complexity of that era and because our main concern is, not to write an essay on the history of his age, but to set forth a general explication of his political thought, to analyze and to evaluate his views, and to discuss the meaning of his beliefs for our age.

Kazantzakis was an abundantly prolific man of letters who lived by his pen. He was widely published and read during his lifetime and, although his ideas generated much opposition within his beloved Greece and from various parts of the political spectrum in Europe, he enjoyed rising fame during his later years. Writing most often in modern demotic Greek, but sometimes in French, Kazantzakis composed essays, newspaper and encyclopedia articles, scenarios and screen adaptations, verse, plays, an unfinished (only A to K) and unpublished French-Greek dictionary, and novels. In addition he translated various classics and carried on a rich correspondence with his first wife, his second wife, and his many friends.

Since the purpose of our inquiry is to examine Kazantzakis' political thought, and not his mysticism, pantheism, or other interests, our greatest attention is given to those writings which are oriented to an exposition of his philosophy. These are *The Fratricides*, the most political of all Kazantzakis' works; *The Odyssey: A Modern Sequel; The Saviors of God,* which gives perhaps the most artistically comprehensive picture of Kazantzakis; *Report to Greco*, in which he reflects on his intellectual and existential odyssey and that of the modern world; *Zorba The Greek* and other novels that collectively contain a comprehensive and systematic statement of his thought; "The Immortal Free Spirit of Man" and other essays that also contain statements of his political beliefs; and his letters, which are of immense importance. Fortunately for those who do not read Greek, most of Kazantzakis' major works have been translated into English. (His "Buddha" is currently being translated by Kimon Friar and Athena Dallas.) Kazantzakis, who was fluent in several languages, collaborated in the translation of *The Odyssey,* thereby enhancing the literal accuracy of the English edition. Also appearing in English in increasing volume are translations, interpretations, and summations of his articles and essays.

Some secondary sources have been examined, though there is a marked lack of analytical material on his thought. For biographical detail, the *Report To Greco,* an autobiographical account subtitled "A Fiction" and written one year prior to his death, is used with appropriate caution. Helen Kazantzakis' *Nikos Kazantzakis* and Pandelis Prevelakis' *Nikos Kazantzakis and his Odyssey* have been consulted, for these writers were closest to Kazantzakis and most familiar with his work. Some analyses of Kazantzakis' thought have been published in the form of critical essays, the best of which are Peter Bien's *Nikos Kazantzakis* and his "Kazantzakis and Politics," in *The Politics of Twentieth Century Novelists,* edited by George A. Panichas; Will Durant's "Nikos Kazantzakis" in his and Ariel Durant's *Interpretations of Life;* and W. B. Stanford's chapter on "The Re-Integrated Hero" in *The Ulysses Theme.* In addition, journal articles have been extensively utilized, particularly those found in the November 1971 issue of the *Journal of Modern Literature,* which is devoted entirely to Kazantzakis, as well as two unpublished dissertations: Andreas K. Poulakidas' "The Novels of Kazantzakis and Their Existential Sources," and Saralyn Poole Hadgopoulos' "Odysseus' Choice: A Comparison and Contrast of Works by Albert Camus and Nikos Kazantzakis." Although these and other secondary works on Kazantzakis have been consulted, chief reliance is placed on those writings of Kazantzakis indicated above.

In view of the general ascendancy of Kazantzakis' reputation in recent decades, it is surprising how little philosophical examination of his thought has been conducted. The major reasons for such an oversight seem to be twofold in nature: (1) his reputation as being an apolitical individual; and (2) the emphasis on Kazantzakis as a literary person, rather than as an imaginative social philosopher. The reputation of being apolitical has clung to Kazantzakis, even though it is not a completely accurate portrayal of his life, and has inhibited analysis of his thought from the standpoint of political philosophy. Actually Kazantzakis, as a Greek and a humanist, was very much concerned with the enduring issues of political philosophy; was involved, if only marginally, in the very bitter debates over various political ideologies which characterized his time; and was a member of the Greek Society of Social and Political Sciences. He briefly held cabinet-level offices twice in Greek governments (although the second such office was without portfolio and of no importance), and served in UNESCO's Department of Translation of the Classics. The interest in

Kazantzakis as a literary artist is legitimate, for he was first-rate in this category. He took great pride in his literary output and ranks among the most accomplished of modern writers, having been repeatedly proposed for the Nobel Prize. Kazantzakis left quite detailed accounts of his view of the role and duty of the artist in society and of the contribution that art can make to improving the human condition—valuable guides for the writer who is involved in sociopolitical themes. There is, however, another equally important aspect of Kazantzakis that has been obscured by the above concerns and remains relatively unexplored. This is the invaluable social and political criticism that he leveled at his age and the philosophical beliefs that he expounded as remedies for the excessive materialism, despiritualization, despair, and societal and governmental wrongs of his day. There is a tendency for the philosophies of those not in the mainstream of Anglo-American/European political thought to be neglected in political inquiry. This may reflect a bias on the part of some political theorists against those whose spiritual and intellectual origins are traceable to Africa, Asia, and the Orient as well as to the West. Whatever the reason, it seems that few have been willing to pay heed to this prophet of the soul. With the increased awareness of the timeless value of Eastern thought characteristic of our age, with the growing indications that the nations of East and West are moving toward more mutual understanding and cooperation, and with the rapidity of translation today, perhaps thinkers like Kazantzakis who have attempted a synthesis of Eastern and Western thought will receive their due share of attention.

The social and political thought of Kazantzakis is understandable and meaningful for the twentieth century more than that of many of the brighter stars in the philosophical galaxy. In an age of ideology, Kazantzakis explored many of the major ideologies. He foresaw with surprising clarity that the secularization and material fervor of life in the modern West threatened to extinguish the spark of exuberance and freedom that gives vitality and beauty to the human soul. He railed against injustice whether carried out by left or right, East or West, and in an age of despair sought rigorously for a higher synthesis of sociopolitical life, a "new decalogue" to provide meaning and purpose in place of the anxiety and absurdity of contemporary life. Drawing from many sources and harmonizing antinomies with a burning humanistic vision, Kazantzakis' politics represents an alternative to ideology and the basis for a politics of existential hope beyond absolutist claims, illusory secular faiths, and destructive nihilistic despair.

Kazantzakis

ABBREVIATIONS

Gr. Passion   *The Greek Passion.* Translated by Jonathan Griffin. New York: Simon & Schuster, Inc., 1953.

Zorba   *Zorba the Greek.* Translated by Carl Wildman with Introduction by Ian Scott-Kilvert. London: The Modern European Library, John Lehmann, 1953.

Freedom   *Freedom or Death.* Translated by Jonathan Griffin with Preface by A. Den Doolard. New York: Simon & Schuster, Inc., 1955.

Odyssey   *The Odyssey: A Modern Sequel.* Translated with Introduction, Synopsis, and Notes by Kimon Friar. New York: Simon & Schuster, Inc., 1958.

Last Tempt.   *The Last Temptation of Christ.* Translated with a Note on the Author and His Use of Language by P. A. Bien. New York: Simon & Schuster, Inc., 1960.

Saviors   *The Saviors of God: Spiritual Exercises.* Translated with Introduction by Kimon Friar. New York: Simon & Schuster, Inc., 1960.

St. Fran.   *Saint Francis.* Translated by P. A. Bien. New York: Simon & Schuster, Inc., 1962.

J-C   *Japan-China.* Translated by George C. Pappageotes with Epilogue by Helen Kazantzakis. New York: Simon & Schuster, Inc., 1963.

Spain   *Spain.* Translated by Amy Mims. New York: Simon & Schuster, Inc., 1963.

Frat.   *The Fratricides.* Translated by Athena Gianakas Dallas. New York: Simon & Schuster, Inc., 1964.

T.R.   *Toda Raba.* Translated by Amy Mims with Afterword by Helen Kazantzakis. New York: Simon & Schuster, Inc., 1964.

England   *England.* New York: Simon & Schuster, Inc., 1965.

Report   *Report to Greco.* Translated by P. A. Bien with Introduction by Helen Kazantzakis. New York: Simon & Schuster, Inc., 1965.

Travels   *Journeying Travels in Italy, Egypt, Sinai, Jerusalem, and Cyprus.* Translated by Themi and Theodora Vasils. New York: Little, Brown & Company, 1975.

As adults, we have forgotten most of our childhood, not only its contents but its flavor; as men of the world, we hardly know of the existence of the inner world: we barely remember our dreams, and make little sense of them when we do; as for our bodies, we retain just sufficient proprioceptive sensations to coordinate our movements and to ensure the minimal requirements for biosocial survival—to register fatigue, signals for food, sex, defecation, sleep; beyond that, little or nothing. Our capacity to think, except in the service of what we are dangerously deluded in supposing is our self-interest and in conformity with common sense, is pitifully limited: our capacity even to see, hear, touch, taste, and smell is so shrouded in veils of mystification that an intensive discipline of unlearning is necessary for *anyone* before one can begin to experience the world afresh, with innocence, truth, and love.

R. D. LAING

≡II≡II≡II≡II≡II≡II≡II≡II≡II ≡II≡II≡II≡II≡II≡II≡II

1

Nikos Kazantzakis

There are individuals, notes Walter Kaufmann in his introduction to *The Portable Nietzsche,* "who can write too well for their own good—as philosophers. Plato wrote so dramatically that we shall never know for sure what precisely he himself thought about any

number of questions. And Nietzsche furnishes a more recent and
no less striking example."[1] Kaufman's statement certainly applies
to Kazantzakis, whose works are characterized by an innovative,
experimentalist style and imaginative phraseology. Indeed, even
if his style were simpler, Kazantzakis' very prolificity inevitably
leads to contradictions and paradoxical puzzles. This makes difficult the logical reconstruction of his political vision. In order to
understand fully such an individual's politics, we must know the
life, character, interests, etc., of that person. We must know the
principles, personalities, and circumstances which influenced his
politics. This knowledge can illustrate his significance by making
clearer the strengths and weaknesses, insights and oversights, of
his thought. The first two sections of this chapter, therefore,
fulfill the necessary prerequisite to an analysis of Kazantzakis'
politics by pinpointing the people, philosophers, and events in-
strumental in the construction of his basic outlook. Influences
examined are ancestral—for Kazantzakis attached much importance to his parental lineage; historical, which includes scientific,
commercial, and religious developments of his age; sociopolitical;
environmental; educational; and dominant intellectual
stimulants—decisive steps. The third section describes, in terms
of these influences, Kazantzakis' essential and over-riding
viewpoint—the Cretan glance.

Historical-Political Environment

Nikos Kazantzakis was born at Heraklion, Crete, on Friday,
February 18, 1883.[2] His mother, Maria, of the Christodoulaki
family, "was a saintly woman . . . she had the endurance, patience,
and sweetness of the earth itself" (Report, 34). The Kazantzakis
family relations were in keeping with the traditional Latin, and
also Oriental, view of the male-dominated, almost master-slave
relationship.

Curiously, Kazantzakis, a rebellious figure who questioned
conventionality, was never to break totally with this "sexist" orientation.[3] In fact many of his female characters are submissive,
secondary, almost dehumanized persons whose primary function
is procreation. However, he was drawn to the opposite in his

sexual relations. Dynamic, vital women who willingly embraced life exerted a magnetic appeal on Kazantzakis—as did, in a similar manner, vitalistic political movements—who often agonized over what he perceived as a lack of dynamism in his own life. This appeal was evident in his relations with Galetea, his very strong-willed first wife; Eleni, his beloved second wife, an active socialist and literary figure in her own right, who overcame periodic physical difficulties to pursue her career; and Itka, Rahel, Dina, most especially Elsa—with whom he fell in love—all whom he met in Berlin between the two world wars.

Kazantzakis' mother occupies in his life and writings a place similar to that of Camus's mother in his life, a much revered, much loved, idealized figure who provided in abundance the warmth that was lacking on the paternal side. On being told of the death of his mother, Kazantzakis wrote: "The loss of my mother was an utterly emotional embitterment: the complaint of a child left alone in the dark when the well-loved hand's out of reach."[4] And, "I hold myself in firmly so as not to cry out. Yet I know that only if I shouted like a wild animal would I find relief."[5] From his maternal ancestors, peasants close to the soil, the seasons, and the rhythm of life, Kazantzakis inherited a sensuous and at times pantheistic love of nature with a profound sense of the relationality of man, plants, and animals—the unity of the organic with the inorganic. He also gained a unique, firsthand comprehension of the flavor of peasant life, which was later explored thoroughly and beneficially in such works as *The Greek Passion* and *The Fratricides*.

Kazantzakis' father, Mihalis, was by Nikos' own account a rather forbidding figure. He was well thought of by his neighbors in Heraklion: "People respected him. . . . Some, the most inferior, rose and bowed when he passed." As a father he was unloving: "I cannot recall hearing a tender word from him—except once. . . . But he felt angry with himself immediately; this display of emotion was a self-betrayal." Mihalis was exceedingly somber and "never laughed . . . his heart never lightened." The elder Kazantzakis was so intolerant of priests that he would cross himself whenever he met one on the street to exorcise the unfortunate encounter. "He never attended Divine Liturgy—to avoid

seeing priests. But every Sunday when the service was over and
everyone had left, he entered the church and lighted a candle
before the wonder-working icon of Saint Minas" (*Report,* 31–33).[6]

The father's influence on Kazantzakis is one source of the
larger-than-life characters who people his works. This is especially
so in *Freedom or Death,* whose central character, Captain Michalis,
is based on a fictionalized portrait of Mihalis Kazantzakis. The
father-son relationship is illustrated well by three bold and undoubtedly dramatized tales that depict the ethic of the *pallikária,*[7]
which the father sought to impart to his son. (1) Told that his son
had caused some difficulty in religion class, the father said that he
cared only if he lied or got a beating: "As for all the rest, he's a
man, let him do as he pleases" (*Report,* 117). (2) During an uprising on Crete against the Turkish rulers that had bloody repercus-
sions, Nikos' father made him promise not to be afraid and told
the family that "if the Turks break down the door and enter I plan
to slaughter you myself, before you fall into their hands" (*Report,*
87). (3) The next day the father forced the child of seven years to
touch several Greek Christians hanged in a tree, reasoning that
"was to help you get used to it" (*Report,* 90).

Nikos was never to become a true *pallikária.* His painful awareness of this occasioned continual soul-searching throughout his
life. Kazantzakis' compassion and sensitivity is traceable, at least in
some part, to the lack of these qualities in his father. The father's
influence is highlighted by the fact that the year of Mihalis' death,
1933, coincides with the beginning of the period that the adult
Nikos would label his period of freedom. Kazantzakis' closest
friend points out the impact of the death of the elder Kazantzakis:
"The man-beast whom Kazantzakis had feared all his life and had
regarded as deathless had collapsed. He had symbolized, while he
lived, the roots, the original beast; the mud of which the son was
destined to make spirit."[8] And Kazantzakis wrote of his feelings to
his wife in such disturbing terms that he asked her to destroy the
letter: "It was not love that united me with Father, but a thick deep
root, which has been cut now. . . . I feel . . . the unholy, horrifying
feeling that I have been liberated."[9]

From imaginative reflection on the lives of his paternal ancestors, Kazantzakis—envisioning them as piratical, warlike figures

who boldly roamed land and sea beyond good and evil—derived a keen love of adventure and travel. He gained a sense of lifelong struggle, for their lives had been touched deeply by the numerous uprisings on Crete. He also acquired from his ancestors insight into the primitive and savage in man. Moreover, Kazantzakis obtained from them empathy, love, and a measure of understanding for non-Western cultures, for he thought his line traceable ultimately to the Arabs who had once conquered Crete; if true, this would have made him truly the child of East and West that he fancied himself to be. He never forgot his diverse ancestry and paid homage as he looked back on his life near the end: "Both of my parents circulate in my blood, the one fierce, hard, and morose, the other tender, kind, and saintly. I have carried them all my days; neither has died. As long as I live, they too will live inside me" (*Report,* 49).

His ancestors lived not only "inside" Kazantzakis but came to life in various characterizations in his works. In *The Greek Passion, The Fratricides, Zorba the Greek,* and other novels and plays, Kazantzakis focused on his ancestors and examined and reexamined their personalities and seemed to believe that through constant refinement of these personages he could gain not only greater self-understanding but perhaps even greater insight into the universals of the human psyche. Just as these dramatic figures were visibly influenced in Kazantzakis' work by the times in which they lived, so was Kazantzakis, a complex man whose concerns at various periods of his life were those of a Greek nationalist, religious ascetic, philosopher, left-wing sympathizer, literatist, and periodic politician, influenced by the more important issues and conflicts that composed the swirling panorama of the years of his life. Many events of the sociopolitical and intellectual milieu of the era, both in the immediate environment of Crete and Greece and in the cultural developments of the broader world scene that would eventually become as familiar to this world citizen as his native Crete, are of great importance to Kazantzakis' thought.

An understanding of the years of Kazantzakis' childhood and adolescent period is crucial for the political analyst; for although Kazantzakis was relatively uninterested in politics until he began

his graduate studies in Paris in October 1907, his writings prior to
this "exhibit themes and concerns which were to be subsequently
repeated in a political context."[10] These themes grew primarily
from the confrontation of a sensitive, intelligent child with the
harsh reality of life on Crete. The impact of his childhood existence was such that he would later say of Crete: "This soil I was
everlastingly; this soil I shall be everlastingly. O fierce clay of
Crete, the moment you twirled and fashioned me into a man of
struggle has slipped by as though in a single flash." (*Report,* 18)

Heraklion, which was Méghalo Kástro (so-called because of the
Venetian walls and battlements) during Kazantzakis' childhood
and in his fiction, is a small port town nestled between the sea and
the mountains and is the chief city of Crete. In his youth it was, if
there is truth in his account, organized along the lines of a garri-
son by the Turkish rulers who controlled passage into and out of
the city during times of rebellion. Both Greek Christians and
Turkish Moslems lived in well-defined and generally fortified
towns. The protector of the city was the wonder-working Saint
Minas, whose icon Kazantzakis' father worshipped. Kazantzakis
draws upon and magnifies the singular traits of the people of
Heraklion for his literary characters. Madame Penelope, fat,
greasy, and continually laughing, and her husband Dimitros,
meek and hypochondriacal, who escaped periodically to the
mountains, reappear in Kazantzakis' novels as does Manousos, a
merchant who beat his sister regularly at noon, and Andreas the
Feeler, who always stepped on the same stones when he walked
down Méghalo Kástro's streets. The inhabitants were poor yet so
inordinately proud that they went to extraordinary lengths to
prevent anyone from discovering their poverty. (*Report,* 60–62,
80–81)

As a child in earthy, sensuous, and vital Crete, Kazantzakis first
developed his concern for the knowledge of the senses and his
abiding adherence to the strictures of the basic elements. He
recounts how, in his childhood, the senses grew strong, captured
their respective spheres of existence, and began to establish order
from chaos. And how the first contact with earth, sea, woman, and
the starry sky filled him with fright and joy:

Every one of my emotions, moreover, and every one of my ideas, even the most abstract, is made up of these four primary ingredients. Within me, even the most metaphysical problem takes on a warm physical body which smells of sea, soil, and human sweat. The Word, in order to touch me, must become warm flesh. Only then do I understand—when I can smell, see, and touch.[11] (*Report*, 43)

Kazantzakis' youth fell in the period when the Greek Christians were finally able to drive the hated Turks from their land. Time and time again, in 1821, 1866, 1878, and 1889, they had attempted this feat. "In this last rebellion Kazantzakis' father fought, and Nikos himself, then a boy of six, began to learn the facts of life." (The Turks departed in 1898, and in 1908 Crete joined the Kingdom of Greece.) Durant describes how this struggle structured the Cretan personality: "pious and somber in the women, violent and morose in the men; all lusty and passionate, all waiting for a chance to strike out for freedom, and readying themselves to kill any available Turk."[12] This political struggle for freedom on the part of his oppressed people so impressed the young Nikos that throughout his life he championed the cause of the oppressed and the downtrodden. It instilled a sense of rebelliousness in his make-up, a rebelliousness that was to take religious and metaphysical as well as political forms. The struggle also conveyed a stark picture of human suffering, degradation, and a sense of duty to humanity—all ideas that Kazantzakis later translated into more cosmopolitan and philosophical political terms. And perhaps most important of all, Kazantzakis gained a burning thirst for liberty: "Freedom was my first great desire." (*Report*, 71)

In addition to Kazantzakis' first contacts with nature and politics, certain religious concepts and ideas current during his childhood influenced him profoundly. He had a mystic sense of his religious mission in life—being born on "the day of souls" (*Report*, 74)—which expressed itself in periodic stays in monasteries, and in profound explorations of Christianity, Buddhism, and messianic Communism. Although religious questions would later take on for him a multifold complexity, the religious teachings of his youth were simple; the two central tenets were that among various mysteries and miracles God "did His share of killing," and as for deciphering God's action's and motives, "We're not supposed to understand. It's a sin!" (*Report*, 55) But for a child with a restless spirit, this admonition only led to further questioning of religious dogma. Another important religious aspect of this period was the intense intolerance all-too-present among the Greek Orthodox, the Catholics, the Jews, and the Turkish Moslems on Crete. It is logical to assume that the bitterness of this bigotry was one impetus to Kazantzakis' consistent and overriding concern for unity among peoples. There also occurred during this time his introduction to the innumerable legends of the saints. This was important first because, just as the political struggle for civil freedom from Turkish rule imparted to Kazantzakis the ideal of a hero, the religious struggle of the saints' legends for virtue and Christian freedom from the baser side of man's nature imparted a complementary ideal, leading to the second great wish, "the desire for sainthood." (*Report*, 71) The unity of vision and purpose of the hero and saint becomes a lifelong quest for Kazantzakis. The saints' legends had another significant influence in view of Kazantzakis' later direction—the introduction to creative writing.

These inspiring saints' tales were augmented with stories of adventure passed on by his ancestors and with the stories of travel and exploration in his schoolbooks. Kazantzakis also attended theatrical presentations, one of which was Schiller's play "The Brigands," by various touring troupes. These awakened in Kazantzakis a boundless imagination. "I read the saints' legends, listened to fairy tales, overheard conversations, and inside me all this was transformed—deformed—into dazzling lies."[13] (*Report*, 72) Later he would learn that this secret elaboration is the essence of literary creation. For Kazantzakis such stories had the delightful quality of transcending the mundane limits of logic, ethics, and rationality. Contrasting this tendency to "creation" and the immediate necessities for struggle on Crete in which his family and friends were involved, Kazantzakis early became aware of the conflict between action and writing, between physical participation in the quest for freedom and theoretical, literary involvement. Once, while at school at nearby Naxos in 1897, during one of the reprisals on Crete, he asked Peré Leliévre, a monk and a friend of his family, about the value of a translation of a French dictionary into Greek on which Kazantzakis was working and was given this warning of the pitfalls along the road of art:

> Take it from me that if you follow this road, you'll never amount to anything—never! You'll become some miserable round-shouldered little teacher with spectacles. If you're really a Cretan, burn this damnable dictionary and bring me the ashes. Then I'll give you my blessing. Think it over and act. Away with you!
>   I went away completely confused. Who was right, what was I to do? Which of the two roads was correct?[14] (*Report,* 97)

Fortunately Kazantzakis did not heed the monk's advice, but he never forgot it. Kazantzakis's continuing preoccupation with the two roads of art and action was a major factor in his development.

Another important event during Kazantzakis' childhood and adolescent period was his confrontation with birth, death, and the mortality of man. During Nikos' early years children were not isolated from these realities and the terror and enigmas surrounding them: "These two, birth and death, were the very first mysteries to throw my childish soul into a ferment."[15] (*Report,* 109) The initial chapters of *Report* abound with instances of youthful confrontation with life and death. These "first mysteries" would lead, with supplementary elaboration by Nietzsche, to a lifelong inquiry into the abyss of mortality, the twin voids of prelife and afterlife that were key concerns of Kazantzakis' mature thought. The question of death and man's attitude toward death is explored repeatedly throughout his work.

It was on the basis of these various influences and events discussed above—political, religious, moral—that Kazantzakis was to build his metaphysics. At this early stage of his development it was basically a metaphysics of rebellion: first, a political rebellion against Turkish rule; second, a religious rebellion against Christian quietism and church hypocrisy—"It was not that I had ceased to believe. I believed, but the saints struck me now as [being] much too submissive. They continually bowed their heads before God and said yes. The blood of Crete had awakened inside me" (*Re-*

port, 78); and third, a far-ranging metaphysical rebellion that received expression when Kazantzakis was told that he would understand as he grew older why people died—"I never did find out. I grew up, became old, and never did find out." (*Report,* 51) This was Kazantzakis' basic outlook when he was introduced, during his adolescent education, to the dynamic intellectual and cultural environment beyond Crete. Truly startling developments were occurring in the world beyond Crete during this period, developments with important implications for the future shape of Kazantzakis' thought.

At the French school of the Holy Cross at Naxos, directed by Franciscan monks, where Kazantzakis studied from his fourteenth to his sixteenth year, "this refugee boy from Crete was suddenly introduced to another world. He learned French and Italian and assimilated the rudiments of Western culture."[16] Early in 1899 he resumed his studies at the gymnasium of Heraklion. Kazantzakis explains the multifold importance of his studies at Naxos: "This was the first and perhaps the most decisive leap in my intellectual life. A magic portal opened inside my head and conducted me into an astonishing world." It was a world of expanded horizons. Kazantzakis learned that Crete and Greece were not the only lands struggling and suffering for freedom: "The world was larger than Greece, the world's suffering was larger than our suffering, and the yearning for freedom was not the exclusive prerogative of the Cretan, it was the eternal struggle of all mankind." Along with this realization came a fierce desire to experience as much of the world and its people as possible. New emotions were aroused: "Only two or three primitive passions had governed me until this time; fear, the struggle to conquer fear, and the yearning for freedom. But now two new passions were kindled inside me: beauty and the thirst for learning." (*Report,* 96)

Kazantzakis' "passion for learning," kindled by the Franciscan monks at Naxos, confronted a world culture experiencing some of the most dramatic and startling intellectual innovations of any similar epoch in the history of man. The time from the mid-nineteenth century until World War I, the outbreak of the latter being approximately the time Kazantzakis completed his formal

education and began systematizing and expressing his basic
themes in a coherent political philosophy, was a vital one.
Kazantzakis recognized the importance of birth in such times:

> The Chinese have an amazing curse: "May you be born in an
> interesting epoch." . . . We are living at a cosmic rate—not
> years—weeks, days, hours. Truly every moment nowadays has the
> value of a century. . . . May you be born in an interesting epoch.[17]

The era under discussion has been characterized as the "Age of
Industrialism"; for, with a surge of technological and scientific
development, industrialization spread from Western Europe, the
northern United States, and Japan to the Balkan states, Italy,
Spain, Russia, Canada, and the remainder of the United States.
Continuing developments are, in our day, carrying industrialization into the former colonies of the world empires—the so-called
Third World. Mark Twain, talking primarily of the American
social scene, termed the period a "Gilded Age," for acquisitive
materialism was, in his view, the dominant ethos of the time. The
bourgeoisie and the *nouveaux riche* were seizing political and social
control and manifesting their often boorish taste in atrocious
monuments and architecture. It has also been termed the "Age of
Nationalism and Power Politics," for Italy and Germany became
unified and national boundaries led to national chauvinism. As
the imperialists' empires became increasingly vulnerable to the
Marxist-Leninist critique and the rising consciousness of the col-
onized, power politics and an amoral "balance of power" experienced its greatest failure in a war of nationalism—World War I.
Yet none of these terms expresses the essence of those years from
1850 to World War I as well as does "The Age of Science." The
more important scientific advances of the age were made in the
fields of astronomy, biology, physics, chemistry, psychology, and
economics. These advances, combined with the important political, religious, and artistic developments, would shape, either directly or indirectly, both the form and substance of Kazantzakis'
and other thinkers' political philosophy in the twentieth century.
    Early in his studies in the gymnasium at Heraklion, Kazantzakis
had come to realize the importance of scientific studies for ethics
and morals: "My soul has been thrown into a ferment by two

terrible secrets our physics teacher had revealed to us. . . . I believe the wounds he inflicted have festered ever since." The first "terrible secret" was heliocentric astronomy—that the earth is only one of the many planets revolving around the sun. This revelation had immediate, personal, and religious implications for Kazantzakis and provided further fuel for his questioning mind: "What was this fairy tale our teachers had so shamelessly prated about until now—that God had supposedly created the sun and moon as ornaments for the earth, and hung the starry heavens above as a chandelier to give light!" The second "great secret" was the evolutionary hypothesis put forth by Charles Darwin in 1859. With the application of the principle of natural selection to human beings, it was asserted that man's ancestors were monkeylike animals. This represented a marked shortening of the distance between man, plants, and animals or, as Kazantzakis would say in more dramatic fashion:

> Man is not God's darling, his privileged creature. The Lord God did not breathe into his nostrils the breath of life, did not give him an immortal soul. Like all other creatures, he is a rung in the infinite chain of animals, a grandson or great-grandson of the ape. If you scratch our hide a little, if you scratch our soul a little, beneath it you will find our grandmother the monkey! (*Report*, 114–15)

Because of his intense concern with the divine element in man, Kazantzakis defied the belittling implications of evolutionary biology by following Nietzsche and consistently emphasizing the boundless potentiality in man. In a like manner, Kazantzakis followed Bergson and attributed to man, and particularly to the artist, the elevating capability to grasp the meaning of the creative life-pulse in the world.

Great strides were being made during this period in the fields of chemistry and physics.[18] In chemistry the foundation for the technological society of the twentieth century was being laid with the increasing sophistication in understanding the atom—evinced by Dmitri Mendeleyev's drawing up a periodic table of chemical elements based on their atomic weights. In physics the rational stability of the mechanistic worldview was being under-

mined by, first, research into thermodynamics, resulting in its
First and Second Laws, which ran counter to the presuppositions
of Newtonian physics and accurately depicted the relation between heat and motive power that provided the technological
base for subsequent industrial inventions; and second, research
into electrical phenomena, making possible certain inventions
that revolutionized man's life and leading to the Curies' work in
radioactivity and the discovery of the structure and potentiality of
the atom—to whose consequences Kazantzakis, with many others,
was to address himself. The final blow to the Newtonian universe
came with Einstein, who in 1905 and 1915 advanced his theory of
relativity, which reoriented man's attitude to the structure and
mechanics of the universe and—with its relativistic implications
being carried into realms other than science—further eroded the
possibility of believing in the "truth" of philosophical, moral, and
even aesthetic concepts.

Still another area of science in which developments were occurring that would be important for the development of twentieth-
century thought was psychology. In 1900 Ivan Pavlov demonstrated with dogs the influence of physical stimuli on involuntary
processes. When adopted in the United States and other countries as the basis for a social psychology, Pavlov's experiments
gave rise to a school of "behaviorism" that reduced man to a
machine responding to stimuli. Sigmund Freud, on the other
hand, illuminated the unconscious aspects of man's psychological
make-up and revealed the intricacies of the human mind—
intricacies that Kazantzakis, like his spiritual predecessors Dostoevsky and Nietzsche, would explore in brilliant fashion.

Viewing these discoveries in their cumulative impact, one can
easily see why they were

> to prove shattering to man's self-esteem and confidence. The evo-
> lutionary theory seemed to have divested man of his traditional
> heritage of having been created by a special act of divine grace.
> Freud's plumbing of man's unconscious mental processes seemed
> to shatter the cherished belief in man's power of reason. The busy
> dismantling of Newton's clockwork universe by Einstein and
> others was to be of great consequence for man's view of the uni-
> verse and his role in the scheme of things. The replacement of

absolute laws by theories of relativity would soon be transferred
out of the sphere of science to the field of morality, with the result
that absolute values and standards would be threatened. How the
mighty Homo sapiens had fallen![19]

These are but a few of the truly important developments that set
the stage on which Kazantzakis carried out the struggle of life.
Considering the brilliance of many of these advances it is little
wonder that the decline of religious faith in an increasingly secularized world was replaced by a proportionate rise in dogmatic
faith in science. Kazantzakis, throughout his life, was scathingly
critical of this new god of the West. He protested the extent to
which he and his contemporaries were influenced by the scientific
ethos. Kazantzakis focused particularly on the devitalization, dehumanization, and destruction of necessary myth, *miranda,* and
symbol of the Western world brought about through scientism.
This critique of scientism is a key element in Kazantzakis' theory
of the transitional age.

These family, sociopolitical, and cultural influences composed
a framework for the development of the basics of Kazantzakis'
philosophy—those decisive steps, Christ, Nietzsche, Buddha,
Bergson, Lenin, and Odysseus—[20] these basics later providing
the metaphysical foundation for his politics. Kazantzakis' Cretan
glance, his ultimate philosophical perspective, is a synthesis of,
first, the influences of his family, his childhood experiences, and
the scientific and political developments of his age, and, second,
the religious and philosophic lessons of the mentors to whom he
paid allegiance. The result was a rich, complex, and harmonious
Weltanschauung all his own.

Decisive Steps: Twentieth-Century Masks

Following the completion of his studies at Naxos and the gymnasium at Heraklion, Kazantzakis left for the University of
Athens, where he studied from 1902 until 1906, taking a
degree with high honors in law. In Athens he wrote articles, plays,
and worked at his first of many stints as a "special features,"
primarily travel, newspaper writer. His father agreed to send him

to Paris for further academic study in 1907. While there he audited courses at the Sorbonne in the school of law, attended Henri Bergson's lectures at the Collège de France, became enthralled with Friedrich Nietzsche's philosophy, and awoke to the dynamic currents then swirling through Europe. Bergson and Nietzsche were to become, at least in Kimon Friar's assessment, the dominant intellectual stimulants for Kazantzakis. "Though scholars may later trace in his thought pervading influences . . . of diverse and contrary strains . . . they will discover, I believe, that the earliest influences, i.e., Bergson and Nietzsche, were the deepest."[21] This is not to say that Kazantzakis was unacquainted with other philosophers. Indeed, he was familiar with most of Occidental and Oriental philosophy. He translated and commented on such varied thinkers as William James and José Ortega y Gasset, Bacon and Dostoevsky, Plato and Machiavelli, drawing intellectual sustenance from all. Because of Kazantzakis' admission that he was deeply influenced by those "decisive steps," critics have viewed him basically in terms of "these thinkers, in the shadow of each predecessor, not as a writer with a shadow of his own. It is as if these critics have tasted a unique dish and, unable to identify it for what it is, they compare it to the individual ingredients it contains."[22] Nevertheless, a skeletal sketch of the "individual ingredients" of Kazantzakis' thought is a necessary prerequisite to an understanding of his politics. Of his philosophic and spiritual mentors, the major contributors, to what was, as Minas Savvas stated, essentially an original vision, were Nietzsche and Bergson.

Much has been written about Kazantzakis's reverence for Nietzsche. Kazantzakis' philosophy was obviously shaped by Nietzsche's for it concerns itself with many of the fanciful, brilliant, and brutally penetrating intuitions and insights of Nietzsche. One observer, who is specifically interested in the manifestation of Kazantzakis' Nietzscheanism in *Zorba the Greek,* says: "A great teacher of Kazantzakis, before he met Zorba, was Nietzsche. . . . This philosopher-poet assisted Kazantzakis in breaking away from the barriers of his tradititional and cultural past."[23] As noted above, Kazantzakis became more deeply interested in Nietzsche's philosophy during his Paris studies.[24] It was an extremely important event for the questioning, youthful Nikos, who saw in Nietzsche's rich metaphysical critique of the despiritualization of contemporary man and his celebration of the giant in man a new alternative to the decadence and bourgeois materialism then so widespread in Europe, and to the blandness and ineffectual hypocritical forms that institutionalized Christianity was taking. "It was solid, leonine nourishment that Nietzsche fed me . . . now I found myself too constricted both by contemporary man in the state to which he had reduced himself, and by Christ in the state to which He had been reduced by man." (Report, 331–32)

Kazantzakis was so moved by the tragedy of Nietzsche that he undertook a pilgrimage to the new Golgotha, as he termed it, to the German village of Nietzsche's birth and to places in Switzerland and France where Nietzsche had lived. Later in his life he translated Nietzsche's Zarathustra and Birth of Tragedy and composed a dissertation and an encyclopedia article on Nietzsche. Kazantzakis not only incorporated many of Nietzsche's themes into his work but also had, throughout his life, a sense of affinity with Nietzsche's dramatic odyssey. During one period he kept a mask of Nietzsche above the door to his study, and he always sought mountain or seashore solitude, as Nietzsche had, for his creative periods. Writing from Zurich in 1917, Kazantzakis acknowledged this identification: "I work alone, wandering through the mountains, and sometimes Nietzsche's face appears before me, disturbing as a painful premonition."[25] It was through Nietzsche's famous proclamation "God is dead!"[26] that Kazantzakis first saw clearly the abyss, the void of nothingness, that he had barely sensed in his adolescence, and first realized the implications therein; for Nietzsche's vivid philosophy portrays the ultimate capacity for man and the potentiality of the world for despair.

Nietzsche, who saw his era as the beginning of a new world—a world without God—sought to describe the manner in which Christianity had enslaved man, had dehumanized and devitalized man, and had ultimately contributed to its own demise. He also sought to prescribe for future man—for "freed man," the Übermensch. Nietzsche gives a concise account of the manner in which Christian ethics dominated man:

1. It granted an absolute value, as opposed to his smallness and accidental occurrence in the flux of becoming and passing away.
2. It served the advocates of God insofar as it conceded to the world, in spite of suffering and evil, the character of perfection—including "freedom"; evil appeared full of meaning.
3. It posited that man had a knowledge of absolute values and thus adequate knowledge precisely regarding what is most important.
4. It prevented man from despising himself as man, from taking sides against life; from despairing of knowledge: it was a means of preservation.

    In sum: morality was the great antidote against practical and theoretical nihilism.[27]

Christianity made man less than he would be, it inculcated into his being a philosophy of servitude, and it acclaimed absolute parameters to his questioning, philosophizing, actions, and expectations. However, in the modern age, with the startling developments in the physical sciences, the increasing stress on man's intellectual capabilities, and such incisive critiques of Christianity as were issued by Feuerbach and others, man became less and less attuned to the dogmatic preachings of Christianity, less receptive to the idea of a governing God, and more aware of his lonely existence in the universe.

    Nietzsche believed that Christian ethics, which interpreted nature, history, and individual experience in terms of God's care and moral order, was now of the past. He concluded from this that "God is dead!" But where is man in a godless world; where are his values, his guides, his aspirations and expectations? Man is alone, according to Nietzsche, and must create from his loneliness, and the accompanying despair and alienation, a new fresh, creative, and more wonderfully human attitude toward life and to the world. He must "revalue all values" in free, forceful, human terms. However, Nietzsche was not so naïve as to think that the revaluation, the passage from subservient dogma-hope of salvation to creative aspirations and realizations, would come easily. The world of man would first pass through an epoch of extreme despair—an era of tortured nihilism: "I see the flood-tide of nihilism rising."[28] In that transitory epoch of despair man—lonely, hopeless, and afraid—casts about seeking something to

which he can attach his hopes, seeking values, seeking to fill his
existence with meaning.

Kazantzakis saw his age as the "transitory epoch of despair,"
and he threw his life into the struggle to aid suffering humanity.
Bien, who translated Kazantzakis' *The Last Temptation of Christ,
Saint Francis,* and *Report,* goes so far as to say that Kazantzakis
"echoes Nietzsche's cry to our times." This echo is perhaps
nowhere more evident than in Kazantzakis' best-known work (at
least in the United States), *Zorba the Greek.* Bien explored in detail
the relationship of *Zorba* and Nietzsche's *The Birth of Tragedy* and
reached the conclusion that "Kazantzakis consciously or uncon-
sciously modeled *Zorba the Greek* on Nietzsche's great work."[29]
Poulakidas, who explored the relationship of *Zorba* and
Nietzsche's *Thus Spake Zarathustra,* drew a somewhat different
conclusion. While conceding the accuracy of Bien's insights into
the influence of Nietzsche's terminology on Kazantzakis' literary
characters, Poulakidas does not accept "that it was *The Birth of
Tragedy* that was the 'model' for *Zorba the Greek.*" He agrees that
theoretically this work may have regulated Kazantzakis' thought
"but in practice and technique, the actual model for the writing of
Zorba the Greek has been Nietzsche's *Thus Spake Zarathustra,* a work
that clearly illustrates and communicates Nietzsche's theory con-
cretely and metaphorically as well."[30] Even in their disagreement,
however, these assessments reflect the wide recognition and con-
sensus that *Zorba,* and by implication Kazantzakis' other works,
are patterned after and centered around many of the primary
beliefs that compose the vivid and compelling philosophy of
Nietzsche (without forgetting the actual, living Zorba as a source).

These and other commentators on comparative literature are
fond of compiling lists of the specifics of Kazantzakis' debts to
Nietzsche. Both Bien and Poulakidas do so in extensive fashion in
places other than the above-cited articles. Friar, however, has best
described the contributions of Nietzsche—in addition to the previously discussed elaboration of the abyss of nothingness and the
accompanying transitory era—to Kazantzakis' *Weltanschauung*:

> Nietzsche confirmed him in his predilection for the Dionysian as
> opposed to the Apollonian vision of life: for Dionysus, the god of

wine and revelry, of ascending life, of joy in action, of ecstatic
motion and inspiration, of instinct and adventure and dauntless
suffering, the god of song and music and dance; as opposed to
Apollo, the god of peace, of leisure and repose, of aesthetic emotion and intellectual contemplation, of logical order and philosophical calm, the god of painting and sculpture and epic poetry
. . . however . . . it was not at all a rejection, but rather an assimila-
tion of the Apollonian vision of life.

From Nietzsche, Kazantzakis also took the exaltation of tragedy as
the joy of life, a certain "tragic optimism" of the strong man who
delights to discover that strife is the pervading law of life. . . . But in
contrast to Nietzsche, Kazantzakis had an intense love for the common man and a belief in socialistic orders which try to alleviate
poverty and lift oppression. . . . It was Kazantzakis' vain dream,
perhaps as it was that of Odysseus and Moses, to make all individuals
into superior beings, to lead them toward the Promised Land and to
test them to the breaking point.[31]

Nietzsche possessed a tremendous capacity to penetrate the
comforting and hypocritical facade of modern life through
evocative epigrams, in defending the higher qualities of man
against a materialistic, corporate political ethos. He sought, basically, to provoke his fellowmen into realizing the true potential of
their existence. Kazantzakis vied against injustice and oppression
sanctioned or perpetrated by the sociopolitical sphere, which
inhibits such realization. But whereas Nietzsche, beginning with
these goals, was led to the "overman" and a lengthy societal
critique that contained little substantive prescriptive content,
Kazantzakis—though never losing sight of the giant potential of
certain superior individuals—was led to, as Friar told us, "an
intense love for the common man and a belief in socialistic orders." He was to take one of the most compelling positions of any
modern thinker. Unlike Nietzsche, Kazantzakis sought some
positive means to better the lot of man. In this quest for an
affirmative philosophy, Nietzsche's teachings combined to give
Kazantzakis' thought undeniable figurative and symbolic brilliance, jarring insights, and a critical faculty that makes possible a
breaking away from the barriers of the past. These facets were
well supplemented by the teachings of the other of those "earliest,
deepest influences"—Henri Bergson.

Bergson's philosophy spelled out a positive, affectionate, and affirmative worldview. Where Nietzsche had stripped meaning from man's history by teaching eternal recurrence and had revealed the abyss with its nihilistic implications (which would be explored thoroughly by Kazantzakis in Buddhism), Bergson taught a creative evolution that provided existential potentiality to history. He showed to Kazantzakis what lies in the void— the Invisible Cry or the life force:

> Deeply imprinted in Kazantzakis' memory were Bergson's lectures that he had attended in Paris in 1907–1908 as well as his works *Creative Evolution, Time and Free Will, Matter and Memory*. In January, 1913, Kazantzakis summarized for the members of the Educational Society the philosophy of Bergson who, in contrast to Nietzsche, was responsible for animating and enriching him with a positive point of view; also, in the January 22, 1913, *Bulletin of the Educational Society* appeared his lengthy article on Henri Bergson.[32]

Further, Kazantzakis translated Bergson's *On Laughter*.

By his philosophy Bergson sought to provide an alternative to the twin culs-de-sac of determinism in which intellectualist philosophies, both mechanistic materialism and absolutist idealism, had found themselves. The proponents of the former of these, mechanistic materialism, seized on things as the ground of philosophizing and replaced the God-ordered universe in the sixteenth and seventeenth centuries with a self-regulating, geometrically predictable system. Thus the dominant strain of English philosophy of the modern period leads from Locke through Hume to an ever-increasing reliance on the ontological and epistemological priority of materiality. Supported by Marx's dialectical materialism of the dominance of the industrial-economic substructure and Darwin's dramatic demonstration of the manner in which life forms are channeled by exterior influences (spread by Spencer, an early mentor of Bergson, as a philosophy of industrialism in which the inertia of things became the essence of life), materialism became firmly entrenched as a truly deterministic view. The idealists' reaction to such a metaphysics received its most profound formulation in the complex Hegelian system, which saw reality corresponding to a unifying Spirit or Idea that operated in history, nature, the mind, or some combination of these, thereby achieving a systemic synthesis of epistemology, ontology, and logic. The implications of Hegelianism compose a doctrine according to which, as one scholar notes, "all history, both what we call past and what we call future, may be considered as a single dramatic whole, not unfinished and in the making, but completely present or 'given' to the cosmic mind."[33] In both worldviews, life is other-ordained, and the choices of men have little effect on the ultimate direction of life.

Another tenet of the materialists and idealists was the mind-body distinction, with the materialists emphasizing knowledge of things gained through the senses and the idealists, particularly Berkeley, seeing reality only as an outgrowth of the mind. The materialists argued that cognizance of reality was possible only through empirical data derived from the senses through the interaction of the body with physical matter. Theirs was a participatorial approach to epistemology in that they believed that only through physical involvement could individuals acquire knowledge—and limited knowledge, at that. Constructs of the mind that went beyond relationality and perception were inadequate, imaginative ideas subject to, and products of, misinterpretations, fantasy, the influence of desire and will, etc. The idealists, particularly Descartes, believed that the reverse was true. Believing that the mind functions not only in a passive perceptive manner but also in a positive, affirmative manner through the formation of conceptions, they contended that only through a spectatorial approach could true knowledge be acquired. The idealists (and rationalists) believed that knowledge of the senses was confused and vagrant and offered no potential for comprehensive contact with being. However, conceptions of the mind could affect this contact once an individual surpassed his ego-centered confusion and arrived at true knowledge in the form of "adequate ideas." Bergson sought, in dialectical fashion, to go beyond the primacy of both matter and idea and the bifurcation of mind and body to a philosophy of transformism that emphasizes wilful transubstantiation, through ideals, of matter into spirit, which is then seen as the dynamic life-pulse of creative evolution.

Life, for Bergson, is not dominated solely by the physical view of the materialists or by the biological view of the Darwinians but flows from, as Kazantzakis relates, inner wellsprings—"always and always the procreant urge of the world." Kazantzakis, in his treatise on Bergson, wrote:

> According to Bergson life is an unceasing creation, a leap upwards, a vital outburst, an *élan vital*. . . . All the history of life up to man is a gigantic endeavor of the vital impulse to elevate matter, to create a being which would be free of the inflexible mechanism of inertia. . . . Two streams, that of life and that of matter, are in motion, though in opposite directions; one toward integration and the other toward disintegration. Bergson thinks of the *élan vital* as a seething stream which in its ebullition distills into falling drops. It is these drops which constitute matter.[34]

For Kazantzakis the *élan vital*, the driving life force, was to be identified in messianic fashion with Buddhism, Marxism-Leninism, Christianity, and (finally) with Odyssean freedom. In this last identification it becomes the Invisible Cry of divinity in man, of the nonexistent seeking realization, of the becoming of life's history:

> When I say the Invisible, I do not mean any priestly version of God, or metaphysical consciousness, or absolutely perfect Being, but rather the mysterious force which uses man—and used animals, plants, and minerals before us—as its carriers and beasts of burden, and which hastens along as though it had a purpose and were following a specific road. (*Report,* 402)

This cry is a personal god in man, nature, and history that takes many forms and masks and that is the divine in man seeking release for the greater perfection of itself. It lacks the teleological finalism of Hegel, for it is infinitely potential. It gives rise to the struggle for the ascent from the strictures of matter to freedom.

The form taken by the *élan vital* in a particular epoch is not discernible, for Bergson, through matter and sense data or through intellect and pure idea but through a combination or synthesis of these, which he terms intuition or consciousness. He argues that this constant stream of change, which is life, cannot be captured by thought, for the very essence of thought is dissection—the static photographing, so to speak, of isolated moments of the life force or reality. Bergson thus equates the aesthetic faculty of the artist with intuition or consciousness as the only means of grasping life in wholes:

> intuition may bring the intellect to recognize that . . . neither mechanical causality nor finality (teleology) can give a sufficient interpretation of the vital process. Then, by the sympathetic communication which it establishes between us and the rest of the living, by the expansion of our consciousness which it brings about, it introduces us into life's own domain, which is reciprocal interpenetration, endlessly continued creation.[35]

Bergson's intuitionist philosophy was not primarily an antirationalist one. H. Stuart Hughes says that far "from being the negation of the intelligence, Bergson explained, intuition, in the sense in which he employed the term, was its parallel and complement."[36] Bergson consciously stressed intuition so heavily in order to correct the imbalance brought about by the stress of the preceding age solely on intelligence.

This endlessly continued creation means there is a constant evolutionary flux: everything is always changing and "the same concrete reality never recurs." Each moment is a discrete, unique epoch of existence that is wonderfully different from all preceding moments, and each moment should be experienced to the fullest. The intellect which focuses on thinking time, those photographed, isolated segments upon which we base our action, deludes us into thinking that reality recurs. But lived time, durational time, transcends this dissection by intellectualism: "As soon as we go out of the encasings in which radical mechanism and radical finalism confine our thought, reality appears as a ceaseless upspringing of something new, which has no sooner arisen to make the present than it has already fallen back into the past."[37] Materialistic and idealistic interpretations of reality do not, therefore, reach the essence of being, for they seize only on segmented aspects of reality, e.g., economics, ideas, morality, etc., as motivations. Kazantzakis, applying this to various analyses of human

behavior by such sociopolitical and religious systems as
Marxism-Leninism, Buddhism, and Christianity, would conclude
that none of them reached the underlying unity behind
phenomena; instead, each seized on only one causal factor, for at
"the bottom of every great and critical human passion lies not
economic or moral self-interest, but Passion—by which we mean a
pre-human tempestuous force that is beyond logic and self-
interest." (*Spain*, 161) This passion, which manifests itself "beyond logic and self-interest," may appear in various guises in
different ages. The difficult task of man is to distinguish the true
face of reality from the bogus ones. Thus Kazantzakis' concern
with the others of those "decisive steps"—Buddha, Christ,
Lenin—that may be either reality's face or bogus "masks."

The symbolic value of masks is relied upon consistently by
Kazantzakis. In the context of Bergson's vitalism, masks are like
"dead" snapshots—they are in the realm of intellect: static, discrete, irreconcilable if contradictory. To Kazantzakis, masks are
great rhythmic, passionate projects with a mythic power over
human existence and thus must be continually forged in response
to changing historical circumstances so as to make them pertinent
to contemporary existence. As noted, Kazantzakis once hung
Nietzsche's mask over his study door.

In a very entertaining article, Adele Bloch discusses the preva-
lence of mask imagery in Kazantzakis' work. Masks "occupy a
conspicuous place in all his novels, his plays, his philosophical
writings, and his romanticized autobiography *Report to Greco*."[38]
She gives as examples Odysseus who—when imprisoned in Egypt
for participation in an unsuccessful revolution—carves a mask of
his fighting god and wears it as he dances a frightening dance;
Manolios, the gentle shepherd of *The Greek Passion* who—when
his face is made repulsive by a psychosomatic skin ailment—
carves a mask of Christ; and Toda Raba, the African chieftain
who wears Lenin's mask in a dance of liberation on Moscow's Red
Square. Masks can be terrifyingly revelational, as in Nietzsche,
and can penetrate the world's superficial beauty, harmony, and
illusion to show the chaos and death that lie at the core of existence. They can be nihilistic, as with Buddha, and become (as for
Kazantzakis in the early 1920s in Vienna and Berlin), a bottom-

less, jet-dark eye in which the world drowned and was delivered, and thereby appeal to the despairing side of man's nature. Bloch implies that Buddha appealed to the introverted, withdrawn aspect of Kazantzakis' personality. Masks can be positive-transcendent, as with Christ, who in his representation by the institutionalized church turned men's eyes from the world and its injustices to a pacifistic awaiting for beatitude and otherworldly salvation. Or masks can be positive-immanent, as with Lenin, who represented for Kazantzakis the new savior created "by the enslaved, hungry, and oppressed to enable them to bear slavery, hunger, and oppression—another new mask for mankind's hope and despair." (*Report*, 369) These are, essentially, the alternative masks that Kazantzakis believes twentieth century man has donned—nihilism-escapism with Nietzsche or Buddha, otherworldly passivity with the Christ of the church, or materialistic revolution with Lenin. Each has its own shortcomings and in some measure fails to express the unity of God and man, of theory and action, of affirmation and destruction, of good and evil, of spirituality and materiality, of the many contradictory, dichotomous themes of man's rich and varied existence.

This paucity on the part of any one mask gives rise to Kazantzakis' attempt to synthesize the masks as an expression of the unifying God, soul, spirit, dynamic principle, *élan vital*, etc., behind the movements in the world: his struggle to unite those "decisive steps." "The great sirens Christ, Buddha, Lenin, they seduced me. . . . all my life I have fought to save myself from all these sirens, without denying any one; I have been fighting to get them together and to make their three unequal voices into a harmony." (*Report*, 369) This dialectical endeavor is Kazantzakis' inner quest to transmute diversity into unity and gives rise to the central tension in Kazantzakis' thought between unmasking and artistic synthesis.

Life is a flowing, expanding, and ubiquitous stream of consciousness for Bergson and Kazantzakis, which forever explores new channels in seeking to join with the rhythmic, oceanic tide of the cosmos. Of the many channels into which life may flow in a particular era, there is only one that is deliverance, and it is Kazantzakis' goal, particularly in *The Saviors of God: Spiritual Exer-*

cises and *The Odyssey,* to depict systematically how an individual may attain the expanded consciousness and proper perspective to discover the true harmonious and unified evolutionary face of his age and thereby save "God," the divine in man. Key elements of Kazantzakis' salvationist perspective are individualism versus community, nihilism and the human condition, atheism and spiritual values, classical versus modern views of the nature of man, and—most important—determinism versus autonomy. Kazantzakis' concern over the mechanization of society, his striving for the true value and meaning of life, and his critique of the ills of the transitional age, coalesce around these elements within the burning, vibrant forge of the artistic, spiritual, and intellectual concepts discussed above to compose one of the most compellingly humanistic and compassionate of contemporary visions. Reflecting fondly on the rich environment to which he was irrevocably attached, Kazantzakis calls his vision the Cretan glance.

The Cretan Glance: Transubstantiation and the General Concepts of Kazantzakis' Philosophy

The Cretan glance is an ontological attitude toward the cosmos that is a synthesis of the varied, antinomial influences of Kazantzakis' experiential odyssey and the spring from which his political philosophy flows. This attitude received its most thorough philosophical expression in *The Saviors of God* in 1923, its most compelling translation into activity in *The Odyssey* completed in 1938, and its most enlightening explication apropos the rest of Kazantzakis' philosophical system in *Report* in 1956. However, the most artistically perfect and hence most powerful expression of the Cretan glance is found in *Zorba,* where the Boss, Kazantzakis' autobiographical spokesman, explains:

> "We are little grubs, Zorba, minute grubs on the small leaf of a tremendous tree. This small leaf is the earth. The other leaves are the stars that you see moving at night. We make our way on this little leaf examining it anxiously and carefully. We smell it; it smells good or bad to us. We taste it and find it eatable. We beat on it and it cries out like a living thing.
> "Some men—the more intrepid ones—reach the edge of the

leaf. From there we stretch out, gazing into chaos. We tremble. We guess what a frightening abyss lies beneath us. In the distance we can hear the noise of the other leaves of the tremendous tree, we feel the sap rising from the roots to our leaf and our hearts and all our souls, we tremble with terror. From that moment begins . . .

"I stopped. I wanted to say 'from that moment begins poetry,' but Zorba would not have understood. I stopped."

"What begins?" asked Zorba's anxious voice. "Why did you stop?"

"begins the great danger, Zorba. Some grow dizzy and delirious, others are afraid; they try to find an answer to strengthen their hearts, and they say: 'God!'. Others again, from the edge of the leaf, look over the precipice calmly and bravely and say: 'I like it.' " (p. 277)

The predicament of those who grow "dizzy and delirious," who "are afraid," derives not from the fact that there is an abyss, a precipice, beyond which there is chaos, but from their reaction to that abyss. We are afraid, we tremble, we surrender, we turn away from the abyss—which is fate/mortality—and conjure up explanations, either ideas, rationality, superstition, or religion, as our ancestors have done through the ages, to deny this reality. We do this because, as Nietzsche realized, we would rather have the void for our purpose than be void of purpose! We deny the void by filling the void, by adding to the precipice that which, since it represents the ultimate reach of man, becomes our moral, cultural, and social circumscribants and determinants. It is at the void that we come against the shock of life's history, that we surrender to and are overpowered by the reality of the precipice, by being so intimidated and frightened by it as to turn to our minds—either in rational or irrational fashion—to construct our unreality. That unreality consequently becomes the guiding and central orientation of our lives and that which we, since we are forever fearful of the void, seek to impose and spread to others. This is evidenced in doctrinaire religious teachings that diverge in startling manner from reality in order to camouflage the void. It is evidenced in philosophic absolutism which seems to force chaotic reality and infinitude into ordered terms. It is evident in conformist societal mores enforced to create an aura of comfort, security, and oneness to communal existence. In dogmatically acquiescing to these we do nothing, we neither negate nor affirm ourselves, our existence; we do nothing; we are nothing; we live dead lives—we are immobilized and devitalized.

As Kazantzakis develops this theme in *Zorba*, he also develops and presents his thoughts on the resolution of the human predicament. This resolution lies in the negation of the negation; in the affirmation of life; in the overcoming of the oppressiveness of the void. It lies in the recognition of fate, of mortality, of the misfortunes of life and the ultimacy of death—the confrontation with the void but not the submission to it. It lies in struggle, suffering, rebellion, in both the affirmation of life and the transcending of the strictures of that life—it is at the same time a negation and creation. It is, as Bien puts it, to "Say yes to necessity, fill the vacuum with joy as Zorba does, or . . . redeem life's anguish by transubstantiating matter into spirit, Dionysiac reality into tragic myth."[39]

The resolution requires an act, an acceptance and avowal of life. It demands a confrontation with mortality. It demands an act of will to life, to life's reality. It demands a facing of the truth that there is no eternity, no resurrection, no afterlife, none of the dogmas with which socioreligious innovators have filled the void, and no earthly salvation to be found in political ideologies—no unity gained through enforced conformity. It requires the Cretan glance, an affirmation that eternity is in every moment and every moment is potential eternity. It is being Zorba and joining with him in his dynamic rebelliousness against staticism; with the "purgation of matter which comes about through suffering, he fulfills the highest debt man owes to God his Creator: he transcends his nature, makes it spirit, and like the butterfly after breaking its cocoon, flies up and effects a union with God."[40] For Zorba, the Cretan glance, the *Übermensch*-like capacity to "love life and have no fear of death," was innate and instinctual; therefore, he needed no enabling guides, either philosophical or theological, to direct him to the proper perspective. But what of us who do not possess this instinctual courage and insight, who cannot naturally effect a union with God, who tremble before the void or surrender to its terror by Buddhistic acquiescence? It is for us that

Kazantzakis expressed himself in his prophetic *The Saviors of God,* to portray how in step-by-step fashion we can join with El Greco, Zorba, and Odysseus, and soar like a winged falcon beyond the delimitations of nothingness.

The Cretan glance, the third eye of the soul, is freedom, the ontological attitude that can grasp life and death—the *élan vital/* life pulse of the universe. It is "that vision which can embrace and harmonize these two enormous, timeless, and indestructible forces, and with the vision . . . modulate our thinking and our action." (*Saviors,* 44) Kazantzakis saw humans as being in a certain unfavorable situation in the world. In his view, they lived in the world disunited from the cosmos, ignorant of the pulsating life force of the world, and uncertain even as to the possibilities of their true existence. In the manner in which they lived in the world, they were bound by and subservient to either phenomena or noumena—to stimuli artificially constructed by themselves. Man must, in Kanzantzakis' view, fulfill three basic duties in the world which reveal different levels of perception before he can escape this unreality.

The first duty is that of epistemological emendation[41] which involves two steps. Man must first explore the realm of the phenomenal with the mind's eye, to impose order, relationships, discipline, law, rationality, to the chaos of things. He must labor with the intellect and the five senses, immerse himself in the transitory world, and say: "That I may not stumble and fall, I erect landmarks over the vertigo; I sling bridges, open roads, and build over the abyss." He must then complete the corollary second step, which is to recognize and glory in the limitations of the mind. At this stage man neither knows, cares, nor asks

> whether behind appearances there lives and moves a secret essence superior to me. . . . I create phenomena in swarms and paint with a full pallette a gigantic and gaudy curtain before the abyss. Do not say, 'Draw the curtain that I may see the painting.' The curtain is the painting. (*Saviors,* 48)

The second duty is to the heart and may be termed ethical emendation. It also involves two steps. The first is to reject the rational boundaries composed by the mind's eye, explore the realm of the noumenal with the heart's eye, and rip away the curtain in order to see the painting behind it. Man must seek truth, essence, being, reality, and the order of the cosmos, and follow his heart "to grasp what is hidden behind appearances, to ferret out that mystery which brings me to birth and then kills me, to discover if behind the visible and unceasing stream of the world an invisible and immutable presence is hiding." (*Saviors*, 51) Again, man must recognize the ineffectiveness of the heart in discerning a purposive essence, a teleological presence, behind the universe and with this recognition comes the anguish which ensues from the attempt to give a human meaning to this superhuman struggle: "To bleed in this agony, and to live it profoundly, is the second duty." (*Saviors*, 50)

The third duty is to free oneself from both mind and heart, from the illusory yet tempting hope offered by the former of conquering phenomena and the equally illusory hope offered by the latter of harnessing the essence. Man must realize that knowledge of the mind, reason and science, is always problematical; for, instead of understanding the nature of things, we organize, classify, hypothesize it, and then appeal once more to the data for verification. Why things are the way they are is unanswered at this level for you do not approach this, you only ask how things are done. Since the self organizes the sense data, man's experience is a solipsistic one. Equally important for man's action and thinking is the realization that ethics derived from the second level of inquiry, that of the heart's vision, is based on knowledge, as one Kazantzakian interpreter opines, of which the heart "apprehended merely a human meaning, a human myth, and imposed this upon the unknowable."[42] The third duty is the metaphysical acceptance of nothingness; the transcendence of ill-fated illusions that hide the nonexistent; the transubstantiation of our materiality through the burning power of the third eye of the soul into free, self-conscious spirit.

> Nothing exists. . . . There is no beginning and no end. Only this present moment exists, full of bitterness, full of sweetness, and I rejoice in it all. . . . I know now: I do not hope for anything. I do not fear anything, I have freed myself from both the mind and the

heart, I have mounted much higher, I am free. This is what I want.
I want nothing more. I have been seeking freedom. (*Saviors*, 59)

In one way such a man is in much the same situation as the
Platonic cave-dweller who on being unchained and led from the
darkness realizes the degree to which his previous existence was
built on reflections, false generalizations, and rules based on
images and echoes rather than reality. Like that philosopher, the
man who has emended his existence has cast off his chains and
emerged from the cave-like cocoon which each inevitably creates
for shelter in the tragic comedy that is existence. His spirit stands
bathed in light. But he is unlike the philosopher in a very important respect. Plato describes this individual as one who descends
once more into the cave only to encounter ridicule, helplessness,
and despair and is it any wonder for:

> while his eyes are blinking and before he has become accustomed
> to the surrounding darkness, he is compelled to fight in courts of
> law, or in other places, about the images or the shadows of images
> of justice, and is endeavoring to meet the conceptions of those who
> have never yet seen absolute justice.

In another passage Plato sees the lot of the just philosopher in an
imperfect world in such dismaying terms that he concludes this
individual quite properly

> holds his peace, and goes his own way. He is like one who, in the
> storm of dust and sleet which the driving wind hurries along,
> retires under the shelter of a wall; and seeing the rest of mankind
> full of wickedness he is content, if only he can live his own life and
> be pure from evil or unrighteousness, and depart in peace and
> goodwill, with bright hope."[43]

Kazantzakis, however, counsels a very different path. This is
not the end of the journey, but only the beginning; for man has
not at this point yet attained the Zorbaic capacity to dance de-
fiantly in the face of infinitude. What he has done at this stage is to
have prepared—the three duties in *The Saviors of God* are found
under the heading "The Preparation"—for the expansion of
consciousness which comes from the ensuing taut, tension-drawn
pilgrimage through life in the forward, ascending journey to

unity with infinity. Man has now reached the point "from which you began—the ephemeral, palpitating, mysterious point of your existence—with new eyes, with new ears, with a new sense of taste, smell, touch, with new brains." (p. 100) Man need not despair, nor must he seek to remain pure by avoiding experience—which to Plato threatened the contemplation of truth—but he should involve himself in the world and affirm life to the utmost. Only this road will lead to the void and enable each to discover within his unique, experiential perspective his destiny or *daemon*. Thus, the next step is the "march" through Ego, Race, Mankind, The Earth, from which comes "The Vision" which enables man to discover the proper relationship of man to man, God, and nature. This precedes "The Action," in which there is a joining of theory and action, that modulation of thinking and behavior which harmonizes the timeless, indestructible forces of growth and decay, birth and death. By this path we are thus led to the peak of "The Silence," from which noble heights man leaps into the abyss of eternity to link with God.

It is this ascending, bittersweet pilgrimage that Kazantzakis envisioned his own life as being, that he believed to be the world's odyssey of the twentieth century, and the great adventure on which he launched Odysseus to illustrate graphically both descriptive and prescriptive elements of his political philosophy for contemporary man. Friar has incisively summarized this journey, which leads to the Cretan glance:

At the start of his journey, he hears an agonized cry within him shouting for help. His first step is to plunge into his own ego until he discovers that it is the endangered spirit (or "God") locked within each man that is crying out for liberation. In order to free it, each man must consider himself solely responsible for the salvation of the world, because when a man dies, that aspect of the universe which is his own particular vision and the unique play of his mind also crashes in ruins forever. In the second step, a man must plunge beyond his ego and into his racial origins: yet among his forefathers he must choose only those who can help him toward greater refinement of spirit, that he may in turn pass on his task to a son who may also surpass him. The third step for a man is to plunge beyond his own particular race into the races of all mankind and to

become identified with all the universe, with animate and inanimate matter, with earth, stones, sea, plants, animals, insects, and
birds, with the vital impulse of creation in all phenomena. Each
man is a fathomless composite of atavistic roots plunging down to
the primordial origin of things. A man is now prepared to go
beyond the mind, the heart, and hope, beyond his ego, his race,
and mankind, even beyond all phenomena and plunge further
into a vision of the Invisible permeating all things and forever
ascending.[44]

At the same time Kazantzakis was marking out this path, Hermann Hesse's *Demian* was traversing a similar one. In pursuing his
daemon, Demian came to realize "to what extent our soul partakes
of the constant creation of the world. For it is the same invisible
divinity that is active through us and nature . . . the soul whose
essence is eternity, whose essence we cannot know, but which
most often intimates itself to us as the power to love and create."
Pistorius, the organist, agrees and tells him that because of this
each carries the world within him—all that was and is—and thus is
at one with the universe and the invisible essence. This being so,
Demian wonders of what value is individuality and "why do we
continue striving if everything has been completed within us?" He
is told as Kazantzakis tells us that "there's an immense difference
between simply carrying the world within us and being aware of
it." At the level at which most men live, they never actualize their
possibilities and thus live in darkness, confusion, and mediocrity.
Nonetheless, "each of them contains the possibility of becoming
human, but only by having an intimation of these possibilities,
partially even by learning to make himself conscious of them, only
in this respect are these possibilities his."[45] Wisdom, courage,
selflessness, and nobleness characterize one who has successfully
completed the journey. Man has then fulfilled his greatest debt to
God, which is the spiritual concept of evolutionary perfection—
the Good, in transforming his mundane existence into a glorious
reign, in releasing the divine within, in furthering the cause of
moral betterment in the world, in upholding his responsibility to
God, man, and nature, in following the worm that becomes a
butterfly, the flying fish that leaps into the air and transcends its
nature, the silkworm that turns dust into silk, and transubstantiat-

ing his materiality into free unalloyed spirit, in joining with the
saviors of God and achieving beatitude:

> And Thrice Blessed Be Those Who Bear On Their Shoulders
> And Do Not Buckle Under This Great, Sublime, And Terrifying
> Secret:
>   THAT EVEN THIS ONE
>   DOES NOT EXIST! (*Saviors*, 131)

The *Weltanschauung* spelled out in *The Saviors of God* in the
1920s, acted out by Ulysses in *The Odyssey* in the 1930s, artistically
depicted in *Zorba* in the 1940s, explained in *Report* in the 1950s,
and adhered to in all other works by Kazantzakis, has obvious
literary, theological, philosophical, and existential significance.
This worldview is also of important political significance. The
vantage point of the Cretan glance, attained through the
expanded consciousness of one who has emended—
epistemologically, ethically, and metaphysically—his existential
insignificance by following the innate divinity within himself, is
man fulfilled. Thus, each individual's fulfillment as a unique
person is, to Kazantzakis, the ultimate end of all sociopolitical life.
All laws, institutions, and mores must conform to that principle.
Kazantzakis' view toward the best manner of attaining that end in
politics passed through a multiphased development. A cognizance of the stages of this development and the causal factors
involved is essential to an understanding of Kazantzakis' mature
political philosophy. Prominent factors influencing Kazantzakis'
changing views are the political manifestations of his agonized
tightrope dance between social activism and literary involvement
and the extent to which Kazantzakis was, to use Camus's phrase, a
historical revolutionist.

"I say it is useless to waste your life on one path, especially if that path has no heart.

"But how do you know when a path has no heart, don Juan?

"Before you embark on it you ask the question: Does this path have a heart? If the answer is no, you will know it, and then you must choose another path.

"But how will I know for sure whether a path has a heart or not?

"Anybody would know that. The trouble is nobody asks the question; and when a man finally realizes that he has taken a path without a heart, the path is ready to kill him. At that point very few men can stop to deliberate, and leave the path.

"How should I proceed to ask the question properly, don Juan?

"Just ask it.

"I mean, is there a proper method, so I would not lie to myself and believe the answer is yes when it really is no?

"Why would you lie?

"Perhaps because at the moment the path is pleasant and enjoyable.

"That is nonsense. A path without a heart is never enjoyable. You have to work hard even to take it. On the other hand, a path with heart is easy; it does not make you work at liking it."

CARLOS CASTANEDA

≡Ⅱ≡Ⅱ≡Ⅱ≡Ⅱ≡Ⅱ≡Ⅱ≡Ⅱ≡Ⅱ≡Ⅱ≡Ⅱ≡Ⅱ≡Ⅱ≡Ⅱ≡Ⅲ

2

Words: Weapons in the Battle

Kazantzakis, whose eye was consistently on the abyss of nothingness, believed freedom to be the essence of man and sought to liberate civilization from the enslaving inhibitions of human mortality and historical temporality. He explored, through his life and art, the advantages and disadvantages of social involvement versus literary activity as weapons in this battle. His view of the means to be used to translate his visionary Cretan glance—the call to the higher man—into reality and thereby to attain freedom evolved through three significant stages. First—and least important for traditional western political theory—there is Kazantzakis' Buddhist phase. From approximately 1918 until the mid-1920s Kazantzakis embraced headlong the Buddhist worldview, which focused not on the political, cultural, and social life of man but contemplated the sanctum of infinity. This period was characterized on Kazantzakis' part by an escapist attitude and a disavowal of responsibility for suffering mankind. The dehumanizing injustices of the finite world of man were as inconsequential drops of rain on the pane of eternity for Kazantzakis during his Buddhism. His was a thoroughly apolitical experience. In the "Berlin" section of *Report,* Kazantzakis reflects on the Buddhist belief that the world does not exist and tells how, through his once-held adherence to this belief, suffering and tyranny were transformed "into a spectacle both ephemeral and vain. I told myself none of this was true. I must not be led astray into believing, like some simple, naive person. No, hunger and satiety, joy and sorrow, life and death—all were specters!" (*Report,* 374)

But in Berlin the Buddhist prism was slowly penetrated by the harsh light of reality, or, to change the metaphor, the curtain of nirvana was parted and the inhuman chaos of the world thereby revealed became Kazantzakis' concern. He realized that he could neither intellectually nor emotionally maintain his aloofness from the political arena when faced with the evils of the misery he found on his arrival in Vienna in 1921 and in Berlin in 1922. With Kazantzakis' acceptance of the world came realization of the "fearful responsibility man bears for all the world's injustice and opprobrium!" (*Report,* 387) That being so, the question confronting Kazantzakis was what should be done to relieve that injustice? In answering this question Kazantzakis would draw from the 1920s to the late 1930s extremely varied if not opposite conclusions turning on the efficacy and desirability of acting versus writing, and physical versus spiritual arms. In what may be termed Kazantzakis' radical phase, lasting until the late 1930s, the efficacy of acting and physical arms was at the forefront of his thought. This period was characterized by intense Marxist involvement, a shrill impatience with temporal injustice, and a lack of concern with the ethics of political means. These traits of Kazantzakis' thought were superseded in his mature stage— mature both in a literary and a political sense—in the late 1930s. As Kazantzakis accepted his literary nature and realized the importance of the spiritual unity of mankind, his political theory took on new depth and more profound dimensions.

Radical Vitalism

Once Kazantzakis had abandoned Buddhist apoliticism and accepted social responsibility for injustice, he threw himself into the battle. On the whole he paid little attention to normal avenues of political change, and even when he did he was rebuffed in his attempt to utilize them. Nietzsche had convinced him "that negativism could be a weapon for the cure of contemporary decadence and need not be a symptom of that decadence."[1] Accordingly, Kazantzakis turned with a rush to vitalistic movements as the best way of destroying the old laws and accelerating the release of the free spirit of man from the forces that oppressed it. Thus was revealed one of the dominant traits both of Kazantzakis' character and of his politics. He was imaginative and telling as a social critic; however, he was also subject to exaggeration, to pushing his basically good intentions and beliefs to extreme and perhaps unwarranted conclusions. There is an excessiveness about Kazantzakis' personality that often distorted his most cherished ideals. This excessiveness was the primary motivational force that led to his extremely radical and violent position in the period under discussion. The only recourse for Kazantzakis, who saw and opposed the evils being wrought through and by bourgeois political systems, was to eliminate them and the outmoded concepts on which they were maintained. In 1922, therefore, when addressing the Congress of Radical School Reformers in Berlin, Kazantzakis argued against piecemeal reform of the school system, which is after all an emanation of society. "If we are going to help society to advance, we must one day make up our minds to sever its rotten roots and free men from their shell, which prevent them from growing."[2] He also sought to ally himself with the Soviet Marxists, for they too were bringing about the destruction of the old forms that must of necessity precede creation of new ones. He could say of World War I, "when the vile war came, it brought one great good: it intensified the process of decomposition." (*T. R.,* 116) He filled the first half of *The Odyssey,* written from 1925 to 1938, with passages acclaiming the necessity of destruction: of the outmoded ethic of a placid Sparta; of the decadent society Odysseus found on Crete, against which he led a successful revolution, placing a companion in charge; of the tyranny of the Egyptian pharaohs, against which he participated in an unsuccessful revolution; even of his ideal city founded on scientific naturalism. At this point in his development Kazantzakis was unconcerned with the ethical implications of political means but cared only for their efficacy of preparing the world for the building of the New Jerusalem of freedom, justice, and virtue. As late as 1937 when, as a corre-spondent covering the Spanish Civil War, he was asked of the communists, "Why did they have to go and burn the churches?," he rationalized such acts as permissible because of previous injus-tices. "Don't forget that if the Reds did burn the churches, the Spanish Catholic priests burned the Church. . . . In Christ's name they have sanctioned and desired a thousand crimes."[3] And when asked by a German philosopher, Dr. Colin Rose, during the same conflict, if he was for or against war, he answered: "Neither for nor against . . . as I am neither for nor against an earthquake." (*Spain,* 163)

While recognizing and taking into account that Kazantzakis was not as bloodthirsty as these remarks paint him, and that he was attempting to surpass his romantic idealism and face a harsh reality, there is still evidenced a disconcerting lack of concern for the use of violence. Kazantzakis' abandonment of his earlier ascet-ic yet compassionate orientation for an identification with and exaltation of the claim to absolute virtue of vitalistic movements, particularly Marxism, in the 1920s and 1930s gives rise to two questions. What lay behind Kazantzakis' deification of activist movements? What are the implications of such a politics of violence? By turning to the issue of Kazantzakis' involvement with activist movements is encountered one of the central, all-important themes of Kazantzakis' life and art—the personal-psychological struggle between actor and writer.

Perhaps the most intriguing aspect of Kazantzakis' thought is his attitude toward physical participation in the quest of bettering the human predicament versus theoretical, literary involvement. Although Kazantzakis is perhaps most commonly thought of, particularly among his English reading public, as being an ascetic, apolitical literatist—no doubt because of the unfamiliarity with his life resulting from the lack of a good English language biography—this aspect of his life in fact was characterized by ambivalence, self-questioning, and conflict. This question and Kazantzakis' ultimate assessment of action versus words is best explored through analyzing his identification with Soviet Marxism in the 1920s; for this is his most intensive, sustained effort at political action and consequently his most extreme betrayal of his literary nature and manifests the important political implication of his internal struggle for Kazantzakis' thought. As noted above, it was the vitalistic spirit of Marxism that appealed to Kazantzakis. Although there is some ambivalence in Marx, there is vitalism, inherited most especially from Hegel, and there is the notion of freedom. This explains why so many twentieth-century intellectuals, including Sartre, have embraced Marx, even though Leninist and Stalinist rigidities appear to run counter to their ontological commitments. There is also, however, in Marx's personality an eschaton, a finalistic static solution. The vitalism stops, and this explains in part the betrayal of that early spirit.

Kazantzakis was introduced to the comprehensive and apocalyptic vision of Marxism-Leninism in Berlin by his fellow idealist (and lover) Itka Horowitz. He became so openly sympathetic to communism that he was the only Greek intellectual invited to attend the celebration of the tenth anniversary of the revolution. His sympathy occasioned several outbursts and letters by Kazantzakis in which there is evident a movement away from the more ascetic, uninvolved, and nonviolent attitude of his earlier Christian-Buddhist religious orientation. They contain a more strident and more emotional protest and are centered around the position Kazantzakis arrived at as he writes Eleni from Russia in 1927:

> I'm deeply affected by setting foot on the Russian earth . . . by gazing at the mute enduring masses. . . . Whatever I've written seems to me unworthy and provincial. My cry has been heard by only a few people . . . because the means I use are weak.
>
> What do art and a beautiful phrase and a good simile and a brilliant line of verse matter? All these things are little; and they don't touch the great waves of humanity. Only religion and action—only a Christ or a Lenin—deserve to live today. The others exist in order to wait for him, or at most to prepare the way for him with their inarticulate, provincial cries.[4]

In addition to the goals of social justice there is evinced in this passage another element of Kazantzakis' attraction to Marxism—his disillusionment at this point with art as a means of effecting social change. This theme will be explored thoroughly a bit later.

Kazantzakis' perception of why the masses silently endured and why his contemporaries sanctioned or at least implicitly condoned such inhumane conditions as existed in Vienna, Berlin, and most of Europe in the mid-1920s is found in various passages throughout his writings and help to explain his attempted movement toward radical activism. This reason lay, in Kazantzakis' view, in the sterility, apathy, and anguish displayed by the men of his day. These undesirable traits permitted the oppressors to carry on uncontrolled by the masses and led Kazantzakis to conclude that there was a need not only for economic and political emancipation but, more importantly, for the "psychological and spiritual emancipation of man." In Kazantzakis' view, his contemporaries were too content to overlook or to countenance those acts of their government that did not directly hinder their daily lives, and they were openly receptive to the espousals of gradualness, of tolerance, of nonviolence, and of order proffered by their government officials for, "Needless to say, the bourgeois regime is striving to stifle this endeavor." [5]

In light of the injustice in the world, the apathetic attitude of mankind aroused Kazantzakis to fever pitch. Kazantzakis' politics, when faced with what he viewed as the oppressiveness of both German and Greek political systems, as well as others, and the dynamic Soviet successes, would eventually move so far from the nonviolent apoliticism of Buddhism as to lead him to a rabid support of Marxism, its means as well as its goals, in his address to the Moscow World Congress in 1927. "Capitalist war is inevitable because the capitalists who are in power have an interest in making war," he declared. "There is only one thing do do: prepare for social war. When the capitalist war comes, it must be turned into a social war."[6]

Kazantzakis' politics represent at this point what seems to be the supreme contradiction of his earlier asceticism. The moral absolutism of orthodox Marxism with which Kazantzakis readily identified and which he exalted directly contradicts the repeatedly stated theme that "it is our duty to stare at the abyss" and not succumb to the false masks of "Buddhas, Gods, Motherlands, Ideas. . . . Woe to him who cannot free himself from Buddhas, God, Motherlands, and Ideas." (*Zorba*, 191) With the identification of the Marxist cause as the *élan vital*, the evolutionary movement of God, and his consequent justification of actual physical interference with those who disagreed with that cause, Kazantzakis' politics reached a nadir of conformism and dogmatism that was at odds with his basic humanistic outlook. He was to acknowledge that certain movements—e.g., Marxism—could embody the moral laws of the invisible lifeforce and was to justify governmental actions, in this instance by Stalin's Komsomol, which sought, by any means, to uphold those moral laws. This was evidenced in 1929 in the break-up between him and his (at that time) fellow Marxist Panait Istrati over the famous Rusakov Affair. Victor Serge, a Trotskyite revolutionary and old friend of Kazantzakis' and Istrati's, was "unjustly treated by the Soviet bureaucracy. . . . Serge was first isolated and then exiled; his wife went mad, his child was left in the streets, his father-in-law [Rusakov] starved to death."[7]

Whereas Istrati became furious at this injustice, protested to the Secretary of the Party, left the Soviet Union, canceled favorable newspaper articles he had prepared about the Soviets, and attacked what he accurately perceived as the beginning of the purges, Kazantzakis continued his travels in Russia; and, rather than protesting the barbaric treatment of the Serges, he protested Istrati's unfavorable statements about Russia.[8] His mystical, fervid support of communism would temporarily lead Kazantzakis to adopt a brutal ideological amoralism: "What interests me is not man, nor the earth, nor the heavens, but the flame that consumes man and earth and heavens." He was interested not in Russia "but [in] the flame consuming Russia. Amelioration of the fate of the masses or of the elite, happiness, justice, virtue: these things that lure so many people do not catch me." (*T.R.*, 94) Perhaps the answer to the question of why Kazantzakis deified Lenin's brand of Marxism is to be found, if anywhere, in the realm of the psychoanalyst and not in that of the political scientist. The most logical answer is that Kazantzakis, the man of words and of strong beliefs, who by his own testimony lived through his heroes and who sought out the dominant rhythms of his age, found in Lenin, the man of action and absolute morality, that unity of theory and action, of the intellectual and activist, for which he had expressed such concern in *The Saviors of God* and other works. "He felt the need for a commitment; and Lenin had now captivated his heart. Not being a man of action, he felt the need to act." [9]

Other than through his writings, his honorary post as cabinet minister without portfolio in 1945, his position with UNESCO as director of the department to translate the classics (which was only offered to him after it had been rejected by another), and his mission as director general of the Ministry of Public Welfare in Greece in repatriating Greek refugees from the Caucasus in 1919 and 1920, Kazantzakis never attained much success in politics. In 1924 he entered into an illegal and unsuccessful political action with the communists in Crete, for which he was arrested (this occasioned his "Apology" to the examining magistrate, after which he secluded himself on the Cretan coast). In 1928 he was charged in Greece with offenses against the state and against religion for his lectures (with Istrati) on socialism and his controversial *The Saviors of God.* In 1929 he planned to present himself as a communist candidate for the Greek legislature and yet failed to do so. In 1940, following Mussolini's attack on Greece, Kazantzakis proposed his great (and somewhat ludicrous) plan for unification of Greece and England. In the 1940s he offered to join the communist partisans only to be rejected, while at the same time the rightist government banned much of his work and investigated his communist ties. Kazantzakis never realized his lifelong goal of leading a communal society of artists; or his proposed Institute of Greek Culture in the United States; or the International of the Spirit that he proposed in the late 1940s. Moreover, his publications and influence were effectively circumscribed by the rightist Greek government.

As these events (and nonevents) demonstrate, he was not a highly successful political actor, yet it was not until his seventh decade, the 1950s, that, as his wife Helen writes, "for the first time I heard no regrets uttered about his incapacity to set himself at the head of a great political movement."[10]

Kazantzakis was unable to head such a movement for essentially two reasons. First, Kazantzakis' philosophy, which stresses living fully in the present, is subversive of the kinds of organizational commitments required for successful political action in a technocratic society. This is not to say that Kazantzakis' was an anarchistic vision with no requisites for a humane community. Indeed, as will become evident, he proposed several criteria for the good society, and his life and art were a witness to these. It simply means that Kazantzakis was more concerned with the values of a political system than with its organization. Perhaps this explains why, paradoxically, Kazantzakis' greatest political influence, both in Greece and in the world, came after his death. The other reason for Kazantzakis' political ineptness was his literary nature.

With this understanding of Kazantzakis' desire for action and his political-religious messianism, it is easily seen why he would find in Leninism an opportunity for participation. He seemed to experience a vicarious pleasure through Soviet Marxism, particularly through Lenin's actions, and so closely identified with the Soviet experiment that in

his third journey to Russia Kazantzakis saw the opportunity for a new test. Was he a man of action? Would he be able to make contact with the revolutionary society, with the god-bearing people, and to

release his powers? While he was still at work on his epic and
without any cause to hope for an escape, he had written to me from
Aegina (August 25, 1927): "As soon as I finish *The Odyssey,* my small
service, I shall give myself entirely to the problem of how to get to
grips with reality and to act. If I live elsewhere, if I find friends
outside Greece, I shall triumph. That is to say, I shall do what my
nature is capable of doing."[11]

There is a haunting and disturbingly tragic aspect to Kazantzakis'
mystical and fervid identification with men and movements of
action, such as Lenin and Zorba, and his misperception of Mussolini, and his soul wrenching yet rather incongruous attempts at
becoming a political activist, revolutionary, and leader. This is an
elusive yet important theme of Kazantzakis' life and work. There
is a saddening distortion of life evidenced by Kazantzakis' attempts to break with his literary nature. There is also a saddening
irony in that he who passionately loved life ("I who love so vio-
lently both the 'yes' and 'no' . . . instead of burning it [life] stingily
and miserably, let's burn it at both ends."[12]) would in reality live a
large part of his life only in words. There have of course been
other cases of men attempting to compensate for life through
constant writing—the case of Henry David Thoreau, for example.

Thoreau, as with Kazantzakis and also Nietzsche, was emasculated to some extent by his writings. Alfred Kazin's discussion of
this devitalizing tragedy of Thoreau's life—his devoted attempt to
create and live a life of words—is instructive. "Thoreau," Kazin
writes, "is one of the most fanatical, most arduous, most tragic
examples in history of a man trying to live his life by writing it—of
a man seeking to shape his life by words." Thoreau, Kazin believes, exercised an exceptionally rigorous control over language
in order to create works that were not mere art but were life itself.
Writing became for Thoreau not "a withdrawal from life, a compensation for life, a higher form of life, all of which it had been for
so many writers since Romanticism identified the act of composi-
tion with personal salvation. It became a symbolic form of living."
The crisp, clean prose that issued from the Concord explorer not
only recorded experiences but became experience. Through his
writing Thoreau transfigured his often lonely, bare life into a

rich, profound existence. He labored long hours over the precise
sentences found in *Walden* and his other works, sentences with
which he forged a lasting legacy that was his greatest aim and
accomplishment. In Kazin's interpretation, those sentences represent the culmination of Thoreau's life, the end product of his

> hallucinated, perfect, all-too-perfect attachment to his local world;
> each was a precious particle of existence, existence pure, the life of
> Thoreau at the very heart. Each was victory over the long uncon-
> scious loneliness—In the end was the word, only the word.[13]

From 1906 until his death in 1957, Kazantzakis left innumerable essays, a goodly number of encyclopedia articles, many newspaper articles, over forty children's classics translated and two
original schoolbooks and a reader, more than twenty other translations of some of the most important works in Western literature
and thought, some twenty-one cantos, at least four screenplays,
nineteen or more tragedies and plays, a dozen or so full-length
novels, the theological-philosophical *The Saviors of God,* and his
obra, The Odyssey, which runs to 33,333 lines. The depth of
Kazantzakis' attachment to his writing surpasses even Thoreau's
literary addiction. This intense attachment of Kazantzakis and
Thoreau to the word led, in a curious sort of way, to an immobili-
zation of each of them in the active sphere of life and politics.
Devotion to writing, in which were recorded all the experiences,
observations, dreams, and aspirations of powerful minds, not
only became a substitute for children and home for Thoreau but
ultimately became "Kazantzakis' means of his own salvation."[14]
Yet underneath this sublimation were strong, uncompromising,
righteous characters who broke through in similar ways.

Thoreau's movement was not Marxism but abolitionism and his
heromartyr was not Lenin but John Brown. Yet when John
Brown was being hanged in Charleston prison, Thoreau could
only write and speak for him: "Thoreau said that 'the cost of a
thing is the amount of what I call life which is required to be
exchanged for it, immediately, or in the long run.' By that test
Thoreau paid much to become the writer he did."[15] Applying that
test to Kazantzakis, we find that he also paid much to become the
writer he did.

This payment became evident when Kazantzakis was confronted with the vital brilliance of Lenin and all the pent-up righteousness, all the moral fervor, all the unused strength of purpose of Kazantzakis' character exploded in orgiastic fury into the only real outlet that it had—the word. The words and essays that issued on the occasion of Kazantzakis' trips to the Soviet Union in the 1920s are described by Prevelakis as possibly the strongest of any of Kazantzakis' writings. They depict the explosive release of all the frustrated violence so often found in man's solitary existence. The Soviets' attack on bourgeois society symbolized for Kazantzakis the basic struggles of good versus evil, of justice versus injustice. It was an apocalyptic event that represented in a single stroke the fruition of the many surface forces and undercurrents clashing in a badly divided and diffused psyche. Prevelakis notes of Kazantzakis at this point:

> His repressed desire for action often appears not only in his letters and in his plots, but also in the style of his language; he had not succeeded in releasing his messianism, but he had preserved its ardor. The drama of Kazantzakis' life up to this time—and even a little later—was that he was setting out in pursuit of his destiny at an age when others have created their work and through it have found release.[16]

Much to Kazantzakis' horror, this movement, which to him represented the highest form of vitality, justice, and morality, was solidly attacked not only by bourgeois forces but also by many socialist forces, as well. This movement, which symbolized to Kazantzakis the inability of the true vision of pure evolutionary morality to compromise with the forces of injustice, and which attempted to crush the evil of bourgeois society, was denounced in his native Greece and throughout much of the world. All the forces and institutions that Kazantzakis most despised rallied their powers and processes to smother the spirit of Marxism. The failure of Kazantzakis' attempt to become a revolutionary activist is signaled by his reaction to this opposition: he turned back to words—speeches (rather ineffectual ones, at that), essays such as the "Apology," newspaper articles, and an attempt to found a socialist periodical—as weapons in the battle. The word was truly action for Kazantzakis, and the word was his only contribution to the struggle. There was nothing else that Kazantzakis could contribute to the battle, for he, like Thoreau, was constitutionally incapable of forceful action. Words were described consistently by Kazantzakis in terms of two interesting and revealing metaphors—as spermatic and as military. Words performed a vital, liberating function for Kazantzakis. By them, through creative literary expression, he freed himself from various agonies and ideas. At one point he says of *Zorba*, in a passage that applies equally well to all his works:

> Mobilizing all my memories, retraveling all my travels, bringing back to mind all the great souls to whom I had lighted candles in my life, dispatching wave after wave of my blood to nourish the seed within me, I waited. I fed this seed with the precious honey I had collected from a lifetime of boring into the most fragrant and venomous of flowers. For the first time I tasted the true meaning of paternal love, and what a fountainhead of eternity a son is. . . . On the basis of this seed, this son, my fate would be determined. (*Report,* 463)

And, regarding the military metaphor, words were in a true sense Kazantzakis' many legions. In *Report* (482) he says: "Under my authority I had nothing but twenty-six lead soldiers, the twenty-six letters of the alphabet."[17] His psychic enrollment of these forces into the battle for negativistic, action-oriented, end-dominated political movements, disregarding the ethics of means, bring up a crucial question for Kazantzakis' thought, that of the implications of political violence.

The Responsibility of Means

The consequences for politics of such a disregard of the ethical and moral aspects of political action are many and far-reaching. The most important implication comes from the act of defining what is politically permissible under one's own subjective conception of the correct goal of mankind. Kazantzakis concluded that, given the imperative need to deliver man from his slavery, the end justified the means. This conclusion and the way in which

Kazantzakis reached it are evident in *Japan-China* (134), written one year after *Spain:* "As in science where a 'hypothesis,' even if it is wrong, causes the discovery of true natural laws, so a 'wrong' religion or political doctrine may give birth to a great civilization."

Though Kazantzakis correctly perceived the need to bring about change, to free the oppressed, and to make the world more just, he failed to see, at this stage of his development, that the political "hypothesis" on which society proceeds is of at least equal importance as the goal it aims for in determining the outcome. The solution to injustice does not lie in the hypothesis of violence as attempted and advocated by the negativists of the world. Neither does the answer lie in standards of absolute eternal laws, or in any assumed right of those who, on the basis of their individual judgments, claim justification to interfere with, and kill if necessary, those who are less perceptive and do not understand "true justice." Abolition of archaic and repressive institutions and making society more just did not justify the wanton slaughter of the Spanish Civil War any more than establishment of a Republican government in France justified the Reign of Terror in the eighteenth century, and any more than establishment of some ephemeral future state justified Stalin's use of terror and liquidation camps in the twentieth century. In his acceptance of the historical inevitability of such events and his eagerness to help speed them along so that a better civilization could more quickly arise, Kazantzakis ignored the need for "limits" in politics.

One of the most eloquent and consistent opponents of this ethic of limitlessness in politics, of absolutist justice, whether preached by governments or individuals, and of the use of political violence, terror, and destruction for the realization of a new, more just order, has been Albert Camus.[18] Like Kazantzakis, Camus addressed himself to the question of social justice on the philosophical level, but he arrived at a radically different conclusion. His most elemental, devastating, and relevant attack on the ethic of murder for the sake of justice was his assertion that "pure and unadulterated virtue is homicidal,"[19] an assertion whose truth was evident in the increasing incidence of violence and murder in the name of morality that had been unleashed in the West by the French Revolution and had been growing worse ever since.

Camus's own philosophy of freedom and revolt was notable for its intriguing view of the inherent limits and values of the two vis-à-vis a resolution of the human predicament. Perhaps the most moving and humanely expressive utterance of Camus on the human predicament and the roles that justice and violence play in it is in one of his "Letters to A German Friend." The contrast of views between Camus and his German friend, who has yielded to despair and surrendered his autonomy in Hitlerian Germany, is crucial for Camus's philosophy in that, to Camus, the fact that "from the same principle we derived quite different codes" summarized the betrayal by his friend of the solidarity, dignity, and courage of man in the face of the realization of the absurd, meaningless character of human existence. This firm elevation of human solidarity, of the value of courage, moderation, and limits in rebellion is applied by Camus to the issue of violent means, as he states his ethics of rebellion. "Does the end justify the means? That is possible. But what will justify the end? To that question, which historical thought leaves pending, rebellion replies: the means."[20]

Camus' writings reflect the most agonizing and soul-searching confrontation of a contemporary humanist with the issue of violence. He sets forth his doctrine of limits with particular reference to political violence. Fred Wilhoite, who has written extensively on Camus's political thought, believes "despite [Camus's] profound attachment to and respect for human life, Camus was not a pacifist."[21] He recognized that to adhere to absolute pacifism was implicitly to sanction the powers, oppressors, and tyrants that may exist at any given time. Camus works out the contrast between that view of violence represented by Kazantzakis and his view in *Les Justes*, a play based upon the Russian revolutionary terrorists of 1905. Stepan, the rabid totalitarian revolutionary, proclaims his absolute freedom and limitlessness of action to those who were morally unable to murder innocent children:

> There are no limits. The truth is that you don't really believe in the revolution. If you believed in it totally and completely, if you were certain that through our sacrifices and our victories we will create a Russia liberated from despotism, a land of freedom which in the

end will cover the whole earth, if you did not doubt that man, liberated from his masters and his prejudices, would then turn toward heaven the visage of a true god, why would the death of two children matter in the least?

Their deaths would matter precisely because ends do not justify any means. They would matter because, as Camus tells us through the young revolutionary poet Kaliayev, though he believes in the revolution:

> life continues to look wonderful to me. I love beauty and happiness. The revolution—certainly! But the revolution for life, to give life a chance. . . . We kill in order to build a world free of killing. We accept our guilt so that the earth may at last be covered with the innocent.[22]

There can be no headlong suspension of judgment about the morality of an act of violence. The demands of the tension that the true rebel lives by and the standard that any such act must not add to the sum total of misery in the world must be observed and fulfilled.

The question that remains for us to answer, sympathizing as we obviously do with Camus's view of violence rather than with Kazantzakis', is this: if one limits, as Camus does, the use of violence as a means to free the oppressed and to better the human condition—which after all was the worthy goal of Kazantzakis— what is one to do in the face of an organized resistance? Wilhoite has addressed himself—at least in an implicit way—to this crucial issue. In his view, Camus saw no justification for men intentionally shattering the "complicity that exists among them by virtue of their sharing a common fate. The simple existence of physical life was in his view unquestionably good; in fact it is the ultimate of human knowledge and experience." Camus's constructive political thought does not represent a program or a doctrine, "but certain values, and above all a spirit of 'measure'—a determination to remain faithful to the limits of human nature. The rebel realized that a quest for total justice inevitably debases men and altogether negates justice."

This does not mean that Camus resigns himself to men's unhappiness, oppression, and injustices. The rebel must, in

Wilhoite's words, seek "a middle way between amoral revolu-
tionism and passively immoral quietism."[23] As a finite being existing within the historical process, man cannot comprehend the
totality, thus he is not justified in coercing his fellows into a
universal mold of behavior and thought. In their failure to realize
this salient point men have committed the grossest of injustices
for the best of intentions. One does not negate the evil in the
world by doing more evil but by exhibiting goodness, courage,
and compassion. One does not render the world better by indulg-
ing in impulsive and headlong, murderous escapades. One does
not lessen the injustice in the world by being unjust, and one does
not lighten the burden of misery that is an essential part of the
human condition by terror tactics. One must not follow the paths of
Camus's German friend who "supposed that in the absence of any
human or divine code the only values were those of the animal
world," or Kazantzakis who, in his moral fervor, exalted in the
dissolution of the hateful institutions of his age: "We can no
longer fit into old virtues and hopes, into old theories and actions.
The wind of devastation is blowing; this is the breath of our God
today. . . . It shouts: 'Prepare yourselves! War!' " (Saviors, 113–
14) Nor is the path of apathy, withdrawal, and "passively immoral
quietism," as Wilhoite aptly phrased it, the proper one for affirming the value of life together, freeing the oppressed, and avoiding
adding to the sum total of injustice in the world. What man must
do, Camus tells us in the concluding passage of The Rebel with
almost unbearable power and beauty:

> At this moment, when each of us must fit an arrow to his bow and
> enter the lists anew, to reconquer within history and in spite of it,
> that which he owns already, the thin yield of his fields, the brief
> love of this earth, at this moment when at last a man is born, it is
> time to forsake our age, and its adolescent furies. The bow bends;
> the wood complains. At the moment of supreme tension, there will
> leap into flight an unswerving arrow, a shaft that is inflexible and
> free.[24]

Fortunately for those who admire Kazantzakis and agree with
Camus, Kazantzakis' mature thought on the means to be used in
bettering the lot of man proved quite different from the position

described so far and, in fact, resembles markedly Camus's position sketched above. (Perhaps this is one reason why Camus remarked, upon receiving the Nobel Prize, that it should have gone to Kazantzakis!)

While it is nearly impossible to identify a certain point in time when an individual's position on any one issue undergoes a transformation, in Kazantzakis' case 1936 to 1938 seem to have been the crucial years during which his earlier amoral, violent, end-oriented approach to political questions gave way to a deeply spiritual, means-oriented approach. This recognition of these years as a watershed of political maturation is touched on by Hadgopoulos who—without fully developing the issue of means and ends in Kazantzakis' thought—describes his changed view. She turns to the *Prometheus Trilogy,* written in 1937–1938, for substantiation. Kazantzakis' Prometheus sought to "destroy a suffering world in order to create a calm world where suffering men could find repose; he had used violent means for a peaceful goal and had failed—as do all such methods which attempt to establish an absolute through totalitarian means." To Hadgopoulos, Prometheus symbolized totalitarianism, which "Kazantzakis comes to reject in the adventures of his Odysseus." Kazantzakis shows with "his Prometheus the idea of terrestrial power (enforced by the mention of the dragon, his symbol of earthly power) as a never-ending fire of violence, the legacy of Prometheus." While the infinitely malleable Prometheus figure symbolized the failure of violent means, Odysseus [*The Odyssey* was completed in 1938] expresses through his adventures, as Hadgopoulos implies, both earlier and later stages of Kazantzakis' thought, with Book XVI—in which the ideal city is destroyed and Odysseus once more resumes his journey—being the fulcrum. The violent excesses that characterized the preceding books no longer appear. Odysseus is imbued with a new spirit of measure, once his city is destroyed and he no longer seeks forcibly to remake the world in a utopian mold. Hadgopoulos continues: "Kazantzakis implies that only the fire of the spirit can lead to true change and that the fire and ax together lead to destruction but not to fruition."[25] This emphasis by Kazantzakis on the forceful power of the fire of the spirit rather than the power of violence becomes a central

theme in his works of the 1940s and 1950s. Thus in the late 1930s
Kazantzakis arrived at the last of his three-staged view—following
Buddhist apoliticism and revolutionary activism—on aiding
mankind in the quest for freedom in which unity and brotherhood as well as individual responsibility become increasingly important concepts in his thought.

Writing to Prevelakis during that period of his life, Kazantzakis
looked back on these developmental stages. First, there was nationalist and Buddhist enthrallment. Next, there was socialism;
"From approximately 1923 to 1933 . . . I was part of the left wing
(never a communist . . . I never caught that *intellectual pox*). The
pale shadow I felt beside me was P. Istrati." After that came the
"third stage—will it be the last? I call it freedom. No shadow. Only
my own . . . I have ceased to identify my soul's fortunes—my
salvation—with the fortunes of this or that idea." He had learned
that "ideas are inferior to a creative soul."[26] Kazantzakis drew
sustenance from the discarded intellectual, religious, and political
husks that he left strewn in his ascendant wake. Bien makes clear
the self-creation of Kazantzakis' journey. Kazantzakis' walk
"through political experience enabled him to meet himself: to
actualize his own personal potentialities for mature, meaningful
idealism; to understand his previous immaturity; . . . to fulfill his
need to transcend the flesh and be free."[27] Kazantzakis walked
through others on the road to himself.

Mature Idealism

The question of means is explored in *The Last Temptation of
Christ.* Judas, the firebrand revolutionary, casts his lot with Jesus
because he believes Jesus has the following and fortitude to lead a
successful revolt against the Romans. Jesus slowly leads Judas to
understand that violent revolution is not the way but that the
spiritual revolution brought about by his sacrifice as God's son will
bring about the desired end of justice: "If the soul within us does
not change, Judas, the world outside us will never change. The
enemy is within, the Romans are within, salvation starts from
within." (p. 347) Therefore, Jesus enlists Judas' aid to ensure the
crucifixion will occur. Other instances in the 1940s support our

theme of change. In the early 1940s Kazantzakis revised *The Saviors of God* and deleted reference to it as a "metacommunist creed." This signaled that his activist, ideological fervor of the mid-1920s, when the work was written, was ended. In the late 1940s upon hearing of Gandhi's murder, Kazantzakis cried out:

> the world has contracted. Four bullets have deeply wounded the worldwide conscience. . . . In such a materialistic, greedy, amoral world as the present one, it was only natural that the hero of nonviolence be killed by violence. . . . The doctrine of peace and love in such a miserable era arouses and organizes hatred, so it seems. The dark forces have been unleashed—the blind Titans— and every noble endeavor increases their fury tenfold.[28]

Still another manifestation of Kazantzakis' increasing allegiance to the moving power of the spirit was his mounting appreciation of St. Francis, of whom he wrote *The Poor Man of God,* and Albert Schweitzer, whom he knew and loved. Linking the two as noble spiritual hero-models of medieval and modern times respectively, Kazantazakis declared that each possessed "the philosopher's stone which transmutes the basest metals into gold, and gold into spirit."[29] Paeans to the spirit also resound throughout both *Report* and "The Immortal Free Spirit of Man." Evident in all these works is Kazantzakis' increasing concern about the responsibility of means. This concern reached its culmination in *The Fratricides,* the last and most political of all Kazantzakis' works, in which is found the most extensive and rewarding examination of spiritual versus violent means and of proper ends.

The Fratricides, a dramatization of the Greek civil war following World War II, centers around two groups in opposition. They are the communist guerrillas, the "red tops," in the hills, and the nationalist troops, the "black tops," of the village of Castello. The captain of the nationalists, and Loukas, assistant to Captain Drakos who leads the rebels, represent—as Stepan represented in Camus' *Les Justes*—the path of violence, hate, and terror. The former, as he slays communist guerrillas, asserts: "The end justifies the means, and our end is the salvation of Greece." (p. 115) The latter, as with equal dedication he kills nationalist troops, argues: "The true communist does not falter when he sees injustice; he accepts it if that injustice helps our cause, everything is for the cause—everything for victory." (p. 235) Captain Drakos, who symbolizes the young Kazantzakis, wavers between Loukas' view and a more humane, compassionate belief. Although leading a fierce band, he experiences doubts concerning their destructive tactics and wonders, "was it possible that this was not the right road." (p. 198) In answering Loukas, who is trying to oust him, partly on account of his doubts, Captain Drakos issues a ringing manifesto to humanity, a declaration reminiscent of Kaliayev's rebuttal of Stepan:

> "That's going to be our downfall!" So the end justifies the means, does it? We should go ahead with injustice to reach justice, eh? We should go on with slavery to reach freedom? I hate to say this, but that attitude is going to destroy the cause. It hasn't been very long since I began to realize that if the means we use to reach our goal are dishonest, our cause becomes dishonest. Because the cause is not a piece of fruit, that hangs ripe and ready at the end of the road for us to pick; no, no, never! The cause is a fruit that ripens with each deed, that takes the dignity or the vulgarity of each of our deeds. The path we take will give the shape and flavor and taste to the fruit, and fill it with either honey or poison. (pp. 235–36)

Drakos, unlike Kaliayev, follows the path of violence for so long that he becomes "poisoned" and when, at the climax of the story, he alone can stop the bloodshed, the fratricidal demon he has nourished within himself screams for blood and the slaughter continues.

Kazantzakis divides characterizations in *The Fratricides* as he did so successfully in *Zorba* in projecting himself partially into all his characters. He presents through the figure of Father Yanaros the divine element in man in opposition to the evil portrayed by the previously mentioned characters. Father Yanaros, who symbolizes the mature Kazantzakis, is the priest of Castello and the natural father of Captain Drakos. His task is to discover God's road to ending the fratricidal horror—whether it be resistance or capitulation on the part of the villagers. Father Yanaros pits the forces of love, brotherhood, and the divine spirit of man against the forces of evil as he turns the village over to the rebels to stop the slaughter. He sees Drakos betray that trust by breaking their agreement and slaughtering several village elders in the name of

freedom and justice. Father Yanaros rails against this—
"Tyranny, force and the whip? So that is how we get freedom?
No, No, I won't accept that." (p. 248) He pays for this opposition
with his life. We must not be misled, however, by Father Yanaros
into believing that ineffectual quietism was Kazantzakis' path.
This is not so, as proven by still another work of the same era, *The
Greek Passion.*

In *The Greek Passion* Kazantzakis pits Greek refugees (the proletariat) against the well-to-do Greeks of the village of Lycovrissi
(the bourgeoisie) and relates how the latter drive away their
dispossessed brethren. Toward the end of the work the refugees,
facing starvation, assault Lycovrissi; they are repulsed, however,
and have to resume their quest for a new community. Thus,
violence has failed to rectify the situation. Like Camus, however,
Kazantzakis does not totally reject violence. The central figure of
the work, Priest Fotis, summarizes Kazantzakis' view in a revealing monologue. "There was a time when I too, used to say: 'Why
struggle for this life here below? What does the world matter to
me? I am an exile from Heaven and I yearn to go home to my
country.' But later I understood." Priest Fotis learned that one
cannot attain heaven unless he has first been victorious on earth,
and one cannot be victorious on earth unless he struggles without
rest against injustice. He discovered that earth is the only
springboard, if man is "to fly up to heaven. All the priest
Grigorises, the Ladases, the Aghas, the big proprietors, are the
forces of evil which it has been allotted us to combat. If we throw
down our arms, we're lost, here below on earth and up there in
the sky." (p. 347) The Greek refugees, under the leadership of
Priest Fotis, exhaust all possible avenues of rectification before
turning to the avenue of violence. With Prometheus, Odysseus,
Jesus, St. Francis, and Father Yanaros, Priest Fotis testifies to
Kazantzakis' abandonment of his youthful end-dominated politics. Theirs are resounding voices lifted in unison on behalf of the
responsibility of means and the moving force of the spirit of man.
The question remaining is: why did Kazantzakis change his position so radically?

There are several reasons for Kazantzakis' turnabout. One is
his gradual return, in the 1940s, to an exploration of Christian

teachings. Another is his insistent concern over the inner man. Also of importance was the widespread devastation of World War II, which Kazantzakis experienced firsthand on Aegina. A more important reason lies in Kazantzakis' twofold realization—perhaps as an outgrowth of the above concerns—of the imperative need for unity and the sobering acceptance of the fact that by acquiescing in that unity in the face of the chaotic nature of the world one necessarily accepts some limits, some measure, on one's egoistic existence. This is evident in Kazantzakis' comments on his friendship with Angelos Sikelianos. Kazantzakis describes Sikelianos as content in the naïve conceit of his superiority as a literatist. Sikelianos does not seek the ascent, the summit, for he believes he has already attained it, and thus need not be concerned with the metaphysical void facing man and history: "I said to him one day, 'The great difference between us, Angelos, is this: you believe you have found salvation, and believing this, you are saved; I believe that salvation does not exist, and believing this, I am saved.' " Believing himself immortal, Sikelianos transformed all questions into egocentric terms, "mine, mine, and me, me was my friend's terrible prison, a dungeon without windows or doors"; therefore, Kazantzakis tries to free his friend by telling him of the highest peak a man can reach, "conquer the self, the ego. When we reach that peak, and only then, Angelos, we shall be saved." This is so because the "Spirit is not called *Me*, it is called *All of us*." (*Report*, 192–96) In this difference of approach by Sikelianos and Kazantzakis lies a crucial distinction between Kazantzakis' changing view of means from the 1920s to the 1940s, a change leading to a more compassionate politics on Kazantzakis' part. Focusing more and more on the unity of mankind, Kazantzakis came to realize that the violence he had sanctioned, inevitable though it might be, irrevocably shattered that unity. Kazantzakis had earlier realized that one must save oneself before he can save others, and with the realization of the imperative need for unity among men came the corollary understanding that "the sole way to save oneself is to save others." (p. 486) But even more important as an explanation of Kazantzakis' political maturation than either his return to Christian themes, or his concern with the inner man, or his emphasis on unity, was his artistic maturation.

With Kazantzakis' reflection on his failure as a political activist came greater self-understanding of his true literary nature. The decade between *Toda Raba* in 1931, which is a novelized account of Kazantzakis' Marxism, and *Zorba* in the early 1940s is one of artistic growth in that Kazantzakis increasingly, though perhaps unwillingly, becomes more and more the artist and less and less the activist. Bien discusses this transition which is, in the main, accomplished by the time of *Zorba*. Kazantzakis accepts his role as artist and much

> subdued now is the hysterical fervor of the early works in which his personal obsessions tended to vitiate the execution and which seemed determined to reform the world then and there. . . . [Zorba] is a crucial fulcrum in Kazantzakis' career since it so openly records his passage from embroilment to serenity: the distanced noninvolvement of the artist, the events and people the book records are Kazantzakis' agonized tightrope-dance between activism and Buddhistic withdrawal.[30]

The immobilizing character of rationality, of adherence to ideas, of compensation for life by intellectual and literary constructs—Thoreau's payment—is a theme brilliantly worked on time and time again by Kazantzakis throughout *Zorba*. The Boss, or Kazantzakis, represents one who has withdrawn into the world of intellectualism, has denied his passions, has become enmeshed by the cumulative socioreligious culture that has been constructed to give purpose to the void, to fill the void. He recognizes this enmeshment as he tries to free himself of "all these phantoms . . . Buddhas, Gods, Motherlands, Ideas. . . . Woe to him who cannot free himself from Buddhas, Gods, Motherlands, and Ideas." He is led to face his surrendered state by Zorba who, uncontaminated by learning and esoteric intellectualism, has instinctively overcome the void and followed the trembling of his passions. Zorba's vibrant, searing personality was, in Poulakidas' view, the antithesis of Kazantzakis'. "In hearing and seeing Zorba's carefree philosophy, characterized by Kierkegaard as the philosophy of the 'existing individual,' Kazantzakis could only laugh at himself and at every intellectual."

The manner in which Kazantzakis expresses and, to some extent, cognitively deals with the problem of the emasculating character of too intense a devotion to a literary life on his part and that of his master, Nietzsche, is dealt with in an intriguing manner by Poulakidas. Zarathustra, who lives isolated from his fellows, "wants to mingle with people. One would dare to say that if Zarathustra would ever act he would be healed of his philosophy, which does not grow out of his experiences and adventures but out of his thought. Zarathustra is primarily a thinker and not a doer." Elaborating on this idea, Poulakidas hypothesizes that had Nietzsche "acted," his pathetic end would have been averted. However, Nietzsche's overman was to be realized only in his work and not in his life. Kazantzakis realized where his great teacher had failed and operated on "Zarathustra, separating his two selves and making both integral, functional, and human in *Zorba the Greek.*" He wed the real George Zorba to Zarathustra's philosophy of the overman, creating Alexis Zorba, who is dynamically aware of life and death. He wed himself to Nietzsche and Zarathustra's inaction, creating the Boss, who lives in his mind and through his words. Zarathustra, Nietzsche, and Kazantzakis dislike intellectual activities that are indulged in at the expense of life, and yet all would agree with the Boss when he tells Zorba: " 'The old goat within me, has still got a lot of paper to chew over.' " They know that "they cannot give themselves fully to life and action."[31]

As Kazantzakis came to a recognition of his literary nature, his work became more sophisticated and more powerful. The "messianic ardor" of which Prevelakis spoke was harnessed to a moving, dramatic, and unquenchable thirst for expression. Thus Colin Wilson could write: "Kazantzakis stands like a colossus, or like a mountain. Everything about him was big. The main difference between Kazantzakis and most of the younger writers is a matter of *will.*" To Wilson, the main defect of most twentieth-century writers lies in their defeatism and despair. Thus, they pale beside this uncouth Greek giant: "But Kazantzakis was not born a giant; he *made himself* into a giant. Again and again he loses confidence, comes to despair, then gradually straightens his shoulders and stretches his arms until his fears roll off his back."[32] It is the colossuslike stature of Kazantzakis, his giant yet compassionate will, his being a "living symbol of man's greatness" in an age of anguish, alienation, despair, and small souls, that makes Kazantzakis' ideas on freedom, unity, and the human condition important for political philosophy.

Significant that this rebellious opposition consciousness [i.e., the counter-culture] should have emerged
most vividly in the arts—and should have largely remained there, giving us our singular tradition of the
artist as outlaw, rebel, lunatic, misfit, rogue. Why
should this be? Perhaps because the burden of alienation weighs most heavily on the creative powers; because the beauties of science are not the beauties of art
but their antithesis. Who recognizes a cage for what it
is? Not canaries of careful Reason who value well-
fortified shelter, but skylarks whose song needs the
space and sunlight beyond the bars. And what does it
tell us about the nature of our religious tradition in the
west that it should be the arts and not the churches that
have produced far and away the greater number of
modern martyrs, persecuted prophets and suffering
saints.

THEODORE ROSZAK

≡║║║

3

Poetry, Prophecy, Political Philosophy

At the end of World War II, Kazantzakis was invited by the
British Council of Letters, an official agency that sends and re-
ceives artistic and intellectual representatives in furthering
British culture, to visit England and survey the intellectual re-

sources of the country. While there he wrote *England,* met the leading minds of the country, and made three addresses over the BBC. One of these addresses, subsequently published in the English periodical *Life And Letters* under the title "The Immortal Free Spirit of Man," included a questionnaire that Kazantzakis directed to writers and men of science, the world over. The title of this chapter is taken from the cumulative picture of Kazantzakis' outlook presented in these questions:

> Therefore, I address this appeal to all intellectuals of good faith throughout the whole world. And I ask the following questions, confident that the answers will facilitate a broad international cooperation of the spirit:
>
> 1. Do you believe we are living at the end of an historical epoch or at the beginning of a new one? And in either case, what do you think are the characteristic traits?
> 2. Can literature, art or theoretical thought influence the present movement of history? Or do they merely mirror existing conditions?
> 3. If you believe that thought and art do influence reality, in what direction do you think they should lead the development of the spirit in your own country?
> 4. What do you think is the positive contribution that British thought and art can offer the world?
> 5. What is the level of contact between the British intellectuals and the large mass of the people? And what could be done to broaden this basis of contact?
> 6. What is the foremost duty of the intellectual and the artist today? How can they contribute to the peaceful cooperation of all peoples?
> 7. Would it be practical to establish an "International of the Spirit"? And if it is practical, are you willing to collaborate in it?[1]

As with so many of Kazantzakis' attempts at political organization, his proposal for an International of the Spirit met with little response. In many ways, however, Kazantzakis' political thought revolves around the manner in which he himself answered these basic questions.

Transitional Age: A Philosophy of History

Kazantzakis placed much importance on one's being born in an "interesting epoch." For many reasons he believed the era of his lifetime to be such an epoch—a crucial age of historical transition. His political philosophy, his literary activity, and his personal odyssey were all deeply influenced by this belief. Kazantzakis brought his sense of historical transition to bear on the problems of his age and deciphered "the painful, inexorable meaning of our time: that we are faced with the end of a civilization and the symptoms that always manifest themselves in times of decadence." (*T.R.*, 116) This view is consistently stated with little variation throughout his works in, among others, *The Saviors of God* (1925), *Toda Raba* (1931), *The Odyssey* (1938) "The Immortal Free Spirit of Man" (1946), and *Report* (1956). There are several intellectual sources of Kazantzakis' philosophy of history and many perceived causes and symptoms of the end of civilization.

Many thinkers contributed to Kazantzakis' concept of the transitional age. Nietzsche reinforced Kazantzakis' instinctual epochal inclinations with his depiction of the death of God and the intermediate age of nihilism. Bergson contributed the idea of dynamic evolution, an idea that implied the existence of crucial developmental stages in world consciousness. Buddha taught that life existed between twin abysses of nothingness and, by inference, that man's history also existed as luminous intervals between nonexistence. In addition, two thinkers with whom Kazantzakis first came into contact in Berlin in 1922 to 1924 presented crucial elaborations of the idea of epochal historical moments. They were Marx and Spengler.

The social revolutionaries Itka, Rahel, Leah, and Dina, with whom Kazantzakis became involved in Berlin, impressed upon him the vigor and dynamism of Marxism. Such vitality proffered a stark alternative to the Buddhist escapism toward which he was then inclined.[2] It was through Marx that Kazantzakis was introduced to Hegel and Feuerbach; for as one commentator on Marxian thought has said, Marxism might perhaps be epitomized as "Hegelianism mediated by Feuerbach's critique of Hegel."[3]

Marx pursued his early studies during a time of nearly com-

plete Hegelian domination of German thought; and if one of
Marx's era was not of Hegelian persuasion, he was at the very least
obliged to focus and formulate his ideas around the arguments of
the Hegelians of the day. Hegel's elevation of man's consciousness, his emphasis on the progressivistic movement of the world
spirit, and his ideas of the transformation of the world were vivid
and controversial. Hegel was radically idealistic, and the extent to
which he rejected the material world is evidenced by his identify-
ing alienation with man's consciousness of his involvement with
the world. One of Hegel's philosophical successors, Ludwig
Feuerbach, reversed the idealism-materialism, other-world versus real-world dichotomies established by Hegel and emphasized
the material, external, natural world in which man lived as the
only proper, truly meaningful locus of man's actions. In a similar
vein, Feuerbach's anthropocentric philosophy of humanism
turned attention away from speculations on an Absolute Spirit,
God, or Omniscient Reason, which dictates and determines
through history the course of mankind. Marx followed Feuerbach's lead in placing man in the world, in turning Hegel on his
head. Yet the comprehensiveness inherent in the Hegelian system and the eschatological bent were both adopted by Marx in the
formulation of his philosophical system. Using Hegel's dialectic
and Feuerbach's materialism, he constructed a revolutionary philosophy of history according to which man creates a new world of
humanism. "The world of phenomena having been shown to be a
world of human alienation, the revolutionary imperative took
shape as a call to end human alienation by changing the world."[4]
From this vantage point Marx made a critique of the historical
predicament that Raymond Aron has called "an analysis and an
interpretation of capitalistic society in terms of its current func-
tioning, its present structure, and its necessary evolution."[5]

Marx based his critique, his revolutionary philosophy, and his
dialectical materialism on the role that labor plays in men's lives:
"the productive life is the life of the species. It is life engendering
life." Using these component elements of his system both as
analytical devices for the past and predictive tools for the future,
Marx issued a grand historical theory that held that class relations
and the religious, legal, philosophical, political, social, ideological

concepts of the "superstructure" are based on the productive forces of the "substructure" in society. Thus man's history moves in accordance with developments in the productive forces always toward a higher integration or synthesis of freedom, with occasional lapses or zig-zags of history, and with apocalyptic epochs of qualitative changes occurring periodically until the final realization of the City of God on earth—the communist society.

> Communism is the positive transcendence of private property, of human self estrangement, and therefore is the real appropriation of the human essence by and for man; communism therefore is the complete return of man to himself as a social (i.e., human) being—a return become conscious, and accomplished within the entire wealth of previous development. This communism, as fully-developed naturalism, equals humanism, and as fully-developed humanism equals naturalism; it is the genuine resolution of the conflict between man and nature and between man and man—the true resolution of the strife between existence and necessity, between the individual and the species. Communism is the riddle of history solved, and it knows itself to be this solution.[6]

Marx' ambitious solution of the "riddle of history" aroused great emotional empathy in the compassionate Kazantzakis in the midst of the squalor and chaos of post-World War I Berlin. He wrote his first wife, Galetea, of the widespread misery, of seeing young children and old people naked and starving: "What misery, my God, and how long will it last? . . . It would be better for the earth to vanish. To have the firmament purged from the infamy of contemporary life."[7] This dramatic combination of intense, dehumanizing poverty and Marx's apocalyptic vision deeply influenced Kazantzakis' view of history.

Oswald Spengler's equally apocalyptic vision to solve the "riddle of history" was the other primary source of Kazantzakis' philosophy of history. The doctrine of the mortality of civilizations was one of the major intellectual developments of Europe in the postwar years. Prevelakis documents how Kazantzakis was repeatedly confronted with this doctrine. He encountered it first in Germany "during the tragic years of inflation and hunger, and he accepted it intellectually with the aid of Spengler, whose *The Decline of the West* (in the German edition of 1923) was one of the books he brought back on his return home"; second, in French thought, "in, for instance such illuminating works as Paul Valery's *Prologue to the Persian Letter* (1926), *Glances at the World Today* (1931), and other *essais quasi politiques*"; and, third in Greece "in a good many of Cavafi's poems, in certain writings of Petros Vlastos and, later on, in the tragedies of Sikelianos and other younger writers."[8]

Spengler surveyed the destruction and chaos rampant in Europe (particularly in his native Germany) in the war years and, drawing upon a mass of data (much of it of questionable value), argued that the crashing wave of European culture was receding. In his view cultures are comparable to living organisms; they are born and cultivated in a particular era, they pass through various stages of aging, and they die, at which time another "organic" culture is born. A culture grows up in a place that is susceptible to precise definition and to "which it remains as faithful as a plant. A culture perishes when the soul has realized all its possibilities, molding peoples, languages, religious systems, arts, states, sciences; it returns then to its primordial psychic state."[9] As one analyst observed, it was Spengler's belief that the era of "individualism, humanitarianism, intellectual freedom, skepticism" was ending, to be replaced by an era of "restrictions on individual freedom . . . a revival of faith . . . and an increase in the use of force."[10]

This cyclical theory, once held in ancient Greece, was not unique to Spengler; it was espoused by many of the leading thinkers of the age. The Enlightenment teaching of the linear progressive betterment of man's lot in history was widely discredited in many schools of thought by the intensity of destruction of World War I. This, combined with nostalgia for a simpler age, an increasing awareness of the values of alien cultures accruing from comparative anthropology, and a reaction against scientific rationalism, made for an intellectual climate favorable to Spengler's theory.

His work received much attention and was the first of "a series of novel and unclassifiable writings that have seemed to mark the end of a cultural epoch."[11] Kazantzakis was one of those who acclaimed Spengler, and many years later he echoed the German historian: "Whatever spirit this world once possessed was expended in creating a brilliant civilization—ideas, religions, arts and crafts, sciences, deeds. Now this world has vented its strength.[12] (*Report*, 420) The sources of Kazantzakis' theory of the transitional age were then: (1) his innate mystical leanings; (2) those decisive intellectual, personal, and religious steps that he found so important; (3) apocalyptic, eschatological Marxism; (4) and apocalyptic, cyclical Spenglerism. Kazantzakis resolved in practical fashion the contradiction between the last two most important sources—that conflict being Marx's linear view and Spengler's cyclical view—by seeing the communists as only temporary, although important, victors in history. With these sources in mind, Kazantzakis perceived several causes and symptoms as manifesting the death of civilization.

The causes of the historical predicament to Kazantzakis are multifold, with the disparity between mankind's mind and soul being one of the primary causes. The paucity of the moral resources of mankind was evidenced by Hitlerian genocide, with six million Jews dead in gas chambers; by American bombing of Hiroshima and Nagasaki, with untold dead; and by similar brutalizing and dehumanizing degradations to which man had stooped in his savage battle for domination. In 1946 Kazantzakis stated in an essay his belief that the chief danger in the world was that the contemporary mind had outstripped man's spiritual development, creating a critical imbalance. "Mind has conquered the cosmic forces and placed them at the disposal of man, who has not yet attained that moral maturity to use them for the service of the world's peace and prosperity."[13]

In "The Immortal Free Spirit of Man" Kazantzakis is concerned with the reconstruction and overcoming of the forces that threaten civilization. He describes a gap, an abyss, that must be transcended by civilization lest its life be extinguished. Believing that behind every economic, religious, and political movement there lies a great moral passion, Kazantzakis argues that civilization must of necessity be based on both intellectual and moral maturity or else it will succumb to the inner barbarians. The reverse occurred in the Middle Ages, according to Kazantzakis, when the Eastern societies, whose moral development had outdis-

tanced their intellectual development, succumbed to barbarian
invasions. A related cause of the world crises was, for Kazantzakis,
the oppression of spiritual values by materialistic values. Hadgopoulos discusses Kazantzakis' symbolic treatment of this theme
in terms of his contrasting imagery of Helen, who epitomizes
spirit, and Eros, who epitomizes matter. Helen's role in
Kazantzakis' world view is

> that of insatiability, both in creation and in destruction; she is the
> bewitching force that leads mankind's spirit to struggle. Her coun-
> terpart, her opposite is Eros, that impetus which becomes en-
> chanted as soon as it casts its glance on matter and then longs to
> impress its features upon it.[14]

Beautiful Helen, the guiding concept or ideal of spiritual ascen-
dence, is mired, in Kazantzakis' eyes, in the chaos of the materialistic West; "Materialistic explanations, which are solid as far as
they go, are used to integrate all human experience, although
they are utterly limited in scope." (*T.R.*, 116) Such an ethos fails to
address itself to the higher needs of civilization and fails to fulfill
the nobler aspirations of the human soul, for a "civilization can
rest only on spiritual foundations."[15] Orthodox communism's
materialistic orientation plays a major role in Kazantzakis' eventual disillusionment with the Soviet experience.

A further cause of the world's malaise derives from
Kazantzakis' concept of God as the Invisible ever-perfecting
Good moving always toward greater realization. Kazantzakis argues, in the terms of his blend of Marx and Spengler, that the
mystical life force, the Invisible, no longer resides, as it once did,
with the bourgeois but rests with a vital new group, "the working
class: workers, farmers, people productive in the spirit." He tells
his fellows:

> We are confronting a spectacle, the likes of which can be observed
> at the end of every civilization. A single class—in the very begin-
> ning, it was the priests and the magicians, then the kings, then the
> feudal lords, then the bourgeois—assumes power, after shattering
> the preceding class. Then, after a time, when it too has passed all
> the phases of the high point and the decline, another class comes
> (fated to follow the same curve) and takes its place. Such is the
> undulating pattern of history.[16]

But, in the face of conclusive historical evidence, the bourgeosie resist, attempting to preserve their power. Their world is crumbling because on an empirical basis its predatory individualism, inequities of wealth, organized violence and injustice, etc., no longer suffice for the social entity, and because on a normative basis there is no unifying Idea or Passion to lead men, for the Idea has passed at this historical juncture to the working class. Counseling civilization that when the old laws or molds of life no longer ennoble men's souls man must create new ones, new forms, Kazantzakis adds to his teachings of love of liberty and scorn of mortality a Nietzschean cry: smash "even the most sacrosanct of the old molds when they are unable to contain you any longer." (*Report*, 440) Kazantzakis here takes a Marxist line, yet he is ultimately saved from dogmatic fanaticism by his very consistency in adhering to his system; for to him the undulating rhythm of history, the movement of the Invisible, never ceases, that is, the world dialectic does not stop with communism.[17]

Although the disparity of mind and soul, widespread materialism, and class confrontation are significant causes of the crises of civilization, there is, in Kazantzakis' view, a more pervasive and important cause. This is the nihilism arising from the fact that the "ancient myths are dead!"[18] Mankind's agony in confronting the scientific evidence of the paucity of the Judeo-Christian worldview gives rise to nihilism.

> In general our age still clings to a leftover ethical system based on the Christian conception of an ordered, benign, providential universe. . . . This condition in which men apprehend the antinomy between ideas and reality is a sickness, indeed the sickness of our age, the *mal de siecle*. It was perceived by Nietzsche even before it had advanced to its present critical state, and is the background to both the negative and positive aspects of his thought. The name of this sickness is nihilism.[19]

The sickness of despair arising from the clash between the increasing impetus of scientism and the accelerating loss of faith gives rise, in Kazantzakis' view, to important historical-political consequences.

Although he never systematically developed this penetrating insight regarding the significance of hope to the Western world,

Kazantzakis hit upon one of the central themes underlying contemporary civilization and thought. This is so because hope in the modern world has been formulated and channeled primarily in the terms, symbols, and miranda of the Western Judeo-Christian God-culture. Through its teachings of grace, salvation, and a perfect order, the Christian myth has influenced in elemental fashion men's capacity for hope or despair. These posited ends or goals of individual human earthly existence are to be realized in the Heavenly City of God and with the Second Coming, whereby the reign of goodness, justice, and love will be established on earth, only—according to Christian teaching—after a progressive betterment morally, socially, and in all other ways, of humanity in history. It is with this introduction into the consciousness of humanity's life history of the notion of an eschatological linear movement with an apocalyptic end/goal to be faithfully believed in and adhered to that Christianity kindled the embers of hope in men's breasts. But, as has become increasingly evident in the contemporary world of the unbelievers, there is inherent in the combining of Christianity's ethical moral teachings with a linear view of history dangerous implications for politics. These arise from the potential consequences of two possibilities. What if one—e.g., Marx—were to kill the ancient myth and yet retain the Judeo-Christian eschatological and optimistic historic sense, then would the new god-man be led to attempt to bring about, with all the absolute freedom and powers at his disposal in a godless world, his own version of absolute justice, order, and morality? Or, what if one—e.g., Nietzsche—were to deny the Judeo-Christian myth with its hypothesis of the progressive betterment of the human situation, then would he, in the despair and nihilism engendered by the meaninglessness of his predicament, vent his frustration, frenzy, and rage in destruction, terror, and nihilistic murder?

From these observations one discovers that in the despair and hopelessness experienced by mankind when it awoke to the death of the "acient myth" lies immense destructive potential. Man can surrender to the oppressiveness of the historical predicament and, in paranoia and futility, turn to nihilistic destruction. Man can surrender to the oppressiveness of the historical predicament

and, in weakness and need, turn to various religions of history for
succor and authority. Or mankind can persevere in the face of
meaninglessness, can wrench hope from hopelessness, can create
meaning in the world. Man can either betray or bear, in Dietrich
Bonhoeffer's phrase, the "cost of discipleship." That is, he can bear
the cross of death with dignity, faith, and an acceptance of the
unity which this cross confers on man with men. Or, he can
succumb to those who, like Hitler, betray that course. This cross
of death, Kazantzakis' abyss, can be not the end but the beginning.
The Anti-Christ, recognizing this, "fights the cross with political
and social ideology."[20] The disciples reject this, look firmly at the
void, accept as Christ did the burden of the Cross, and gloriously
fulfill their self by resolutely entering the fray for mankind. They
cultivate the creative energy of freedom and emphasize with
Kazantzakis that

> it is our duty to stare at the abyss . . . with dignity and faith. To be
> sure the present moment and the one immediately ahead are
> horrifying and will become increasingly so . . . But the moment
> further on in the distance will be utterly brilliant. I'm certain that
> the human species has not yet revealed all its rich potentialities.
> The belly of the earth is still full of eggs.[21]

Further, the "anguish which at present grips every man worthy of
the name is lined with a great hope, more precisely, with a great
assurance: Evil always ends up by succumbing to the slow but sure
omnipotence of the Good."[22]

Kazantzakis' perception that the "present moment and the one
immediately ahead are horrifying and will become increasingly
so" is borne out by recent events. We have failed, in the present
age, to uphold the dignity and spiritual duty of man. We have
witnessed the idiocies of nations in a "cold war"; we have lived
with the constant knowledge and consequent fear that man may
at any time succumb to his fratricidal urgings and blow the world
to nothingness; have endured and contributed to the unbeliev-
able horrors and inhumanities carried out by the world's most
powerful nation (the United States) against a gentler people of
another culture (Vietnam)—and consequently we find
Kazantzakis' wrenching and exhaustively hopeful cry for

strength, courage, and perseverance an increasingly difficult burden to bear. For those who have suffered the violence of bigotry, the totalitarianism of technology and bureaucracy, the curious and deadly logic of the politics of fear, ideology, and emotionalism perpetrated on a worldwide scale in the name of progress, commerce, and civilization, Kazantzakis' theory of a transitional age of history characterized by despair seems all too plausible. The sufferers wonder, with Kazantzakis, not only how long such a civilization can or will endure but even whether in fact it *should* endure! So many faiths, hopes, and value-systems of the past century having failed, to what does mankind look for solace and inspiration? If in the West, the answer to Kazantzakis' critique is distressing; and if alienation, isolation, futility, and frustration permeate and circumscribe the day-to-day existence of Western man, where does the source of resolution of this bleak historical predicament lie? The major vehicle to which twentieth-century man has, in Kazantzakis' view, attached his hopes for deliverance has been "science."

Science As Deliverance

Through a thorough critique of science as an avenue of deliverance from the historical predicament, Kazantzakis arrived at a position quite at odds with the mainstream of Western thought. He finds that the uses to which science has been put, and the reasoning behind such utilization, may spell doom for mankind rather than deliverance. The central purpose of Kazantzakis' examination is to set forth an explication of the results that have accrued from the technological-scientific ethos. Once these results have been defined, they are then explored in terms of their causes and their import.

According to Kazantzakis the principal results of the adulation of science and technology have been: (1) excesses in fulfilling the basic "outer," material needs, leading to a situation in which these needs are all-determinant and in which there is a consequent deadening of the creative desires of man and a lack of aspirational challenges; (2) a failure of the morally indifferent scientific ethos, which destroyed much of the historically viable authority of the

Christian myth, to supply a new normative myth-ideal; (3) a rise to the fore, in this anormative vacuum, of temporal leaders— politicians, technicians, economists, etc.—while spiritual, artistic, and intellectal leaders go unheeded; (4) the failure of scientific rationalism to lend adequate support to creation of the good life of the polis; (5) the rise of a new barbarism as a result of the cumulative failures of technicism and scientism.

Kazantzakis' was a forceful voice raised in defense of man against the often inhumane forms that scientific "progress" was taking throughout the world. His attack on this front was two-fold. He leveled his criticisms at the artificial needs that were created by an increasingly scientific-technological-industrial cul-ture and that led man from the realization of his higher, spiritual potentialities by diverting his attention from the real values of life; and he condemned the dehumanizing manner in which scientific and technological innovations were utilized to produce these material "needs."

At first glance one is tempted to reject Kazantzakis' criticisms, for on the superficial level they seem merely atavistic and there-fore, to a large extent, useless. His interest in and love of nature and his periodic asceticism coupled with his obvious primitivism have led to this misinterpretation of Kazantzakis. Upon closer scrutiny, however, one discerns that Kazantzakis was not con-demning scientific-industrial progress per se, for he acknowl-edged that "to turn backward is utopian";[23] rather, he was attacking what he saw as a perversion of civilization and an ever-increasing submersion of the individual to technological forces. As is evident from the briefest survey of Kazantzakis' writings, he condemned many of the modes of production of technological society, but not from the position that they were inherently threatening to man. What Kazantzakis railed against as he toured the English cities in the mid-1940s was that the "machines had triumphed. . . . In his enthusiasm over his possession of his new iron slaves, the man of the nineteenth century, kindled by irra-tional hopes and naive optimism, had rushed headlong to con-quer matter." (*England*, 93) This was the wrong, the perversion that had deluded man into scientific technological enslavement. Kazantzakis did not repudiate the possible advantages, though so dearly bought, which the scientific mind of mankind offers. Indeed, he believed that civilization begins only when those outer, materialistic needs of man are provided and there is occasion for leisure, art, music, sport—all the elements of culture. Kazantzakis turns to the archetype of the scientific man, Prometheus, to explain this belief. Prometheus, after teaching man how to order phenomena and conquer the material world, is asked to teach men music and answers:

> Holy moment that I have desired for years! Now
> my complete work is crowned. . . . Till now, bent
> over with effort, I taught you the tools of peace or
> war—how to save the pale body from the wild beasts:
> the frost and the sickness. We couldn't spare the
> space of a breath to play on the grass. Yoked all
> day to wild necessity, we hadn't time, careless,
> to raise our hearts and eyes on high. We must live!
> We must live! God surrounded us to devour us! But
> now, you blessed brave heart of laboring mankind,
> we have passed beyond necessity and breathed the
> free air of beauty. . . . We have left from the
> animal, a new light-bathed path stretches before us
> to carry us from the animal to humanity.[24]

Merely attaining the plateau of opportunity for culture is not enough however. The crucial issue is the goal to which the leisure time is spent.

Along with the cultural liberation of freedom from want promised by rational scientism, we have found that, in Kazantzakis' view, rather than merely meeting materialistic needs we have created an immoral materialistic culture that leads man to the submission of the spirit to the flesh. This is what Kazantzakis means by his curious elaboration on a quotation from Henry Miller concerning poverty in Greece: "Poverty, when it is not excessive and does not reach the point of hunger and misery, is really well suited to any people or any individual averse to weighing the spirit down with the flesh."[25] The satiation of man in advanced technological society has given rise to a situation in which man no longer struggles to release the divine element of his being—that spiritual nobility which to Kazantzakis is the Cry of

God and man's evolution within each man. He has succumbed under the paternalism of the scientific-technological society to the stagnation of the status quo. Kazantzakis describes this deadening of the inner struggle from England: "our own spirits are far more insatiable, far closer to the abyss than the English. Here one finds a great weariness and much control—control that is not the outcome of some great force controlling itself but of weakness that is easily controllable."[26]

A strikingly similar although more empirical analysis of this point that may illuminate the discussion is found in the thought of an even more fervid critic of the scientific-technological society, Herbert Marcuse. Viewing the development of modern technological society, Marcuse argues that it has given birth to "one-dimensional man"—as seen in the laborer who has been emasculated by the "good life" and has abdicated his revolutionary role. He has fallen victim to the policy of "containment," as Marcuse puts it, because the techniques of oppression developed by advanced technological society—which is founded on highly administered economies that must of necessity operate at high levels of production and hence of affluence—are so subtle as to harness and channel the creative energies of the laborer "into the handling of goods and services which satisfy the individual, while rendering him incapable of achieving an existence of his own, unable to grasp the possibilities which are repelled by his satisfaction." For Marcuse, as for many others, the Western dream has become a technological nightmare. Human dignity is affronted, real needs go unfulfilled, and the determining quality of life is organized necessity. Under such conditions a repressive framework functions as efficiently as the technology from which it arose. The repression is two-fold. Externally, the vested interests and the manner of production, however subtly, repress the ordinary man. Internally, individuals, their so-called "needs" having been satisfied, willingly submit to their one-dimensional existence. They think, live, and act only in terms of the diffused life in which they are placed: "The inner dimensions of the mind in which opposition to the status quo can take root is whittled down."[27] It is precisely to this concern with the "inner dimension of the mind" that Kazantzakis addressed himself at the end of

World War II. Calling for a revitalization and regeneration of man Kazantzakis counseled, "make no mistake about it . . . the only true, solid reconstruction is man's inner rehabilitation."[28]

The failure of science to effect the inner rehabilitation of man results primarily from its inability to provide a normative goal for man. Kazantzakis implies that science functions primarily in a negative manner, that is, it disproves many assumptions of the Judeo-Christian value system. However, all scientific attempts to formulate a viable replacement for the Judeo-Christian system have failed because science can never answer the "why" of things. Darwinism, which was proffered as an answer to the enduring questions, in fact blocked all chance of hope by demonstrating not the cause or end of evolution but only the manner or mechanism. Kazantzakis realized that many new value-systems had been attempted in order to fill the void left by science's killing of God— Comte's elaborate scheme, the adulation of reason, the socialist utopias, and Marxism, among others. As these endeavors failed, revealing the ethical bankruptcy of science, thinkers like Bergson forced the scientific advocates to admit that they could not and cannot answer the eternal questions.[29]

At this point Kazantzakis aims a blazing critique at the West's adoption and constant advocacy of the method of scientific rationalism as a means to the resolution of sociopolitical problems. Scientific rationalism, beginning in the fifteenth and sixteenth centuries and reaching its peaks in the philosophy of Descartes and Spinoza in the seventeenth century and its utilization as a directing principle in the French Age of Reason in the eighteenth century, has had many profound effects on Western life. Western democracy's embodiment of that scientific outlook—evident in all aspects of life—with its inherent progressivistic hopefulness, led to formulation of a pragmatic sociopolitical worldview that in itself, and even more so in its reverberations in other areas of twentieth-century life, neglected the potentiality for despair that existed within its optimistic premises. Leading exponents such as John Dewey in the United States would contend, and other scientific sociopolitical philosophers would certainly agree, that the

problem under discussion is precisely how conflicting claims are to be settled in the interests of the widest possible contribution to the interests of all—or at least of the great majority.

To Dewey, the democratic method, i.e., organized intelligence, exposes these conflicts "where their special claims can be seen and appraised, where they can be discussed and judged in light of more inclusive interests than are represented by either of them separately."[30] What Dewey and his colleagues failed to do, however, in their progressivistic faith, was to recognize and take concrete steps against the grave implications for political life of the exclusion from the mediative process of significant ideals, creative aspirations, needs, and myth. In a dialogue with Unamuno, the great Spanish literary giant, Kazantizakis contends that

> today the dialectical mind [by which Kazantzakis meant the scientific, analytical mind, as opposed to the artistic] has gone too far and is no longer helpful for life. We no longer believe in myth and for that reason our life is barren. I think the time has come for the dialectical mind to fall into a deep sleep—to sleep so that the deep creative powers of man can awaken. (*Spain,* 176)

By stripping away the masks of traditionalism in politics, custom in culture, and Christianity's authority in religion, science revealed the chaotic reality that lay behind man's artificial and superficial attempts at creating order. Priest Fotis in *The Greek Passion* (266) says the "world is a mystery. . . . The motions of God's will seem complicated to man's narrow brain." Kazantzakis believed that it would take something in addition to the scientific brain to discern the true face of God's will (i.e., reality) in the world and thus recreate a viable order.

In the anormative vacuum in which we live, and which lacks guiding myths, beliefs, or ideals, temporal leaders such as politicians, technicians, economists, and others who deal in matter and fact rather than in spirit and value have become, in Kazantzakis's view, all-powerful. They have at their disposal the tremendous powers of modern science, yet they do not have the compassionate moral sensibility needed to use these powers for the benefit of mankind. The beast in man dominates as exemplified by such

developments as the Americans' discovery of a poison so potent
that "with 9 grams of it they can in one fell swoop kill all of the
inhabitants of the United States and Canada (i.e., Russia). The
gorilla, you see, without taking the time to become a human
being, has discovered fire and is going to burn the world."[31]
A central element in the rise to power of the temporal technicians is the intellectuals' abandonment of a critical perspective
and their turning away from a theoretical outlook: "theoretical
thought has gone bankrupt and has turned into a tool applied for
destructive purposes, or an aimless, foolish toy in the hands of a
magician." (England, 8) Kazantzakis has unerringly proceeded to
what is increasingly recognized as perhaps the most crucial issue
facing modern civilization. Of others who have explored this rise
to the fore of technical, means-dominated thought, few has done
so more perceptively than Paul Tillich.[32]
In his analysis of this issue, Tillich finds a vital distinction
between metaphysical and ontological reasoning to be the source
of the problem. In Tillich's view, metaphysics concerns itself only
with method and stresses form or intelligible structure. It is an
analysis or critique of intelligible structure rather than an experiencing of being. He sees modern scholastic metaphysics as less
perceptive than ontology and more argumentative, for it is technical reason, not ontological reason. Technical reasoning is not
perception of being but ratiocinative process concerned only with
discovering means for ends. (By contrast, ontological reason deals
with the ends themselves, being-goodness-unity, and goes directly to these primary ends and principles themselves.) Technical reason is reasoning about objects rather than understanding
and perceiving them. Ontology is the foundation of metaphysics
because it concerns content, whereas metaphysics concerns
method. This experiential approach to the study of being dominated philosophy from the time of Parmenides to that of Hegel.
Ontological understanding is the faculty for apprehending actual
existence—to know is to be. In Tillich's view, there is an insepara-
ble connection of mind and being, for the very structure of the
mind enables it to transform being. Ontological understanding is
useful both practically and aesthetically. It is an intellectual force
uniting mind and emotion as the highest form of rationality. God

is being itself and, in Tillich's assessment, is contacted only by
ontological reason; therefore without it we are cut off from life.
Intellect is thus the power for knowing being or what is.

Ideally, ontological and technical reason go hand in hand, and
when they are so combined, reasoning is used to fulfill the needs
of reason. If they are separated, however, the results are disas-
trous. Tillich believes that, since the mid-nineteenth century,
technical reason has been severed from ontological reason
through the development of positivism. The result is the devising
of ends by nonrationalistic forces serving power-domination
rather than insight-enlightenment. Examples of this are the
military-industrial establishment (in which technology undeniably rules), our loss of control over norms and ends and the
chaotic condition of our priorities, the dehumanization of life
accruing from positivists' refusal to heed and understand any-
thing that is not available through human reason, the modern
attempt to control nature rather than know it—in sum, the technocratic way of life: exploitation, control, management—the very
apotheosis of technical reason whereby we know not merely to
know but in order to exploit.[33] In such a civilization, controlled by
technological irrationality, "to discern spirit is considered a mor-
tal sin. . . . The free-thinking man cannot even attempt synthesis." (*England*, 7)

The import of the above deficiencies of the scientific ethos is
that the good life of the polis cannot be built solely on the basis of
scientific knowledge. This is powerfully depicted by Kazantzakis
in Books XV and XVI of *The Odyssey*—Kazantzakis' imaginative
reflection on his disillusionment with the scientific socialism of
Marxism-Leninism—in which Ulysses constructs his ideal city
only to see it destroyed. Ulysses based his city on the scientific
necessity of nature, and Marxism-Leninism was based on the
scientific necessity of history; the former perished, and the latter
was perverted. Ulysses' utopia is built, with elements from Plato
and More, on a firm foundation of barbaric coherence with blind
natural necessity symbolized by a wild pear tree:

"Fellows, at noon today, on my God's rocks, I saw
a tough and twisted pear tree blossoming in the sun;

its leaves and flowers shook, then sang with human voice:
'How long shall I deign to guide you, fool? No matter how
you boast, disdainful man, or strive to shake your yoke,
you'll still plod, shackled, round and round man's threshing floor.
Accept your fate with no false shame, and you'll surpass her!
What else did you expect from the rank herd of man?
Their hearts are airskins, their brains mud, their loins manure,
but yet I love them and I like the stench of earth;
I know well how the spirit blooms, how God is shaped,
what filth my black roots browse on in the darkest gloom.
See how I milk the rock, suck up manure, and turn
all into flowers with patience, with despair, with love,
and now I stand firm in your path, a blossomed pear;
behold me, take me for your model, start your work!' " (Book XV,
  460, lines 375–90)

However, the underlying theme of Social Darwinism, which led
Ulysses to the drawing of organic analogies and a belief in brutal
evolutionary survival, proved insufficient for the governance of
the city. Therefore, Ulysses, after first heeding the teachings of
the model of nature—

Whatever blind Worm-Mother Earth does with no brains
we should accept as just, with our whole mind, wide-eyed (465, lines
  600–01)—

rejects it when the city is destroyed by natural calamity. Ulysses
rages against destructive necessity, with its belittling implications
for man's stature and potentiality;

"Never shall I forgive and bend down to that vain,
that senseless dark which blots the holy light of man!"
Then he thrashed out with rage against his ruthless god:
"You fool, how in your greatest need can you abandon
most glorious man who lives and fights to give you shape?
You fill our hearts with cries and vehement desires,
then sink your ears in silence and refuse to listen;
but man's soul will fight on, you coward, without your help!"
His heart leapt high, spurned Death, and in the black air cut
a thousand roads to fly through on a thousand wings,
then, screeching like a hawk, strove to unwind what fate had
  woven. (484–85, lines 1450–60)

Ulysses came to realize that the polis must be built on something more than scientific emulation of organic nature. Kazantzakis implies that in a similar manner Marxism-Leninism suffered its perversion because of blind adherence to its scientific historical-materialistic aspirations. Just as Ulysses' dogmatic following of empirical nature left no room for individual initiative, so does Marxism, a professed humanistic theory, overlook the individual as a viable participant in achieving his own redemption. While not wholly deterministic, Marx's system is so geared that human initiative as a decisive factor is not given much credence. Redemption is seen as coming in scientific fashion when the economic forces bring it about, and when that happens humans will become human and not before. In practice this denial of human capability opened the door to the most oppressive applications of Marxist ideology.

In his denial of individual participation, Marx opened the way for Lenin and Stalin to deny that the individual was capable of contributing productively to bringing about the socialist society. The communist party, under Stalin, justified its existence and hegemony by the argument from scientific socialism that the forces of production and the consequent factors of class structure were not at a sufficiently advanced level to birth the true socialist society—the classless society. This was a perversion of Marx's thought, but a logical one. Marx's denial of human accomplishments and his view of humans as tools of history opened the door to Stalin's similar denials of human rights and his similar use of humans as mere tools. Marxist doctrine teaches that what is inevitably fixed may yet be unveiled and people will be assigned their functions. Those later Marxists of totalitarian leanings emerged, through their claims as possessors of the only scientifically valid doctrine, as the unveilers of the new order. They and they alone were fit to guide society along the right path to socialism, and they tolerated no deviations. In fulfilling their role they assumed responsibility for assigning all individuals to their proper functions in the transitory stage. This resulted in oppression and injustice, all in the name of some future utopia. Kazantzakis, though intensely involved with Leninism during the 1920s and momentarily unalarmed by Mussolini's fascism, correctly characterized both Lenin's and Mussolini's rule as: "The same suppression of individual liberty, the same faith in a better future."[34]

Finally, surveying the results of the adoption of scientific-rationalism in the union of capitalism and experimental science and the union of socialism and analytic science, Kazantzakis would say in a comprehensive summation that in the generations ahead the mind was going to be "obliged by the pressure of history to forget its independent theoretical function." The most immediate and imperative pressure that he foresaw was that of making propaganda for the historical contest between capitalism and communism and preparing techniques—e.g., lethal weapons, poison gases, etc.—for annihilating those on the opposite side. We thus arrive at a situation in which "science, on which poor miserable man has based so much hope for deliverance . . . and for an answer to the agonizing questions of his spirit, has become the most formidable and immoral weapon of a new form of barbarism, the most horrifying form, the scientific." Kazantzakis concludes that science's moral bankruptcy is evidenced by the numbers of dead in World War II. Science and morality are not only diverging; it seems that the "more science progresses, the more morality retrogresses, until the moral degradation of man reaches a state of primitive bestiality. Vaunted progress has also proved one of the most menacing myths of the modern world." (*England*, 8)

This rise of a new barbarism, in both East and West, was likewise traced by Ortega, one of Kazantzakis' spiritual colleagues, to experimental science and technicism. The impetus that technicism provided to the rise on a mass scale of the new barbarians was, for Ortega, of two sorts: quantitatively, with the proliferation of man, and, more importantly, qualitatively; that is, "the actual scientific man is the prototype of the mass man. . . . Science itself—the root of our civilization—automatically converts him into mass-man, makes him a primitive, a modern barbarian."[35] Owing to its very nature, modern science produces, in Ortega's and Kazantzakis' view, men who have no sense of intellectual and social relatedness and tolerance, men who have no historic-social appreciation, men whose minds are dogmatic and inflexible.

Concerned as always with the evolutionary movement of world reality—with which sociopolitical forms should follow—Kazantzakis concludes, apropos of science, that "in order to comprehend the *élan vital,* the human intellect is necessary, the examination of created things, the history of our earth as our scientific researches show them; but that is not enough."[36] Scientific progress as an avenue leading mankind from the horrors of the transitional age is, to Kazantzakis, a circular route that ultimately turns back into the chaotic quagmire. Further, because of the increased potential for destruction made possible by scientific discoveries, and especially the lack of a corollary development of compassionate sensitivity to that capability, the roadway of science may lead to the dead end of nothingness. If man is to avoid this destination, he must find another road to salvation. Within the exciting and imaginative capability of art lies, for Kazantzakis, the best hope for world deliverance and betterment.

Art As Deliverance

It is not surprising that Kazantzakis, a student of Bergson, a disciple of Nietzsche, and a gifted literary artist, believed that through art one could effect a contact with reality. He expressed his artistic allegiance in various ways. Art is "a mysterious science, a veritable theurgy. Words attract and imprison the invisible spirit, force it to become incarnated and to exhibit itself to man." (*T.R.,* 90–91) "Like Buddha, the artist lives completely liberated and completely liberating matter." (*Gr. Passion,* 63) One must learn "that art is not submission and rules, but a demon which smashes the molds." (*Report,* 503) An artist is "a sort of angel. Well, not exactly. There's a little something lacking. Look here: there are animals—asses, mules—and there are human beings. And then, above them, there are the artists and higher still the angels." (*Freedom,* 118) And an artist, like his "grandfather" El Greco, "divines the future and immortalizes the past." (*Spain,* 207) It is this latter capability of the artist at one and the same time

to assimilate, overcome, and transcend God-father-ancestors
ideas in the forge of creativity and sow the seeds of the son-
future-new values that has import for political thought.

Kazantzakis believed that a new consciousness can be ham-
mered out by the artist beyond the bounds of dry logic and
historical-contemporary inhibitions. In the continuously creative
artistic process of contrasting the old and new, the limits of the
possible are forever shattered and enlarged. Kazantzakis' favorite
symbol for the artist is Akritas—the sentinel. As a sentinel the
artist sees new developments, new potentialities, new realities
before those in the interior do. Two special talents possessed by
the artist make this unique role possible. One of them is his
imaginative capability.

Wilson discusses this dimension of the artist as exemplified in
Book XVII of *The Odyssey,* which is acted out in Ulysses' imagination: "Ulysses has stumbled on the profoundest of all evolutionary truths. The mind is actually a new *dimension* of life, distinct
from the physical world and our responses to it." But, adds
Wilson, because we are still primarily animallike machines that
react to stimuli outside ourselves, we fail to understand this third
dimension of life. With the exception of those rare, ecstatic moments experienced by mystics and poets, man does not
operationalize the tremendous freedom made possible through
the mind's dimension. "It is a realm that he could enter and make
securely his own, if only he became conscious of its existence. His
main problem is that he does not know who he is; he continues to
think of himself as a creature, an earthbound animal."[37]

In addition to imagination-intuition, Kazantzakis ascribes to
the artist a special sensitivity that gives him a greater existential
awareness of the vibrations of cosmogenic evolution. Although
every living man experiences to a degree the fate of his times, the
creator does so "most of all. There are certain sensitive lips and
fingertips which feel a tingling at a tempest's approach as though
they were being pricked by thousands of needles. The creator's
lips and fingertips are of this kind." (*Report,* 449) Therefore art,
with these special capabilities, is the best way to philosophize. Art
allows one to rise above the boundaries of science, reason, empiri-
cism, logic, etc., and to experience being/reality and thereby pro-

vides the best possible answers to the enduring questions of the
spirit of man. Art looks beyond phenomena and transubstantiates
matter into spirit.

> Once again art is beginning to be dissatisfied with external
> phenomena, is beginning to seek, to find the essence; is abstracting
> as much substance as possible from physical bodies, is searching for
> a line, a color, a motion capable of expressing the inexpressible,
> this being the only thing worthy of expression. Rather than what
> the corporeal eye sees, art renders what the restless eye of the soul
> can surmise within this visible world. (*Spain*, 100)

The inexpressible essence that art captures has two components:
(1) the soul of man, which takes on different attributes and forms
in different ages, and (2) the evolutionary God/spirit of time,
space, history, and nature. In capturing these, art makes possible
creation of the new myths, legends, symbols, etc., needed by
twentieth-century man to give meaning, order, coherence, form,
direction, and purpose to his sociopolitical existence.
Kazantzakis, believing the artist possesses these truly powerful
creative tools, addresses himself next to the duty of the artist
apropos of suffering mankind.

Kazantzakis relates how he once asked Unamuno what the
artist concerned with the suppression of the free spirit of modern
man in the transitional age must do. Unamuno responded:

> "Nothing!" he roared. "Nothing!" The face of the truth is terrify-
> ing. What is our duty? To hide the truth from the people! The Old
> Testament says: 'He who looks God in the face will die.' Even Moses
> could not look God straight in the face. He looked at him from
> behind and saw only the edge of His robe. Such is the nature of
> truth! We must deceive the people; deceive them, so that the poor
> creatures can have the strength and cheerfulness to go on living. If
> they knew the truth, they couldn't go on living. They wouldn't want
> to anymore. (*Spain*, 175)

Aware of the shock of scientific revelations of the disparities of
traditional religious "truths," Kazantzakis agreed that the
dialectical-analytical confrontation of the masses with naked, godless reality had created much of the havoc and barrenness of

modern life. However, he reached a different conclusion from Unamuno.

Kazantzakis came to have a comprehensive belief that, far from doing nothing, the artist has a demanding duty and responsibility to aid man once more by filling creatively the void brought about by the dialectical-scientific mind. In fulfilling this responsibility, it is not the artist's duty to look only to the past, symbolized by the Father, or only to the present, symbolized by the Son: "If man can grasp and express nothing but the Son, he creates a merely superficial work of art; if he expresses nothing but abstract ideas, nothing but the Father, he produces not art but metaphysics." (*T.R.,* 90) This meaningful synthetic reconciliation of past and future in the overcoming and surpassing of the former by the latter is the true purpose of the artist. Kazantzakis repudiates those who would say that the duty of the artist is merely to create beauty. In fact, Kazantzakis dwells at some length on the chief danger of art: its beauty can camouflage and cover up the perversity, suffering, and injustice in the world. This concern is revealed in a conversation in Berlin with Itka, who scorns Kazantzakis' naïve adulation of beauty: you (Kazantzakis) "have the effrontery to speak—about poverty, oppression, and villainy. By transforming our pain into beauty you get it out of your system. Damn beauty, when it makes a man forget human suffering." (*Report,* 388)

Responding to this criticism, Kazantzakis foregoes a strict adherence to the demands of beauty in the quest for helping achieve a new, higher existence for man. This gave Kazantzakis' literary output a jarring lack of balance that gave rise to questions about his literary competence. Whatever he wrote—poems, plays, or novels—they took on, without conscious effort on his part, a dramatic rhythm, "full of mutually clashing forces, struggle, indignation, revolt, the pursuit of a lost equilibrium; full of portents and sparks from the approaching tempest. . . . In spite of my wishes, the peaceful voice I desired to emit became a cry." (*Report,* 449)

In a similar vein he scoffed at the debates over the artistic merits of *The Odyssey,* contending that literary critics and historians who follow the artist and measure his work according to previous molds are of no importance to the artist. The artist has a creative prerogative to go beyond set molds: "This is what creation means—to break them by creating new ones. When a vital soul feels, without previous aesthetic theories, the necessity to create, then whatever shape his creations take cannot help but be alive."[38] Just as the artist's duty is to rebel against the demands of beauty and artistic critics in the pursuit of honesty, so it is his duty never to acquiesce in the sociopolitical injustices of the status quo. The writer is of a more sensitive nature than his fellows and "cannot repress his indignation or shirk his responsibility. He is duty bound not to sleep; he must keep his people on the alert." Kazantzakis fervently believed that "this role of the writer as agitator is indispensable in all countries ruled by injustice."[39] Kazantzakis' life, and particularly his arrival at this view toward art portrays, after a fashion, Soren Kierkegaard's magnificent view of the journey to the self.

Kierkegaard believed most men lived on one of three levels, the aesthetic, the ethical, or the religious, but it was possible for some men to pass through all three stages, incorporating the lessons of each in reaching self-actualization.[40] For Kierkegaard, the aesthetic or poetic approach to life is distinguished by a concern with power, an adoration of being and immediacy, a focus on outwardness, a contemplative detachment from life, a superficially descriptive time-frozen attitude, and a lack of concern with universals and norms. These characteristics result in a conquering nature constantly outside itself with an external but no internal history: "But since external history is the one kind of history which can without detriment be concentrated, it is natural that art and poetry choose this especially for representation, and hence, choose likewise the unopened individual and everything that has to do with him." The aesthetic-artistic approach is only a partial attitude to life; for it does not induce understanding of internal history, of selfhood, openness, and the deeper, tragic meanings of life. The aesthete uses the categories of fortune, fate, despair, etc., in his art only to abstract an unrealistic ideality within the immediate, finite world; but "to comprehend misfortune, to come to an understanding with it, to turn everything upside down and to make suffering the point of departure for a view of life, is something he cannot do." In Kazantzakis' terms the aesthete creates beauty through art to cover up injustice.

A more profound level of understanding is to be attained through the ethical attitude to life. This is evidenced in the philosopher who knows the good. The ethical man is of a possessive nature which rests within itself. He is an open individual concerned with inwardness, universal rules, and lived time. He goes beyond description to involved understanding of the tragic-comic existence of man. Where the aesthete describes humans as they are, that is, both good and evil, the ethical individual, in Kierkegaard's view, takes man from this medium and "places him in existence: ethics will at once demand that he be pleased to become, and then he becomes—either good or bad." In addition, ethics "rejects every explanation of becoming which deceptively explains the coming within being, whereby the absolute decision that is rooted in becoming is essentially revealed, and all talk about it rendered essentially nothing but a false alarm." Ethics has no truck with "chance" or excuses and therefore places a heavy responsibility on finite man. It "invites one to believe in reality and to have the courage to fight against the afflictions of reality, and especially those ghostly sufferings which man answers on their own responsibility." Further, ethics "warns you against those cunning calculations of reason which are even less trustworthy than the oracles of antiquity." An ethical attitude engenders a compassionate battle to relieve human suffering and may be said, to be represented, in the development of Kazantzakis' life and art, by his conversion to the humane goals of social justice espoused by Marxism.

The ethical is deficient, however, in at least two respects. For one thing, it is not universally open to all. For another, even those who attain the knowledge of the good are not necessarily led to will it. Hence we move upward to the religious individual who is essentially neither a genius nor a poet. He is, rather, the true individual who loves everyone and who lives by virtue of the absurd. "In infinite resignation he [the religious individual] drains the dark waters of melancholy to the last drop; he knows the blessedness of infinity." Kierkegaard describes the religious person as one who "remains in the finite without betraying any signs of his weary and tortured training, and yet rejoices in it with so much assurance that for him there appears to be nothing more certain."[41]

It is small wonder that Kierkegaard never found such a person. The religious individual, when faced with dilemmas to which no ethical norms or blueprints applied (for no ethics can cover all life's possibilities), would confront them with the trembling religious center of life and would choose. This person is the exception to all rules, but he breaks none arrogantly. His exceptionality is distinguished and made noble, as Barrett says, by his not denying the "validity of the ethical: the individual who is called upon to break with the ethical must first have subordinated himself to the ethical universal; and the break, when he is called upon to make it, is made in fear and trembling and not in the callous arrogance of power."[42] The break is made on the principle that the individual is ultimately superior to any collective universal, yet the ethical rule must be incorporated before it can be rightfully transcended. Beyond aesthetic art or Marxist ethics, Kazantzakis' latter years were the most intensely religious—in the highly personal sense in which Kierkegaard uses the term—of any period of his life. He sought to expand the frontiers of his age for a new existence. Kierkegaard says that the truly religious artist knows that religiosity is not a formal exercise but is "existing; so that the poetic productivity, if it does not cease entirely, or if it flows as richly as before, comes to be regarded by the individual himself as something accidental, which goes to prove that he understands himself religiously."[43] Within the framework of this assessment, the last two decades of Kazantzakis' life and art truly display his passionately religious sense of responsibility for saving mankind.

In upholding this responsibility, Kazantzakis utilized two primary neans. First, he sought to sensitize his being completely to all the currents of his age. He delved into nature, man, ideology, God, religion, etc. He traveled continuously over the earth seeking experience, knowledge, and insight. He traveled within his mind seeking truth, reality, creation, and more. He surveyed wars at first hand and lived in a monastery on Mt. Athos. He did all these things believing that if he could capture them in words, he would "be able to help shorten the agony of other kindred spirits who have set out along the same path. . . . I am not making Art. I am only letting my own heart cry out." (*Spain,* 11–12) Kazantzakis sought to experience all of life and deny none of it and through the alchemy of his sensitive, creative chemistry to convert that experience into knowledge, truth, and mobilization of the spiritual forces within man.

The second avenue that he chose to follow in order to fulfill his responsibility was immersion in the lives of his historical, religious, mythological, spiritual, and literary-hero predecessors. Throughout his work, Kazantzakis dwells on the great tormented souls who had loved and suffered exceedingly in their lives, who had impudently contended against God and destiny. "I fought to drag them up from Hades in order to glorify their pain and struggle—mankind's pain and struggle—in front of living men." (*Report,* 451) This is evident in, among other works, *The Odyssey,* when Ulysses meets, in his travels, Christ, the Poet, the Primitive Man, and Don Quiote, among others. In addition to these figures, Kazantzakis attached importance to Prometheus; Nicephoros Phocas, an ancient liberator of Crete and a great figure in Byzantine history; Hamlet and Faust, and more.

This attempted immersion in the lives of his heroes is a very important aspect of Kazantzakis' art and thought. This is displayed in a very revealing passage in *Spain* where Kazantzakis compares Cervantes, Dante, and Quevedo, the great seventeenth-century Spanish poet, philosopher, and political writer whose satire of Philip IV cost him four years of imprisonment, broken health, and an early death, in order to illuminate the specific manner in which the artist can create a "new riverbed of the spirit" into which sociopolitical reality can flow. Cervantes

> had been able to define clearly the spirit of his race and so save it from compromise and destruction. Magic the power of speech that is capable of creating the thing, or of enclosing the created thing within clearly defined limits, so that it cannot overflow or shrink and loose its original form. Perhaps Quevedo, Cervante's contemporary, is a more powerful writer—richer, cleverer, more forceful with his broad humor and pathos and his violent love of life. But in none of his works could he immortalize the twofold essence of the Spanish spirit. Not capable of saving, he was not saved. But Cer-

vantes, with his Don Quixote and his Sancho, saved the spirit of his
race from being destroyed by time, and he too was saved along with
her. Dante, centuries after his death, effected the unification of
Italy by having coerced her in his strict *terza rima* to be a united
Italy. Just so, Cervantes expressed in speech the hidden or still
unfathomed characteristics of his race. He made them crystal-clear
and fixed, and the Spaniards, seeing this most perfect expression
of themselves, were coerced into conforming to their own racial
character. Such is the difficult, dangerous, utterly mysterious responsibility of the great creator. (p. 44)

Through their lives and art, Dante and Cervantes expressed
those central themes and counterthemes, ambiguities and con-
stants, characteristics, and mysteries that composed the essence of
their age. By doing so, they surpassed their time and cleared a
pathway to the future. The intensity of Kazantzakis' belief in this
ennobling capability of art is demonstrated by his eulogizing El
Greco—a native Cretan, a gifted artist, an enormously imaginative and vital individual who also, in Kazantzakis' view, lived
during the transitional age—as one who, like Dante and Cervantes, wrought a creative conformation of reality "within clearly
defined limits." He describes an El Greco painting as laying bare
"the whole fate of man, the entire soul of the world, flooded with
the tragic-comic powers of good and evil. . . . From every perfect
work of art rises a cry of pain, joy, hope, strife. And, above all, the
unchanging cry of liberation." (p. 102) The perfect work of art
portrays the unity of man with nature, God, animal, man, and life
and death. In doing so, it liberates man by revealing the flow of
the creatively conscious movement of man's history. Paradoxically, it also determines and channels (to an extent) that history.

Art has, therefore, important implications in politics. This is so
because political reality is a central element of the historic flow.
Kazantzakis reflected on this and concluded that the "genuine
role of the politician is not to stop history but to work in harmony
with it." (*Spain,* 251) (This explains to some degree his acceptance
of violence.) Underlying his thought at this point is the belief that
the political and the artistic must work hand in hand, with the
former following the lead of the latter. He speaks wistfully of the
royal Arab courts of old where "the poets were in the ascen-

dency. . . . [and] were not parasites and buffoons, as they were among the Byzantines and the Franks." (p. 109) In *England,* a young writer tells him that, in this chaotic age,

> eventually our poets emerged from their splendid isolation and began to mingle with the main currents. They gave up struggling for the most rare form of expression and began to seek the most responsible and most representative form, the one most universally human. (p. 116)

And in the "The Immortal Free Spirit of Man," where he speaks of the crucial sociopolitical questions facing a war-weary world, he again evinces his belief in the illuminating potential of the poet-artist in the sociopolitical arena:

> Let all those of us who believe in spiritual values unite. Let us, clear-minded, look at the dangerous times we are going through and let us see what is today the spiritual duty of man. Beauty is no longer enough; nor is theoretical truth, nor passive goodness. Man's spiritual duty today is greater and more complex than in the past . . . he must formulate a new universal rallying-cry, able to establish unity—that is, harmony between man's mind and heart. He must find the simple words that will once more reveal to man this most simple truth—that all men are brothers.
>
> As in all past creative ages, the poet is again identified with the prophet. Let us have faith in the spirit of man; in the most difficult moments, when the fate of mankind hangs in the balance, the spirit takes over responsibility.[44]

Just as great artists of the past had affected a union of poet and prophet and thereby opened riverbeds into which reality flowed, so Kazantzakis sought to do. He evinced his immense faith in himself in a letter to Prevelakis:

> It's as though we are the first specimens of some future race, and the physical and psychological conditions around us are still hostile. Neither the air nor the aspirations nor "human beings'" thought are our "climate." This is not "romanticism" or "revolte" or weakness or merely strength. I felt that it is something deeper, more mystical, more organic.[45]

Bringing this view to bear on the anguish of a civilization struggling for deliverance from the many oppressive political, religious, and philosophical masks that dominated it, Kazantzakis reversed Plato and contended, "I chanced to be born in an age when this struggle was so intense and the need of help so imperative that I could quickly see the identity between my individual struggle and the great struggle of the contemporary world." (*Report*, 452)

Whereas Plato thought it possible to discover justice, harmony, and virtue in the individual by reading them as "writ large" in the state, Kazantzakis believed it possible to discover the locus of the world's anguish and the path to overcoming it by reading it indelibly written in the suffering and rebellious torment of the life of the sensitive, creative individual. Kazantzakis saw his personal passage from birth to death in terms of this thesis. His entire life is a portrayal of the path to freedom, to a higher human existence beyond hope and rationality, and despair and nihilism, through overcoming the many obstacles within the contradictions of word-action, mind-flesh, good-evil, mortality-immortality, etc., and becoming a higher man of unity with diversity and honesty. His is an unceasing battle with the abyss, an unceasing quest for immortality in an age when man has succumbed to the masks and is enslaved, like Kazantzakis' childhood Crete, to outer and inner Turks. His cry—in a time of bombs, wars, rationality transformed into irrationality, violence, church hypocrisy, scientific excesses, despiritualization and blandness, ideological ferment, etc.—is one of the maintenance of tension when confronted with the void; not escape from freedom but courage, compassion, fortitude, transubstantiation, transcendence. Kazantzakis cries out against these perversions and for the Invisible, for the future man, co-creation, deliverance, harmony, unity, union with God and nature, reconciliation of flesh, soul, mind, and world spirit; it is an individualistic rebellion and reorientation with important communitarian overtones—a quest for existence beyond nihilism. By organizing, assimilating, and ordering the stimuli of one's experience, Kazantzakis believed, we could "not only come to know ourselves. Far, far more important, we are able to transcend our own insanely proud egos; plunging them and tempering them in the tormented itinerant army of Man." (*Spain*, 11) Kazantzakis' view was an elevating one of the worth of each individual's capabilities for aiding in the world struggle. He consistently held to his oft-stated faith that every

> man has a cry, *his* cry, to sling into the air before he dies . . . this cry may scatter ineffectually in the air, that there may be no ear either below on earth or above in heaven to hear it. No matter. You are not a sheep, you are a man, and that means a thing which is unsettled and shouts. Well then—shout. (*Report*, 478)

In another work, he said that "the bloodstained endeavor of the Spirit in whatsoever field of the earth, is a universal human endeavor that bursts out and goes on indestructibly inside every human being who continues the struggle." (*Spain*, 37)

I submit that Kazantzakis' "struggle" has much to offer for political philosophy, but there are those who disagree. Bien, for example, argues that Kazantzakis was only circumstantially and never essentially concerned with politics, which Bien defines as the technics of "how men behave in groups in societies: how (to go to the root of the word itself)—they build and maintain their cities, developing all the delicate compromises that enable masses of people to reside harmoniously together and prosper." He contends that this was so because Kazantzakis was concerned primarily with his own salvation and not with the welfare of society. He holds that political involvement was for Kazantzakis only a path to individual salvation: "We may speak, therefore, of 'Kazantzakis and politics,' but not of Kazantzakis as a political writer."[46]

This analysis of Kazantzakis' politics makes a distinction without a difference. It is true that Kazantzakis was not immediately concerned with the intricacies of political institutions, but this alone does not disqualify him, as Bien implies, as a valuable source of political thought. Kazantzakis brought an artistic vision to political theory. It was not that of the technical analyst. He expressed his view thus: unlike science "art, on the contrary, has its first source in an intuition, establishing a contact with the great reality. A vision. And then quite simply and effortlessly all the details fall into place and find expression."[47]

Many of the great figures of political thought, from the pre-Socratics to Cicero and Augustine to Hobbes to Nietzsche, to name only a few, have evinced a similar disregard for political mechanics. Like them, Kazantzakis was not only circumstantially but also essentially concerned about the mores, values, goals, priorities—the *"whats"* of a political system—that determine, to a marked degree, how "men behave in groups and build their cities." Thus, although Kazantzakis' focus was not on the mundane stuff of everyday politics but rather was on the ideals, values, etc., of political society, he was still very much a political writer. Reviewing his interrelated artistic-political role as sentinel, seer, value-giver, creator, agitator, and rebel, Kazantzakis realized the grave sociopolitical responsibility that this denoted:

> If we open a riverbed by writing or acting, reality may flow into that riverbed, into a course it would not have taken had we not intervened. We do not bear the full responsibility naturally, but we do bear a great part.
>
> Writing may have been a game in other ages, in times of equilibrium. Today it is a grave duty. Its purpose is not to entertain the mind with fairy tales and make it forget, but to proclaim a state of mobilization to all the luminous forces still surviving in our age of transition, and to urge men to do their utmost to surpass the beast. (*Report*, 450)

Two apparent inconsistencies are brought to light by the foregoing discussion. First, has not Kazantzakis told us that we must strip away debilitating masks and stare into the void? Yet now he proposes that an artist has the responsibility of creating a new "riverbed of the spirit" (or myth) to channel reality. Is not this filling the void and thereby deluding man and devitalizing existence? Or, and this seems more correct, does it not simply reflect Kazantzakis' realistic recognition that man's inevitable lot is to seek direction through myths and visions, a recognition that has led him to propose that the artist must be above all else (to use Tillich's phrase) an "authentic guardian of the void" who continually scrutinizes and synthesizes the masks or myths that are offered to man as sociopolitical, religious, and philosophical camouflage to hide the void?

A second problem with Kazantzakis' position is the obvious "elitist" aspect. Can only the gifted stare into the void? While this may seem implicit in Kazantzakis' position, it is mitigated by his thoroughgoing populism and faith in the common people, his oft-stated view that the Spirit is in every man, and his belief in the humanistic responsibility of art, all of which shine through both his life and work. Bien misinterprets Kazantzakis' avowed goal of self-transcendence as being a denial of concern for others. Actually, as the passage quoted above demonstrates, Kazantzakis believed individual and societal salvation to be inextricably entwined. Those who, like Quevedo, cannot save themselves cannot save others. The former is a necessary prerequisite to the latter. Thus, when Kazantzakis sought salvation through his art, it was not merely an egocentric, self-concerned exercise on his part but also an attempt to help all mankind achieve salvation from injustice, cruelty, and suffering. Even Bien acknowledged this in an apt passage toward the end of his essay, a passage that vitiates somewhat his earlier denigration of Kazantzakis' political writing. Kazantzakis' heroes, Bien writes,

> are models of spiritual achievement, encouraging reality to reach them in some undefined (and constantly receding) future. They die and sometimes in dying help to inspire others to live better and make better societies, but probably even more important than this, they voice—and leave behind them—a cry. This, though intangible and spiritual, is their right art, the one that will do most to bring an end to the injustices and chaos of the transitional age.[48]

There remains, however, the nagging problem of translating Kazantzakis' "cry" into practical political solutions. That is, how is an anthology of salvation actually to be made applicable to contemporary politics? Is it to be through revolutionary resistance and ultimately anarchism? Or is it to be through a rebellious challenge to all systems to transvalue their values according to his prognosis? This is an important question of tactics that visionaries—even those who are committed artists—often fail to answer—and Kazantzakis is no exception. Perhaps all one can say of this immensely complex thinker—even though it is not wholly satisfactory—is that he seemed to accept both the notion of revolutionary resistance and the possibility of a new form of community.

Those who, like Bien, see Kazantzakis as basically unpolitical could make a stronger case by pointing out the contradictions in the label "political writer." That is, it may be possible to say that to be truly political *and* a writer in the ideal sense of the word (an accomplished "literatist" etc.) is simply not possible. The argument could be waged on three levels (and on the first of them Kazantzakis would be particularly vulnerable!): first, that a concern with politics inevitably lessens the scope, worth, and durability of a work of art; second, that rather than art decisively influencing politics, just the reverse seems true; third, that art can do little for the common man: who reads Kazantzakis or looks at an El Greco—the peasant?

In his intriguing essay on art and culture, T. S. Eliot addressed just these points. Eliot believed a supranational network of artists to be essential to the transmission of ideas and the advancement of culture. Political differences in the late 1930s destroyed, in Eliot's view, the vital supranational harmony within the artistic community that was the basis for his review, *The Criterion,* a vehicle for the interchange of ideas. European literature between the two World Wars was weakened in part, he contends, "by the obsession with politics. . . . A universal concern with politics does not unite, it divides."[49] Political division places artists in propagandistic confrontation with each other, resulting in a dilution of artistic quality. *Toda Raba,* for example, which is Kazantzakis' most uncritically Marxist work, is less than successful from an artistic perspective. Political themes thus led, in Eliot's assessment, to a lowering of the standards of European literary output of that period because of the intellectual anxieties and pressures placed on "political" artists within a world of contesting nations and ideologies.

Addressing himself to the second point, the interrelationality of art and politics, Eliot implies that art may be more strongly influenced by politics than vice-versa (as Kazantzakis suggests). This is so for several reasons. In today's large societies, Eliot says, "the professional politician has too much to do to have leisure for serious reading, even on politics. He has far too little time for exchange of ideas and information with men of distinction in other walks of life." A related and perhaps more important factor in the lack of influence of art on politics lies in the tendency for the public to distort and assimilate lesser ideas far below the best and wisest that the leading artists offer. The practical politician, even if he is aware of this trend, must deal with and accommodate the widely held concepts propagandized through mass art "as if they were the constructions of informed sagacity, the institutions of genius, or the accumulated wisdom of ages."

Other factors vitiating the influence of art over politics are the difficulty of travel and the expense of art. These have led to a reduction of "private" art and an increase in "public" or government-subsidized art. This is especially visible in the vital interrelations among artists of differing nations. What with the immense work being done in comparative sociology, anthropology, and political theory, all nations have become extremely culture-conscious. They have established official agencies to assist in the arts and sciences. Many, like the British Council, send and receive representatives—as exampled by Kazantzakis' visit to Britain following World War II. With the cold-war restrictions on travel, the increasing culture consciousness, the increased expense of art and research, and the lessening of private patronage, governmental discretion over art has expanded enormously. Eliot offers, as prophylaxis against this political control, recognition of the need for artists to travel as private citizens to meet one another without official approval. Further, "Some safeguard may be provided, against increasing politicisation of the arts and science, by encouraging local initiative and responsibility; and, as far as possible, separating the central source of funds from control over their use."

A further reason for the influence of politics on art is the resource weakness, particularly in crisis times, of the artistic community in terms of the political community. This was displayed in 1940 when the artistic community shut its borders and turned within itself. There was "a gradual closing of the mental frontiers of Europe. A kind of cultural autarchy followed inevitably upon political and economic autarchy."[50] Eliot obviously wages powerful and logical assaults on the Kazantzakis perspective concerning this point. And in the short run, Eliot may well be correct. Over a long span of time, however, Kazantzakis' belief that politics follows art has much merit, as testified to by the growing importance of his vision for radical politics. Today, Roszak, William I. Thompson, and Marcuse, and others point to a need that was the focus of Kazantzakis' work from the late 1930s on. Also, on the last level of the argument, which is over the question of what art can do for the common man, and which in many ways is the crucial issue, Kazantzakis is much less vulnerable.

Eliot believed that art directly benefited and was understood by an elite. He believed further that without contact among the members of this elite—scientific, artistic, philosophical, political, and religious groups—a society may disintegrate. This group's unity spanned national boundaries through its grounding in the three great sources of Western civilization—Israel, Rome, and Greece. Yet, Eliot argued, in somewhat contradictory fashion, that for the permeation of ideas a noneducated language of the common people is vital. Speaking of Welsh in this particular sense, Eliot says that for the maintenance and transmission of a culture "there is no safeguard more reliable than a . . . literary language—not necessarily a scientific language but certainly a poetic one; otherwise the spread of education will extinguish it."[51]

This espousal of an artistic-poetic people's language as a necessary vehicle for transmitting culture—a directing force of destiny—was supported in stirring fashion by Kazantzakis. His Cretan birth among the common people, his mistrust of pseudo-intellectuals and self-serving politicians, and his maltreatment at the hands of various academics and literary critics, all led him to identify himself with the people and their language. Kazantzakis tells how impressed he was, during a Russian trip in 1929, upon meeting one hundred and fifty Greeks and discussing world issues with them: "If I were Christ surely my apostles would be people like these. Love, warmth, trust. The intellectuals are barren, dishonest, doomed. I had felt tired and sad. And with these simple people I regained my confidence in man."[52] And, comparing the people of his native race with their leaders, he found in the people "great virtues and human depth. But their leaders are a disgrace to them." Kazantzakis discovered among the intellectuals "a few young people full of aspiration, intellectual curiosity, and disinterested love. The older ones are all lost."[53] Thus Kazantzakis' personal answer to the fifth question he posed to the British (and indeed to all) intellectuals: what can be done to broaden the basis of the contact between intellectuals, artists, and the people?, was in terms of Eliot's analysis of the need for a *people's* literary language:

> In the critical evolutionary stage through which our demotic language is passing it is natural, essential—and extremely useful—for a creator to treasure avidly and to save as much linguistic wealth as he can, as in similar periods of Dante, Rabelais, and Luther. Our tongue, because of the laziness and linguistic ignorance of the 'intellectuals,' and because of the linguistic corruption of the people subjected to faulty schooling and newspaper jargon, is in danger of being deformed and impoverished. The creator is more anguished by this danger than anyone else, and because for him every word is a part of the spirit he knows that the greatest responsibility falls to him, he opens the doors of his works wide in order that the nouns and adjectives may find a refuge there. This is how it has always been; the creator, in these endangering periods, even though he knows that his vocabulary may become overladen, wants to receive under his roof (he cannot, he must not resist) all the homeless linguistic refugees who are in danger of dying. Only in this way can the constantly increasing linguistic wealth be saved, that is to say, spiritually.[54]

Kazantzakis chose to write his modern sequel to Homer and other works in an extreme form of the Greek demotic language, that of the peasant, fisherman, and worker, rather than the "pure" Greek of the intellectuals. For this reason Kazantzakis' popular reputation abroad, as well as in Greece, has always been greater than his critical one. This is evident in America in the lack of significant criticism until recently, even though a great many people have seen the Broadway musical and Cacoyannis' film version of *Zorba,* plus Dassin's rendering of *The Greek Passion* in the film *He Who Must Die,* and millions have read the English paperback editions of his novels. In Greece this disparity is evidenced by the fact that the three hundred copies of the original edition of *The Odyssey,* issued in 1938, did not receive wide acclaim and in fact did not even sell out for quite some time after their appearance.

Kazantzakis explains this phenomenon: "The intellectuals of Athens cannot understand this; I give it to the boatmen and the fishermen, and they have no trouble."[55] They, the "boatmen and fishermen," likely did have some trouble paying for the original addition, which was very expensive! This is surely one reason why the copies sold so slowly.

Kazantzakis' adoption of the demotic as the literary vehicle for carrying his thoughts to the people had the effect of reinforcing his identity and sense of unity with the common man. In the same manner in which he rejected the pseudo-intellectual, academic-literary language that ignored the people's needs, he rejected political solutions that did not involve the people of Greece and that were not wrought through and by the people. In *The Fratricides,* Kazantzakis relates through Father Yanaros his belief that of the three possible roads out of the Greek civil war on which the book is based, God's intervention, the leaders'—kings, politicians, bishops, revolutionaries, and intellectuals—good will, and the people's path, only the last offers any hope.

"What third road? There is no road! It hasn't opened yet. We have to open it with our labor, pushing onward to make it a road. And who are the 'we'? The people! This road begins with the people, goes ahead with the people, and ends with the people." (p. 155) Kazantzakis' tenacity in living by the dictates of the people's needs and his addressing his art to those needs in terms the common man could comprehend represents the populist alternative to Eliot's elitism and the only feasible manner of reversing the modern trend and preparing for the influence of art over politics. Drawing on his Greek origins, the Judeo-Christian tradition, his many travels and experiences, and his wide learning, Kazantzakis showed the road of salvation to rich and poor, intellectual and peasant, master and servant.

One traverses this road by saving God.

The future is beyond knowing, but the present is beyond belief. We make so much noise with technology
that we cannot discover that the stargate is in our
foreheads. But the time has come; the revelation has
already occurred, and the guardian seers have seen the
lightning strike the darkness we call reality. And now
we sleep in the brief interval between the lightning and
the thunder.

W. I. THOMPSON

≡III≡III≡III≡III≡III≡III≡III≡III≡III≡III≡III≡III≡III≡III≡III≡III≡III

4

Order from Chaos

In diagnosing the ills of contemporary Western civilization
Kazantzakis believed that the widespread suffering, injustice, and
despiritualization derived from, first, man's escapist surrender to
the masks of ideology and the hypocrisy of institutionalized reli-

gion, both of which stifle the spirit rather than release it; second, the dominance of the technocratic-materialistic ethos, with its many dehumanizing aspects; third, the paucity of synthesizing vision among men of the spirit—artists, intellectuals, prophets, and religious leaders; fourth, the eagerness with which man abdicates his burden of freedom; fifth, the explosive increase of violence in the world. Believing this and viewing his personal salvation as an artist and humanist to be at one with that of the world, Kazantzakis could say, through Father Yanaros, "Now, all is chaos, and I, the worm, must bring order." (*Frat.*, p. 177)

It is this attempt to bring order—Kazantzakis' theoretical prognosis, if you will—which is the heart of his political philosophy. Kazantzakis proffers his prognosis as an exit from the transitional age (and really from any transitional age) made possible through the process of "saving God."

Any philosophy of politics such as Kazantzakis' must necessarily be tested, not only for the perceptiveness and accuracy of its analysis but also for the accuracy, meaningfulness, and utility of its proposed solutions. While Kazantzakis' prognosis for Western civilization is rather mystical and ultimately demanding of men, it is rich in insights, wholly operational, and answers uniquely the central problem of modern man, namely, that of how to resolve constructively the contradiction between the boundless freedom that is his and the deterministic forces that are at play in mass, technological society. For this resolution Kazantzakis attempts in effect to render the individualist Zorbaic-Odyssean vantage point of the Cretan glance into a vibrant communitarian perspective, realizing that "a new decalogue is absolutely necessary." (*Report*, 232) There are several major tenets of his new decalogue for saving God and man, as well as a search for valid humanistic political criteria applicable to that process. By following the logic of this basic metaphysics to its political conclusions, one discovers Kazantzakis' new messianic ideal-order for modern man, for "His politics grew out of his metaphysics, his metaphysics out of his politics."[1]

Saving God: A Political Metaphysics

Spinoza once wrote, "All things, I say, are in God." From this basic cornerstone of his geometrically precise philosophy, he derived proof of God's omnipotence as free cause unhampered by intelligent, purposive, or moral restrictions. Given the infinite potency of God/substance, all real possibilities will be actualized. Spinoza emphasized God's activity as cause—cause infinitely, unconquerably, and exhaustively actualizing potentiality. Man's role in the scheme of things was in no way participatory. His duty was the passive one of emending his intellect by striving for self-actualization through the intellectual love of God. From this intellectual love would come "adequate ideas" of God. These ideas, attained at the third, highest level of Spinoza's hierarchy of knowledge, would enable the mind to conceive things in aspects of their eternality, drive the emotions to subservience and control, and know that "our salvation, or blessedness, or freedom consists in a constant and eternal love toward God, or in the love of God toward men." Spinoza's was the most profound, comprehensive, and rigorous formulation of the ultimately deterministic conclusions logic of the Platonic-Christian ontology. The implications for man of this view are many and far-reaching, the most important of which comes from the elevation of the force of God as necessity and the corollary deemphasis on the capability of man for creative, constructive, and affirmative freedom. If one accepts the Spinozistic-Christian view that "all things follow from the eternal decree of God."[2] and that all men are finite expressions of the essence of God so far as he is extended substance, then man exists in a truly determined world. All men have a broad base of "common notions" on which they not only should rely but upon which they must eventually agree.

One would think, in reflecting on all this three centuries after Spinoza, that if there were such a broad base of common knowledge available to men, if the world were so ordered as Spinoza believed, if adequate ideas were accessible from which and through which we could perceive the essence of the world, and if man was determined by all these things, then man would have made much more progress toward achieving a larger degree of stability and unity in his world than he has in fact done. If Spinoza was right, then it is difficult to account for the fact that, as Kazantzakis observes, most human beings are submerged in the inferno of hatred, barrenness, absurdity. They are like people who cannot read, who can make out only a few letters, but still try to read from the Divine Song. They mix up these letters and link words or phrases analogous to their own humble desires—food, women, wealth, logic. It is like reading some superb work in a drowsy state. Here and there they distinguish a word and then fall back to sleep. (*England,* 84)

Spinoza explicitly explains away the source of much controversy, but he at the same time implicitly does grave damage to the possibility of diversity among men. The existence of diversity and the capability of spontaneity of men are the two most powerful forces in the creativity and vitality of men. Spinoza, with his powerful emphasis on adequate ideas and reason, had taken from man much that is of value to him and much that allows him the flexibility and adaptability to cope with a world that is just not so well-ordered, so rational, so easily understandable, so easily explicable as the Platonic-Christian ontology would have us believe. Taken in its entirety, Spinoza's system has obvious weaknesses, although there are several points of his thought that lend themselves readily to contemporary analyses (such as Kazantzakis') of the human predicament.

It is equally valid to view Spinoza's philosophy on ontological, logical, or epistemological levels; however, he offers perhaps the most sustenance today, particularly in view of the deficiencies in his ontology and epistemology, when discussed on the ethical/moral level apropos of the problem of freedom. Spinoza's frequently cited principle to the effect that "freedom is the recognition of necessity" is particularly meaningful for man who lives on this side of Marx, Freud, and the Industrial Revolution. This is so because we have come to realize, under the leadership of these men and the force of these events, that we are indeed determined to a dramatic extent—culturally, genetically, socially, by our unconscious drives, etc. In view of this, Spinoza's counsel that we must gain adequate knowledge of external determinate causality seems a sound piece of advice, if we are to understand these determinants and our own fate. However, Spinoza's fatal error—and by inference that of the Platonic-Christian ontology—lay in the stricture that man is only a perceiver who, once he recognizes external God-necessity from which (according to that cosmology) all things flow, must submit to that determination. Kazantzakis borrows from "the thrice holy ascetic, Spinoza" (*Spain*, 120) in reacting to the negative role assigned to man through this error and arrives at a more viable, dynamic, man-centered ontology with decisive political import. Taking Spinoza's basic insight into the recognition of necessity, Kazantzakis constructs a system in which man creates his own fate and that of God through saving God.

The basic cornerstone of Kazantzakis' philosophy was a reversal of Spinoza; God "huddles in a knot in every cell of flesh." (*Saviors*, 91) Further, "this world is not His vestment, as I once believed; it is God himself. Form and essence are identical. . . . Zorba knew this, but could not say it. He danced it. I thought to myself, if only I can transform this dance into words." (*Report*, 468) Kazantzakis derived from this reversal of the Spinozistic-Christian cosmology proof of the lack of God's omnipotence and emphasized the world of things and men as free cause unhampered a priori by otherworldly intelligent or purposive restrictions. This is to say that all real possibilities, both good and evil, can and may be actualized; for nature has no morals. What man must do is to actualize the good. He does this by saving God. As pointed out in the discussion of the Cretan glance, God is the divine, spirit, the good and also the evil, the élan vital, and many more things. Will Durant discusses these varied meanings of God for Kazantzakis. Sometimes Kazantzakis describes "a mystical vision: 'I felt a command . . . to become one with the fearful enticing Lover who lies in wait in the darkness and whom we call God. . . . I felt that love, death, and God were one and the same." Sometimes he "united God and Satan in a 'new synthesis' expressing the moral ambivalence of a world fluctuating between good and evil." At other times Kazantzakis "identified God with the Heracleitian flux, almost with revolution: 'God is not the power that has found eternal equilibrium, but the power that is forever breaking every equilibrium, forever searching for a higher one!" Or, like Thomas Mann, he often "offered God as the progressive 'spiritualization of matter' by the heroes of man's mental and moral growth; these nobles of the soul gave developing form and substance to man's ideal; they were the 'creators of God.' " Whatever its meaning " 'God,' which had expressed the highest ideal of men through groping centuries of myth and hope, must not be allowed to die because one of its forms has faded from the minds of educated men." Kazantzakis never ceased " 'longing for God.' "[3]

The question which presents itself in view of the importance of the concept of God in Kazantzakis' system is whether Kazantzakis can accurately be described as an atheist. Opinion is divided on this question with a majority—four of whom are Bloch, Prevelakis, Friar, and Helen Kazantzakis—portraying Kazantzakis as a pure atheist, while some—Poulakidas and Stavrous among them—believing that Kazantzakis may have returned to Christian membership late in life.[4] It is perhaps more correct to say that once Kazantzakis had passed through phases of Nietzscheanism, Buddhism, Marxism, and Hellenism, he was, because of his background, his concern with the soul, and his evaluation of the moving power of the Christian myth, brought back to Christian themes, which is not to say a belief in the Christian faith. Although Christian beliefs do not constitute the totality of his philosophy, he adopted certain Christian postulates, late in life, from a non-Christian perspective.

It is possible that Kazantzakis was—as someone, Proudhon perhaps, once said of Nietzsche and Feuerbach—an antitheist. That is, like them, he opposed not so much the idea of God but the interpretations and usages to which the idea was put by God's earthly followers. Like them, he was avowedly anticlerical and relentlessly battled the institutionalized church. While it is not possible to resolve this question definitively, Helen's recounting of Kazantzakis' death would seem to indicate that he persisted in his antitheism, if not outright atheism, through his later years, especially when faced with the abyss. On the day of his death, Saturday, October 26, 1957, when the Protestant pastor and the Catholic priest came into his hospital room, Kazantzakis turned his face to the wall. " 'Nikosmou,' I scolded. 'What you've done isn't polite. It's Saint Dimitri's Day; the poor men wanted to please us.' He didn't say a word. He only turned his face toward me and asked for a drink."[5] Such nullifications of the Christian cosmol-

ogy carry with it many profound consequences. The most important of these lies in its nihilistic potential.

Kazantzakis' nihilism has been and is at present a hotly con-
tested issue. There are commentators on both sides of the issue,
and they usually—as Kazantzakis was at no time concerned with
conciseness or consistency—support their respective cases quite
well from his writing.[6] Kazantzakis' ascetic inclination, his Buddhism, and his idealism all lead to a tendency to negate the reality
of the world; however, he ultimately rejected the nihilist solution.
His firm adherence to the potential goodness in the world and the
duty of men to realize that goodness through affirming life is
expressed in his emphatic loyalty to his task of saving God.

Kazantzakis states this allegiance to his concept of saving God in
various passages in virtually all his works. In *The Last Temptation of
Christ* (p. 17) Judas cries out: "Man must fight to bring about the
Messiah." Odysseus says:

> I know that God is earless, eyeless, and heartless too, a brainless
> Dragon Worm that crawls on earth and hopes in anguish and in
> secret that we'll give him soul, for then he, too, may sprout ears,
> eyes, to match his growth, but God is clay in ten fingers, and I mold
> him! He spoke, and his ten fingers shaped the empty air. (*Odyssey*,
> VIII, 250, lines 831–36)

He hears God's cry, "Help me, my son. I'm caught in your dark
loins! I groan!" (XIV, 442, line 1052) In *Report* (291) Kazantzakis
says, "Blowing through heaven and earth, and in our hearts and
the heart of every living thing, is a gigantic breath—a great
Cry—which we call God." In such a view God's existence is tenu-
ous at best. His light is perishable. It is to man's support that God
must look for preservation. In transitional times God's survival is
particularly perilous: "Returning from Mount Athos, I felt for
the first time that Christ wanders about hungry and homeless,
that He is in danger, and that it is His turn to be saved—by man."
(p. 236)

One commentator, in analyzing this concept, links Dostoevsky
and Kazantzakis as "friends of God" and traces such friendship to
its founding on two basic ideas. The first of these involves the
irresistible change in man's analysis of creation from objective to

subjective grounds. Man, "from accepting an objective world in which God (who had created him) existed, ultimately thought of himself as the creator of the idea of God (who therefore joined the subjective world within the mind of man)." The second idea is "the subsequent assumption by man of a sense of responsibility, or concern, over the position and merits of a transcendant Being within a solely subjective world which was created by man and must therefore be sustained by him."[7] Thus, armed with this knowledge and responsibility, Kazantzakis, who realized with Zorba and Odysseus that the great, sublime One does not truly exist, turned away not from the world through nihilism as some would have it but to the battle for creating and sustaining God. "The major and almost the only theme of all my work is the struggle of man with 'God': the unyielding, inextinguishable struggle of the naked worm called 'Man' against the terrifying power and darkness of the forces within him and around him."[8]

In this struggle Kazantzakis put man at the center of the universe. He gave man both individual and universal significance, "enabling an individualistic voluntarism to serve transindividualistic ends. By realizing their own potentialities, by overcoming sluggishness and exerting our vitality whether sexually, martially, or mentally, we save God and push evolution forward."[9] For Kazantzakis the forward push of evolution by man for transindividualistic ends can come only through one system—submission to a new harmonious and unifying visionary ideal that "summons and commands all our forces: viz., we must follow a rhythm that is higher than ourselves. Only in this way can man's existence become noble and integrated. Only thus can his energy transcend the stifling limits of the individual." (*Spain,* 62) Kazantzakis believes that only those who find and obey such a rhythm attain true consciousness.

A rhythm may call for action, e.g., communism, or it may call for contemplation, e.g., Buddhism. It is not necessarily logical, but it will concern itself with earthly existence. Belief in a rhythm constitutes faith, which is important because "only through faith can the masses be elevated. What do we mean by their being 'elevated'? We mean the subjection of their desires and needs to a hyperindividual, or rather, to the deepest human rhythm." The only way to fulfill our duty of allying with the rhythm of our generation is to transmute matter into Spirit. This process is highly complex and difficult, in Kazantzakis' view, for matter and Spirit are not always distinguishable: "Whatever was once a movement or an impulse upward in the foregoing generation— whatever was once spirit—becomes, in the subsequent genera- tion, motionless, stifled, heavy, and in time reacts like substance." (p. 63) Examples given are race, religion, nationalism, and vari- ous other ideals. These rise up, in Kazantzakis' analysis, as new life forces to hold sway for a certain period, after which they become material obstacles to new rhythmic life forces which ap- pear on the horizon. There is a linkage of Kazantzakis' metaphysics with his theories of history and politics in this duty of each man as a savior of God to identify and ally himself with the God-rhythm of his generation. For the spiritual rhythm will lead from the transitional age; and, if not wholly political, it will of necessity take political forms for efficacy and comprehensiveness.

Two important questions immediately arise concerning Kazantzakis' politics of salvation. First, how does one identify this "noble rhythm," or, put another way, is there a universal theme underlying all the various political faces that the Spirit takes? Second, will saving God help man to overcome Spinozistic neces- sity and contemporary technological, economic, historical, and sociological realms of determinism? If so, how? And if not, then of what liberating value is the concept? The latter of these ques- tions will be taken up a bit later. As for the former, in addressing it, one is led again to Kazantzakis' Marxism. Just as Kazantzakis' psychic struggle between writer and actor propelled him to Mar- xism, so did his concept of saving God.

Marxism, in Kazantzakis' terms, seemed to embody the God- rhythm. Wilson observes of *Toda Raba* and *The Saviors of God*:

> Like Sartre, he seems to have accepted that Marxism is the most typical and basic philosophy of our century. And where Sartre has attempted, in *The Critique of Dialectical Reason*, to broaden and deepen Marxism, Kazantzakis has attempted to create a new reli- gion based upon the anti-Christian ideas of Nietzsche and Marx. He declares, in effect, that man must cease to regard himself as a slavish creature of God, and recognize that he is God's co-worker.

In fact, more than this; without man's creative effort, God dies;
through the god-like act of creation, man becomes the Saviour of
God. The idea is tremendous and powerful—and, of course, in
total opposition to the self-pitying pessimism that has become so
fashionable in the 20th century, from Andreyev to Beckett.[10]

He was attracted to Marxism by its activist messianism and by its
equalitarian economic, political, and philosophic appeal. Postulated as that alternative philosophy of salvation for which
Kazantzakis was seeking, he was dismayed to discover that, in
practice, Marxism took on many of the aspects of bourgeois
Christianity, the inquisitional religion that he opposed. Like
many of his more sensitive and compassionate contemporaries,
Kazantzakis saw communism as a religion endangered "by materialistic emphasis. He rejected the materialistic bias of communism, but similarly rejected the dogmatic anthropomorphic
God of the Christians as equally materialistic."[11] In the name of
the City of God, the later Marxists used injustice to bring about
social justice, the murder of heretics to attain brotherhood, and
intolerance and oppression to achieve equality, thus bringing
about a tragic conflict between the idea and its realization. Marxism became more than a necessary ordering ideal of men's lives
when it claimed to be the sole and absolute vehicle for man's
salvation on earth—just as religions claim to be the absolute,
hegemonous vehicle for man's salvation after death. Centralist,
compulsory means were used to assimilate society and the individual into a collective machine in order to restructure and recreate everything and everyone in the name of a future eschaton.
This claim to absolutes allowed for no deviation, no spontaneity,
no freedom. The later Marxists committed the fatal error of
attempting to stop history! Following his intense involvement
with Marxism, Kazantzakis became disillusioned with Soviet
Marxism, with all its materialism, bureaucratization, and moralizing, and—because of these—its loss of dynamism. He never,
however, abandoned socialist goals.

Kazantzakis had rejected as outmoded the Christian ontology
and the bourgeois ethic built on that worldview when he formulated his alternative concept of saving God, only to see the first
sociopolitical application of his new view fail with the in-

stitutionalization of Marxism. He had emphasized commitment
and choice and yet proffered no guides for such choice. In this
respect, at least, he was vulnerable to Camus's criticism, as related
by Wilhoite, of Sartre's brand of existentialism: "Sartrean existentialists present no criteria for evaluating personal choices, much
less for justifying their own political and ideological alliance with
proponents of a deterministic view such as Marxism." In a highly
paradoxical fashion "they seek to actualize their boundless freedom by aligning themselves with a movement which claims the
authorization of history for its total freedom."[12]

Do success, vitalism, and vigor, representing the "authorization
of history," provide the viable criteria for one's commitment? Is
this how one tells a liberating ideal from an oppressive one?
Kazantzakis addresses this issue in *The Fratricides*. Leonidas, a
sensitive young nationalist soldier, writes to his love:

> Why am I fighting? For whom am I fighting? They say we fight to
> save Greece, we, the Royal Army, the blackhoods as they call us;
> and that our enemies in the hills—the redhoods—fight to divide
> and sell Greece. Oh, if I could only be sure! If I only knew. . . . Is it
> possible that we are the traitors, the ones who are selling Greece,
> and can the so-called traitors in the hills be the armed moun-
> taineers and the rebels of 1821? How can I tell justice from injus-
> tice, and decide with whom to go, and to which side I should give
> my life? There is no greater torment, to a fighter, than this doubt.

Leonidas, who symbolizes Kazantzakis, realized that sincerity in
one's commitment as expressed through individual bravery and
fortitude represents a possible evaluative standard. Yet when his
group captures five young rebels the prisoners, rather than join
the nationalists, choose to be executed; "so courage and faith is
not the infallible test." Leonidas wonders how, then, "can I separate the truth from the lies? How many heroes and martyrs have
sacrificed themselves for some damned ideal; God has his pure
heroes and martyrs; Satan has his pure heroes and martyrs; how
can I tell them apart?" (pp. 102–04)

Following his disillusionment with Marxism, Kazantzakis,
perhaps unlike Sartre, came to appreciate fully—as evidenced by
Leonidas' agonizing—the political cul-de-sac of solipsistic rel-

ativism that his saviors faced. In seeking valid criteria to replace that relativism, he cast about for enlightenment and turned (or perhaps more accurately, returned), as have so many others, to the two most enduring and powerful of Western traditions: Greek classicism and Christian doctrine. As Bien states, "Kazantzakis seems unable to avoid Christianity and Hellenism when he bodies forth his visions of future man."[13]

The Human Condition and the Classical View[14]

Seeking universals for his saviors, following his Marxist disillusionment, Kazantzakis focused in the 1930s an encompassing gaze on his Greek heritage in much the same manner as he had once focused on his Cretan ancestry. For his most ambitious work, *The Odyssey,* completed on Aegina, Kazantzakis went for sustenance to one of the fountainheads of Greek culture, Homer's *Odyssey.* The novels of the late 1930s and after provide ample evidence of his Greek enthrallment; *Zorba, The Greek Passion, Freedom or Death, The Fratricides* are all set in Greek locales, and *Report* abounds in praises to Hellenism. Bien notes this return to Greece and its effect on Kazantzakis' life and art. By relaxing sufficiently so that Greece could embrace him (to Bien "rootedness demands humility and passive acceptance"), Kazantzakis "was able to introduce into his works a natural, unforced and therefore convincing particularity which they had hitherto lacked, a particularity which no amount of universalizing could then erase." In enabling Kazantzakis to go beyond the confines "of Mind and Self, this rootedness had the additional effect of allowing a true sense of community to an *oeuvre* which had tended formerly to individuation and indeed to solipsism."[15]

This solipsism was precisely the crucial political-philosophic problem of Kazantzakis' concept of saving God. There is evident in Kazantzakis' return to Hellenism for criteria, for the exit from the transitional age, a mystic love of the Greek spirit and country, but he was not returning to the political view that "during the decade from 1912 to 1922 may be summed up as 'aristocratic nationalism'." Rather, in his Greek heritage, Kazantzakis sought for his saviors insight of universal, internationalistic validity. Prevelakis sees this internationalism as the central manner in which Kazantzakis' *Odyssey* differs from the literary stereotype of the nationalist genre. Kazantzakis' Odysseus "would not be a national hero." In fact, the reverse was true: "The arena of his actions would be the whole world. Instead of the friendly setting of his native land, there would be threatening horizons. Instead of well-known faces, there would be magic masks."[16] Bringing this internationalist inquiry to bear on his Greek heritage Kazantzakis discerned valuable criteria for his saviors' struggle within the two central missions of Hellenism—liberty and the reconciliation of East and West.

Kazantzakis believed with Augustine that "every great people has its own bluebird, the supreme and mystical ideal in which all its urges coalesce. Ancient Greece had beauty; Rome, the state; Jews, divinity; the Hindus, Nirvana; Christianity, the everlasting Kingdom." Approaching the cumulative experience of the Hellenes in this fashion he discovered the "beloved bluebird, bloodstained but immortal, that first on this planet built its nest in Greece—freedom." (*England,* 280) This immortal bluebird was the Hellenes' hallmark; the overriding "mission of the Hellenic race: Man's struggle for liberty." (*Gr. Passion,* 305) The Greeks sought, as Stanford suggests, to fulfill their mission in many ways, both politically and spiritually. "Freedom, *eleutheria,* has long been the political and spiritual ideal of the Greek mind—at times a deluding will-o'-wisp, at times a spur to greatness." They have demonstrated their allegiance to this goal from the time of Socrates to the Greeks of the campaign against the invaders in World War II; "these, and many more, at different times and in different ways, spent their lives in seeking freedom."[17] Greek political quests for liberty from ancient to modern times are well documented. It was to the spiritual-religious quests that Kazantzakis, in keeping with his continuing search for directional aid in saving God, turned his attention. In Kazantzakis' view, the primary spiritual manner in which the Hellenes have sought freedom involved the transformation into Greek terms of the God figure of the Jews. On Crete and Greece "the Greek soul accomplished its destined mission: it reduced God to the scale of man." (*Report,* 151) Thus, God was rendered a dynamic concept and with the

wedding of classical Greek thought, politics, art, etc., which represented the high point of Western culture, to the God-Christ
myth, the tempo of Western civilization was set. In leaving behind
the transitional age the saviors must reaffirm this basic Nietzschean truth; again the "time has come when we must make Christ
laugh; yes, must! No more scourgings, weeping, or crucifixions.
Christ must once more bind the strong, happy gods of Greece
inside him; He must assimilate them all. The time has arrived for
the Jewish-Christ to become a Greek." (*Report*, 208) The other-
worldly God, the slave ethic, the crucified Christ of humility, will
all be transvalued into an affirmative man-god. Through such
reaffirmation will come a release of the spirit, joy, happiness, and
a resurrection of civilization. This resurrection will be made even
more meaningful if the second mission of the Hellenes is fulfilled.
This corollary task was to synthesize Eastern and Western concepts of life, that is, to "give features to the featureless and
measure to the measureless, balancing the blind clashing forces,
such is the mission of the much-buffeted sea and land known as
Greece." (*Report*, 165–66)

Situated geographically at the historic crossroads of the world,
Greece represents the meeting place of East and West. For
Kazantzakis this meeting is symbolized as the interaction of
Apollo, God of the West, and Dionysos, God of the East. Apollo
"dreams of the world's harmony and beauty, beholding it in
serene forms. Entrenched in his individuation, motionless, he
stands tranquil and sure amidst the turbulent sea of phenomena."
Apollo's look is "full of light; even when sorrow or indignation
overcome him, they do not shatter the divine equilibrium." On
the other hand, Dionysos is the God who seeks to

> shatter individuation, flings himself into the sea of phenomena
> and follows its terrible, kaleidoscopic waves. Men and beasts be-
> come brothers, death itself is seen as one of life's masks, the mul-
> tiform stalking-blind of illusion rips in two, and we find ourselves
> in breast-to-breast contact with the truth . . . that we all are one,
> that all of us together create God, that God is not man's ancestor,
> but his descendant.[18] (*Report*, 323)

This fusion of Apollo and Dionysos provides important revelations for Kazantzakis' saviors. Historically, in this process the

"turbid, unsettled cry of the Orient grows pellucid when it passes through' the light of Greece; humanized, it is transformed into logos—reason." Greece is "the filter which, with great struggle, refines brute into man, eastern servitude into liberty, barbaric intoxication into sober rationality." (*Report*, 165–66) This filtering process unites radically different *Weltanschauungen*.

Eastern and Western outlooks on life represent contradictory concepts of humanity. Eastern values are the primacy of the state, the people as mass, the superiority of the idea over the individual; self-sacrifice before a dispassionate God; obedience to an omnipotent Creator; and the calm, unquestioning acceptance of human suffering without justifying it as having an intellectual place in the world. Western values, on the other hand, are the primacy of the individual over the state, the mass, and the idea; pride in the potential of man; resistance to God, in whose image man is made; the rigorous search for truth, depicted metaphorically in the highest symbols of the West—Prometheus, Odysseus, and Faust; and finally, a questioning spirit, an inability to accept calmly life's suffering, injustice, inhumanity, and ignorance. The Westerner, who is both the creator and the product of the West, is normally pragmatic, realistic, and sure that life is real, actual, and worthwhile. The Easterner insists that life is merely a dream and that actual experiences which have happened will happen again in the same fashion. To the Westerner each moment and action is novel; to the Easterner each action is insignificant because if life is dreamlike and cyclical, then fate does not admit any unique quality or essence to particular events.

Kazantzakis uses this conflict between the dream world of Eastern withdrawal and the actual world of Western commitment as the foundation of his new synthesis.[19] Hellenism's synthesis of these produced a paradigm of harmony and creativity, in contrast with the present one which is the paradigm of disharmony and destruction. In that taut, symbiotic moment in time, Apollo and Dionysos collaborated to produce a wedding of the divine and the diabolic, irrationality and reason, beast and god; and Thanatos was brought under the control of Eros for a spiritually creative civilization.

Kazantzakis' reliance on this ancient synthesis is evident

throughout the section in *Report* entitled "Pilgrimage Through Greece." By viewing the temples, myths, and heroes of the various regions of Greece, Kazantzakis believed he could see the manner in which the spirit had passed over and bequeathed the suitable soul to each. Thus he attached importance to the insights attained through a receptive, openly sensitive journey through Greece. Such a journey passes from spiritual victory to spiritual victory in an uninterrupted and magic unity. (*Report*, 157) This unity is demonstrated by Greece's temples, art, and architecture, through an ideal organic linking of spirit and matter, myth and reality, tragedy and beauty, individuation and unity, love and struggle, effort and serenity, discipline and passion, etc. In ancient Greece more than in any other place man most truly succeeded in "imposing order over chaos, in establishing a 'cosmos'—and cosmos means harmony." (*Report*, 164)

Today, as in ancient times, contradictory Eastern and Western forces are clashing—individuality and community, quest and acceptance, Nirvana and secularism, dream and commitment—

> New forces are rising from the East, new forces are rising from the West. . . . Following the tradition of reason and empirical inquiry the West bounds forward to conquer the world; the East prodded by frightening subconscious forces, likewise darts forward to conquer the world. (*Report*, 175)

The saviors must use the lessons of ancient Greece in the task of once more wedding these chaotic forces and creating order. Hellenism's examples are not, however, in and of themselves, complete and infallible guides; for the creative equilibrium of Hellenism—of mind and body, East and West—was but a momentary one (as are all syntheses). Hellenism's transformation was wrought in the uninspired Hellenistic period through the surrender of the Hellenese to the extremes of mind, that is, rational extirpation of reality, bodily, bestial desire, or both. Kazantzakis, echoing Plato, ascribes the fall of Hellenism in part to the domination of the appetitive pleasures of the body. At the time of Greece's initial decline, the athlete's body began to hypertrophy, killing his mind. Kazantzakis cites Euripides and Galen as having been among those who protested and denounced this development. Heracles, the great martyr, demonstrated this decline as he gradually degenerated into a huge-bodied, low-browed drinker and glutton. Greece thus arrived at the realistic, magniloquent, and faithless Hellenistic era that had no suprapersonal ideals. Emotions and passions dominated. The free individual lost his discipline, and the bridled instinct that maintained necessary balance became runaway depravity.

Following the Peloponnesian War, Greece began to disintegrate. Belief in the fatherland was no more as individual self-sufficiency triumphed. The protagonist on the stage was not god or the idealized youth but the wealthy citizen, with all his lascivious passions and pleasures—a skeptic, materialist, and libertine. Genius had already been replaced by talent; then good taste replaced talent. Children, coquettish women, and realistic scenes filled art. Men were portrayed as being either brutal or intellectual. (*Report*, 169–70) As Nietzsche taught, those who betrayed the delicate balance through excessive intellectualism murdered that mythical tragedy that was the highest expression of Hellenic civilization

> by logical analysis. Socrates, with his dialectics, killed the Apollonian sobriety and Dionysiac intoxication. . . . Would the Socratic spirit—in other words, science—keep Dionysus forever in chains? Or, now that human reason recognized its own limits, might a new civilization perhaps appear with Socrates as its symbol—Socrates at long last learning music. (*Report*, 325)

Consequently, Kazantzakis would conclude regarding the relevance and utility for his saviors of the legacy of ancient Greece: "Here lies the danger and the price of the love we bear Greek civilization. It is difficult to distinguish which elements are still useful and which will remain forever a divine spectacle devoid of practical relevance." (*T.R.*, 207) One "still useful" element of Hellenism manifests itself in Kazantzakis' thought as a passionately daimonic quality. This important theme becomes evident when Kazantzakis' system is discussed within the framework of Rollo May's critique of the contemporary predicament.

May, who once visited Greece's holy Mt. Athos (where Kazantzakis and Sikelianos had spent forty days), based his critique on the insights of Greek mythology. Like Kazantzakis, he sees an important role for the artist rather than the scientist in this transitional time. "Our curious predicament," May argues, "is that the same processes which make modern man so powerful—the magnificent development of atomic and other kinds of technical energy—are the very processes which render us powerless." This is so because man's will is undermined by the impersonal technical power spheres within which we exist—mass advertising, drugs, machines, and the rest—that separate us from one another and from nature. This vacuity of will occurs precisely at the time when we must take ever-increasing responsibility for crucial choices in leisure, sex, politics, and everything else; and when—in this transitional time—the symbolic valuative and normative criteria for responsible choice are chaotic: "We are caught, as [R. D.] Laing puts it, in a 'hell of frenetic passivity.' " The perimeters of our captivity have been portrayed by Dostoevsky, Kafka, Beckett, Sartre, and others as despair, anxiety, and alienation.

May suggests that the essence of this entrapment is apathy—the lack of feeling, passion, emotion. To him the opposite of love and will is not hate and indecision but the detached, indifferent, uninvolved apathetic attitude that we have adopted in order to maintain "sanity" in an age of insanity. This apathy is translated into noninterference in incidents of street rape and murder, withdrawal, etc. It is intimately related to violence. In the mid-1960s, "this problem erupted in the form of several incidents that shook us to the very foundations. Our 'emptiness' has been turning into despair and destructiveness, violence, and assassination; for it is now undeniable that these go hand in hand with apathy."[20] The dialectic of apathy and violence proceeds unabated. It nourishes on the multifaceted deterministic cooptions of our era and the corollary despairing sensation in the pit of our stomachs that life has passed us by. May asserts that it is solely through a reinvigoration of will undergirded by forward-looking intentionality that man can reformulate his values, transcend the impersonality of his predicament, and attain freedom. Drawing from the Greek synthesis that Kazantzakis relied upon, May concludes that the only way to reconstitute our will meaningfully (as intentionality) is through an erotic, vibrant, integration of the daimonic. The elaboration of this integrative process is May's chief concern and has important implications for Kazantzakis' thought.

The daimonic, which May uses according to the classical Greek meaning (as distinguished from modern perversion of the term), is "any natural function which has the power to take over the whole person." Examples given are sex and eros, anger and rage, and the craving for power. The daimonic has both constructive and destructive elements. It can engender creativity and evil. A person's daimon confers creativity when confronted and evil when repressed, projected onto others, or both. This process is applicable on a societal scale. In analyzing the daimonic as both good and evil, May observes: "All life is a flux between these two aspects of the daimonic. We can repress the daimonic, but we cannot avoid the toll of apathy and the tendency toward later explosion which such repression brings in its wake."

The mythology of ancient Hellenism portrays par excellence the recognition of the imperative need to integrate the daimonic. Such integration underlay and gave rise in part to the symbolic richness of Greece. In the Hellenistic and Christian periods, this integrative synthesis dissolved. There was a splitting of the daimon into concepts of good and evil, passion and rationality, eros and sex, death and life, etc. The early Christians and Hellenistic Greeks gained a great deal in moral dynamism "by this splitting of the struggle of good and evil into devils and angels," but they also lost something. "And what is lost is important; namely, the classical organismic concept of *being* as combining both good and destructive possibilities." The loss of this concept of being has extracted heavy payment down through the centuries. May cites approvingly Rilke's epigram: "If my devils are to leave me, I am afraid my angels will take flight as well."

We moderns have sought to deny and repress our devils and have discovered the truth of Rilke's statement. Our angels have left us also. Thus, in this century we have waged the most intensely destructive, fratricidal wars in history. To reverse this trend we must undo the damage done in the Hellenistic period and at the time of the early Christians and emphasize once more the Hellenistic knowledge that good is possible and constructive only in symbiotic fusion with evil within the self. Good is, as St. Thomas Aquinas taught, recognizable only with reference and in relation to evil. To be good is to overcome evil. Yet overcoming evil must not lead one to suppose that evil has been eradicated, for then one loses both the sense of direction imposed by the potential for evil and the depth of experience that is required for a total appreciation of the complexity of human existence. We must recognize the daimonic, therefore, as an element of human experience and not as a force outside ourselves. We must live with the daimonic, which is our own human capacity for cruelty, aggression—evil, if we are to live creatively. "Not to recognize the daimonic itself turns out to be daimonic; it makes us accomplices on the side of destructive possession."[21]

The inspiring recognition of the daimonic is a vital lesson that Kazantzakis, Zorba, and Odysseus teach. In the prologue to *The Last Temptation of Christ,* Kazantzakis explains this common life-dominating inner struggle—the Supreme Duty, to reconcile the divine and the daimonic:

> I loved my body and did not want it to perish; I loved my soul and did not want it to decay. . . . The struggle between God and man breaks out in everyone, together with the longing for reconciliation. Most often this struggle is unconscious and short-lived. A weak soul does not have the endurance to resist the flesh for very long. It grows heavy, becomes flesh itself, and the contest ends. But among responsible men, men who keep their eyes riveted day and night upon the Supreme Duty, the conflict between flesh and spirit breaks out mercilessly and may last until death. (*Last Tempt.* pp. 1–2)

Theirs is the example of one who confronted and listened to the daimonic and thereby integrated it into the self. Recognizing the daimon of his time—"Our age is a savage one; the Bull, the underground Dionysian powers, has been unleashed; the Apollonian crust of the earth is cracking."[22]—Kazantzakis sought to harness the destructive, diabolic elements of his age to the constructive ones. Faithfully following his daimon, his Dionysian *élan vital* (May says of the daimonic, "It is nonrational in its resembling the 'Dionysion' of Nietzsche and the *élan vital* of Bergson"[23]), called the voice of God, the tigress, the spirit, Kazantzakis searched for a valid, whole existence. He discovered in a dream that the one who attains a redemptive manner of life is "he who perceives, loves, and lives the totality."[24](*Report,* 367) In living the totality we must not deny instincts or the underground powers. We must be open to all passions or these daimons will exact their revenge.

Kazantzakis relates a tale of his meeting in an abbey in the Sinai Desert with one Father Joachim. This holiest of men, who spoke only to God, passed on to Kazantzakis the fruit of an entire life spent in apprenticeship to flesh and spirit.

> "Angels are nothing more—do you hear!—nothing more than refined devils. The day will come—oh, if only I could live to see it!—when men will understand this, and then . . ."
>
> He leaned over to my ear. For the first time, his voice was trembling.
>
> ". . . and then the religion of Christ will take another step forward on earth. It will embrace the whole man, all of him not just half as it does now in embracing only the soul. Christ's mercy will broaden. It will embrace and sanctify the body as well as the soul; it will see—and preach—that they are not enemies, but fellow workers. Whereas now, what happens? If we sell ourselves to God, He urges us to deny the body. When will Christ's heart grow sufficiently broad to commiserate not only the soul but also the body, and to reconcile these two savage beasts?" (*Report,* 303)[25]

Kazantzakis lived this counsel and incorporated the daimonic— the devils as well as the angels—in an existence exactly opposite to that May describes as characterizing our existence.

This insight of Kazantzakis—that we must recognize the savage Dionysian powers within each of us individually and within all of us collectively—is the antithesis of apathy and of the denial of eros and passion. It is a demonstration of the path out of the dialectic of apathy and violence through love and will, and thus one of Kazantzakis' most important borrowings from classical Greece.

Several more "still useful" elements for Kazantzakis' saviors— in addition to the recognition of the daimonic—are derived from his exploration of ancient Hellenism. As previously noted, the new visionary rhythm that we must find in order to save God and achieve deliverance from the transitional age has to be such as to ennoble man's mundane life when confronted with the twin, terrifying abysses of human mortality and historical temporality. From Hellenism one learns that for worldwide applicability this aspirational ideal must incorporate the wisdom of both East and West. It must fill the demands of community—to provide coherence and individuation—to allow spontaneity. It must also incorporate, as did Greek tragedy, the insight of art, the arena of imagination, intuition, and predictive foresight, and dialectical science, the arena of intellect and analysis. And it must heed, as well, the lessons and wishes of the heart. The ideal must maintain the proper harmonious balance between mind and body. This ideal order must be founded on a comprehensive understanding of the natural world and human nature—the diabolic as well as the divine. As its essence, the vision must possess a universal normative-ethical schema cognizant of the natural-historical milieu in which humanity's life exists. It must follow faithfully the "immortal bluebird" of liberty. Ancient Greece's failure to persevere dynamically in the pursuit of these goals, owing to the staticism of later Hellenism, rendered the noble synthesis vulnerable to dismemberment in the Hellenistic period and ultimately made Greece easy prey for the Macedonian conquerors.

Hellenism's insufficiency in meeting these many demands caused Kazantzakis to research the other of the two dominant sources of his view of future man—Christianity. He sought not to negate the lessons of ancient Greece but rather to augment them with the spiritual criteria of Christianity. His success in that endeavor is signaled by his having written Prevelakis in 1950, while working on *The Last Temptation of Christ,* that "the old antinomies are beginning to become organized into an organic synthesis. . . . I've found the solution I have outside the realm of intellect or analysis—i.e., beyond the purlieus of 'Satan.' "[26]

Christianity: Criteria of the Spirit

Noting the importance of certain Christian teachings, as exemplified by the Christ figure, for Kazantzakis' thought, Blenkinsopp observes:

It may seem strange at first sight that Kazantzakis finds a place for
Christ in his dialectical scheme of reality, and yet it is precisely here
that he differs from his mentor Nietzsche. He followed the same
road as Zarathustra but further along it he rediscovered Christ as a
traveller who had gone before him. Like Joyce and many others
before and since, he had bad luck with the particular form of
institutionalized Christianity in which he was raised. He rejected it
and it rejected him; the Greek archbishop would not allow his body
to lie in church chiefly because of *The Greek Passion* and *The Last
Temptation of Christ,* and the last named novel was, for good measure, put on the Roman Catholic index. He has some hard things to
say about conventional Christianity as a "well-organized fairy tale
promising paradise and immortality" and the churches are
"taverns of hope where you go to forget your real duty." Yet his
work, like that of Joyce, is pervaded with Christian symbolism and
the action in almost all the novels is played out within the time
sequence of the Christian calendar.[27]

Kazantzakis had looked at the often horrid record of institutionalized Christianity and seen that the church was at times
guilty of dehumanizing actions. However, it became increasingly
obvious to Kazantzakis that the Christian myth was of the utmost
importance: "Like Dostoevsky, Kazantzakis regarded the Christian myth and the existence of God as indispensable to human
sanity; both saw nothing but chaos without them."[28] Believing
this, Kazantzakis rejected tradition and institutionalization and
chose the resurrected Christ, not the crucified one, as the embodiment of Christianity.[29] He cut away the layers of judgmental,
devitalizing crusts covering the true power of the myth, and
looked to the positive, ennobling elements of Christianity.

Kazantzakis rejected the dehumanizing hypocrisy of the ethic
of humility. "I am less afraid of the major vices than of the minor
virtues . . . because these have lovely faces and deceive us all too
easily." After failing to castigate a deceitful monk, Kazantzakis
would say: "For my part, I want to give the worst explanation
because I want to shame my soul and keep it from doing the same
thing again."[30] (*Report,* 213) The minor virtues, in Kazantzakis'
view, can imprison man in a cage of habitual cowardice and
expediency. Focusing on the Christ figure, Kazantzakis sought,
particularly in *The Last Temptation of Christ,* creatively to "renew

and supplement the sacred myth that underlies the great Christian era of the West." He endeavored to "reincarnate the essence of Christ, setting aside the dross—falsehoods and pettinesses which all the churches and all the cassocked representatives of Christianity have heaped upon this figure thereby distorting it."[31] For this immensely creative process Kazantzakis emphasized, therefore, the affirmative existential possibilities for man in a chaotic, materialistic transitional age that lay within the actions of Christ. These actions are lessons that teach that if man is to save God, he must uphold the freedom to do as Jesus did and choose one's path to God; human dignity, pride, and the soul; brotherhood and the force of love. Kazantzakis consistently called on his fellows to realize their immense potential through a joining of these within and among themselves as ennobling prerequisites to saving God. The first of these lessons, the capability of choice—freedom of the will—is a logically essential precondition to saving God.

If we are to save God, which is the cause of moral goodness in the world, a necessary prerequisite is that we must, as Kazantzakis recognized, be able to choose the commitment that enables each in his own way to liberate the spirit. A person who rejects the power to choose between alternatives, between doing and not doing, could not logically believe in the existence of the creative potential of man and the responsibility of each person for advancing the divine. For if there be no such thing as free will, if the slaveholder and Hitler, who actualized not divine but diabolic potentiality, could not have avoided their acts of tyranny and oppression, then they would have no responsibility for evil, and they could not therefore reasonably be the objects of moral blame and indignation. If the will is not free, then no one is morally responsible for his acts, be they good or bad. The men and the nations that stifle the spirit of the Good are no more justly liable to condemnation than an earthquake or a hurricane. The point is that if the will is not free, no ethical appeal can reasonably be made to those attempting to halt the flow of *élan vital,* the life force—the bourgeoisie, the technocrats, etc.—to refrain from their suppression. They can logically reply that they are not free to refrain. On the other hand, those who struggle to transubstantiate matter into spirit cannot logically have recourse to moral indignation, for both groups are victims of forces over which they have no control.

Obviously, most people, in their everyday conduct, judgment, and attitudes, act as if they believe in free will and yet some reject it in theory. By this rejection they inevitably weaken their belief in internal and external freedom. In applying this theoretical assumption to political situations, they are logically prevented from moral opposition to men who destroy political and social liberty. They cannot rationally denounce a Hitler if the man possesses no free will and is therefore presumed to be inevitably compelled by character and circumstance to fall under the domination of motives that irresistibly force him to conquer and kill. An evaluation of his conduct must be stated in terms not of blame but of regret. Thus the practical effect of denial of free will is to render man incapable of condemning violations of political and civil liberties.

In creating and keeping alive the belief in free will, "Christianity," in the words of one observer, "has exercised vastly more influence than all other social forces combined."[32] The entire body of the Christian religion is based on the presumption that man has free will, at least in some respects. Certainly man is free to choose God. There is no hint of circumstance or of inevitable force that shall cause man either to choose or reject God. This is the basic right of all men and cannot be taken away from man by man. As stated in the New Testament, "whosoever will, let him take the water of life freely."[33] In Kazantzakis' system this prerequisite act, from which all else follows, is cast as the freely chosen commitment to save God. Zorba chooses to dance and affirm life, for that is his manner of spiritualizing his being. On a higher level, El Greco chose to paint penetrating and beautiful portraits of the spirit hidden deep within men's souls. And, on a still higher level, Jesus chose the cross when faced with the alternative of human happiness, for that was *his* way of saving God. Chilson says, "the actual path to salvation appears to depend upon the individual . . . there is no universal pattern for salvation." Because of this Odysseus "finds it impossible to agree totally with any of the Saviors he met in his later journeying. He cannot take the path of Buddha, Faust, Don Quixote, or Christ; he must find his own way."[34]

Finding one's path is made much more difficult by the complexities of transitional times.[35] Kazantzakis relates, in the last summation of his life and work, how he tried the paths of love, science, philosophy, social activism, and, finally, poetry, before discovering his God on Mount Athos and thereby choosing the intent and purpose of his creative actions. "When I saw that all these led to the Abyss, fear would seize me, and I would turn back and take another road." Despairing of salvation he sought refuge in prayer and chastity in a hermit's retreat on the holy mountain where no female had ever set foot. Enduring cold, hunger, thirst, sleeplessness, and similar privations, he disciplined the body to obey the spirit. And he disciplined the spirit to reject easy virtue, false hope, cheap joy, and the minor passions. By purifying his existence in this manner he finally saw the "red ribbon left behind him in his ascent—within us and in all the universe by a certain combatant; I clearly saw his bloody footprints ascending from inorganic matter into life and from life into spirit."[36] From that time on Kazantzakis sought forever to follow those footsteps and appealed to his contemporaries to do the same.

The efficacy of Kazantzakis', and all men's, actions in fulfilling this quest is dependent upon, interrelated with, and made viable by the second postulate—pride and the power of the soul. Kazantzakis saw men as endowed with potentially powerful souls that are born with them and remain so long as life remains. Historical neglect of this tremendous potential does not diminish it, for "man's soul is omnipotent." (*St. Fran.*, 102) Fulfilling the commitment to freeing Crete, Captain Polyxigis charges into battle chastizing those who timidly hang back: "The holy splinter, you idiot, is the soul of man. I know of no other." (*Freedom*, 296) In *Report* Kazantzakis tells of the lesson of his Vienna illness:

> Ever since that day I have realized that man's soul is a terrible and dangerous coilspring. Without knowing it, we all carry a great explosive force wrapped in our flesh and lard. And what is worse, we do not want to know it, for then villainy, cowardice, and falsehood lose their justification; we can no longer hide behind man's

supposed impotence and wretched incompetence; we ourselves
must bear the blame if we are villains, cowards, or liars, for although we have an all-powerful force inside, we dare not use it for
fear it might destroy us. But we take the easy, comfortable way out,
and allow it to vent its strength little by little until it too has
degenerated to flesh and lard. How terrible not to know that we
possess this force! If we did know, we would be proud of our souls.
In all heaven and earth, nothing so closely resembles God as the
soul of man. (*Report*, 357)

This omnipotent, divine soul lays the basis for the worth of each
human being.

The power of the soul and consequent moral dignity of the
human personality is another elementary lesson of Christ. Christianity teaches that man is created in the likeness of God and
possesses an immortal soul. Man is made free through this likeness and given worth by it as related by Paul, "where the Spirit of
the Lord is present there is freedom. All of us, then, reflect the
glory of the Lord with uncovered faces; and that same glory,
coming from the Lord who is the Spirit, transforms us into his
very likeness, in an ever greater degree of glory."[37] The possession of an immortal soul and the likeness of man to God connotes
basic human dignity, which means that the human being is an end
in himself and is not to be used as a means or instrument to any
other end. Each man possesses great stature in Kazantzakis' eyes
because of his moral dignity as a person; and although recognition of this stature may be prevented by external force or internal
incapacitation, men who realize their potential will answer their
oppressors as the nationalist soldier Ninios, in *The Fratricides*,
answered his rebel capturers: "My dignity as a man does not allow
me to be forced into obedience." (*Frat.*, 247)

St. Augustine had stated the traditional Christian view of man's
image and soul: "God made man in his own image. For he created
for him a soul endowed with reason and intelligence, so that he
might excel all the creatures of earth, air, and sea which were not
so gifted."[38] Kazantzakis' heretical theme, that man now possesses
the capability to surpass God and in fact creates God in the image
of man, was anathema to the church (which was still tied to the
Augustinian view), but not to many of his contemporaries.

Bonhoeffer, for example, also sought to strike the chord of man's greatness.

Bonhoeffer sees the dominant movement since the thirteenth century toward the autonomy of man as reaching a certain completion in the twentieth century. This is evidenced in religion with the substitution of reason for revelation; in ethics with the substitution of moral principles for the ten commandments; in politics with the substitution of reasons of state for religious morality; in international relations with the substitution of the law of nature for divine law; in philosophy with the substitution of mechanism for providence; in science with the substitution of infinitude for a finitely created cosmos. There is no longer any need, says Bonhoeffer,

> for God as a working hypothesis, whether in morals, politics, or science. Nor is there any need for such a God in religion or philosophy (Feuerbach). In the name of intellectual honesty these working hypotheses should be dropped or dispensed with as far as possible. A scientist or physician who seeks to provide edification is a hybrid.

Christian apologetics have tried in various ways to oppose this recognition. They have confronted the self-assurance of the modern world with the needed tutelage of God to answer the ultimate questions of death and guilt. The secularized offshoot of that movement, the existentialist philosophers and the psychotherapists, attempt to talk to man about God by demonstrating to him that he knows nothing, that he is unhappy, and that he is in severe straits. Bonhoeffer sees these approaches of the Christian apologetics as pointless "because it looks to me like an attempt to put a grown-up man back into adolescence, i.e., to make him dependent on things on which he is not in fact dependent any more, thrusting him back into the midst of problems which are in fact not problems for him any more"; as ignoble "because this amounts to an effort to exploit the weakness of man for purposes alien to him and not freely subscribed to by him"; and as un-Christian "because for Christ himself is being substituted one particular stage in the religiousness of man, i.e., a human law." Such attempts present Christ as undynamic, inflexible, and in opposition to the autonomous development of man. Writing from prison in Nazi Germany, Bonhoeffer argues that if we are to be faithful to man, avoid the counsel of despair and false emergency exits, and maintain our intellectual sincerity, there is only one valid way: "that of Matthew 18.3, i.e., through repentance, through ultimate honesty. And the only way to be honest is to recognize that we have to live in a world *etse deus non daretur* [even if God is not there]."

With Kazantzakis Bonhoeffer sees the present world as existing before God. This recognition teaches that God expects us to be able to live without him. "The God who is with us is the God who forsakes us [Mark 15:34]. . . . Before God and with him we live without God." Christianity, in Bonhoeffer's view, is distinguished from all religions by God's weakness. In his distress man prays for help from God's power in the world, but the Bible depicts a powerless and suffering God; "and that is exactly the way, the only way, in which he can be with us and help us. Matthew 8:17 makes it crystal clear that it is not by his omnipotence that Christ helps us, but by his weakness and suffering." Thus, Bonhoeffer concludes that the process he has described "by which the world came of age was an abandonment of a false conception of God, and a clearing of the decks for the God of the Bible, who conquers power and space in the world by his weakness."[39] Working before and with God, we must wreak the creative ordering of the world. This creative ordering, in which choice and free will are logically essential and which relies on the potential of man's divine soul, is given ethical and moral unification, in Kazantzakis' view, by the demands of brotherhood and love.

Kazantzakis' view of the role of love in saving God is revealed in *Spain,* where he speaks of God "astride his Pegasus, Love." (*Spain,* 128) As God's Pegasus, love aids man's efforts to save God. It provides an ethical-moral starting point: "Love is the beginning; it is not the end. I cry 'Love!' because man must begin with that." (*Frat.,* 69) It is also a means to personal salvation: "Ah! An erotic love, a passion for something other than yourself—I believe, Genossin, there is no other salvation."[40] In addition, through love is attained—as Saint Francis demonstrated—the crucial uniting

of man with his fellows, nature, and the cosmos, leading to insights into solutions for mankind's perpetual problems:

> Saint Francis becomes contemporary both because in his own
> heart he had realized the perfect union with the cosmos—to which
> present-day science is leading us along other roads—and also be-
> cause his heart had found the solution to the problems that are still
> insoluble: poverty, injustice, violence. Only the love preached by
> him could bring us to a solution of these problems.
>
> Who was the woman saint who ran through the corridors of his
> monastery uttering a piercing cry, "There is no love for love"? In
> our own epoch there is no love for love. And this is the only key
> which can unlock happiness on earth.[41]

Surpassing the ego, men should love others as themselves, as
persons having the same dignity, the same potential, the same
needs. Perhaps the greatest of these needs is immunity from
interference in those creative activities essential to life and the
development of the personality, such as freedom from "poverty,
injustice, violence." While the postulate of brotherly love and
cognizance of the needs of others is knowable by reason, it owes
most of its force and appeal to the lesson of Christ, whose life's
testament equated the love of neighbor and the love of God.

It is widely felt that if the tenets of Christianity were reducible
to one word, that word would be "love." The doctrine of love is
expounded throughout the New Testament. Christian believers,
followers of Christ, are warned—as Kazantzakis warned his
friend Sikelianos—against self adulation and are told that "thou
shall love thy neighbor as thyself."[42] This love is seen as freeing
man from the artificial entrapments that he is so prone to devise
for himself. While this concept has been neglected, it would, if
adhered to, free man from his passionate and often self-destruc-
tive quest for power, dominance, and economic superiority. The
force of love is heavily relied upon by St. Augustine, who sought
to turn the Romans away from their transgressions. He felt that
the perversion of goals in the later Roman empire led to ever
greater desires for conquest and domination of other people.
This destroyed, to a great extent, the love of man for man.
Augustine denied that any state was able to aid man in his true aim

of salvation and tried through the advocacy of the permeation of
brotherly love throughout Roman society to free man from his
often fatal fratricidal struggle. He conceived the Christian's role
as patiently bearing wickedness so that he might render good to
the evildoer. The just and pious must not seek revenge and
thereby join the wicked, but must adopt a benevolent, brotherly
attitude toward all men. The Christian, through love of God and
love of his brother, is freed from the fight for earthly want and
earthly power to seek an increase in the number of those who
worship God, i.e., to give God his due.[43]

Kazantzakis would agree—recall his thoroughgoing critique of
materialism—that man should forego such goals as economic or
political dominance, but he would turn the force of love released
through this process from the heavens wholly to the world:

> Love wretched man at last, for he is you, my son.
> Love plants and beasts at length, for you were they, and now
> they follow you in war like faithful friends and slaves.
> Love the entire earth, its waters, soils and stones;
> On this I cling to live, for I've no other steed.
> (*Odyssey*, IV, 477, lines 1165–69.)

Kazantzakis' opposition to the other-worldly emphasis of traditional Christianity is endorsed by the theologian Harvey Cox, who
rejects a passive role for the Christian in the twentieth century. He
desires to paint a more vivid, live picture: thus his conception
parallels Kazantzakis'. With Augustine and Calvin, Cox emphasizes that man should love his brother as in a similar manner he
loves God. However, Cox seeks to refute the dominant transcen-
dent aspect of this love and to turn man's attention primarily to
the world and to the many social problems confronting the world.
He is much concerned with the inequality in the world and with
the polarization of people in the world. Cox views the teachings of
the Gospels and the role of the church as reconciliation, freedom,
and hope, and thinks that an emphasis on brotherhood would
hasten the actualization of these teachings into reality.[44]

Unfortunately, all too many people agree with the old archon
Patriarcheas; brotherhood is "very fine when it's said in church,
when the priest pronounces it on Sunday from the pulpit. But you
Manolios, blessed sucker, you must be completely cracked to put

it in practice!" (*Gr. Passion,* 123) If it were put into practice, however, it would, as Cox and Manolios know, forcefully advance the cause of the good because, as Father Yanaros recognizes, "Love is a sword, Andreas, my son; Christ had no other sword but love, and with that he conquered the world." (*Frat.,* 216) Kazantzakis' is truly a provocative and "a precious message of love to come in our time of disparity, what warm affirmation of life, not unrealistic, for a world of anxiety, bitterness, disaffection, frenzied rejection and predilection."[45] It is a positive inspirational vision which rebuts the negativism of both modern conservatives, those individualists who preach the doctrine of extreme self-reliance, and modern liberals, those pragmatists many of whom preach the doctrine of extreme relativism.

In answer to the former, an admirer of Kazantzakis might cite a further passage from St. Augustine, that is, that justice, peace, and brotherhood are not served through alienated human relations but in "that a man, in the first place, injure no one, and in the second, do good to everyone he can reach."[46] To the latter, one might offer Camus's cry that the demands of humanity are not met through abdicating our responsibility for rigorous choice by scientific or ideological idolatry but through basing our actions upon the realization that "something in it [the world] has a meaning and that is man. . . . This world has at least the truth of man and our task is to provide its justification against fate itself."[47] There is, as Kazantzakis knew, no other justification.

Freedom of choice, the recognition of man's divine soul, and love—these are, then, the important criteria of the spirit based on and made effective by the example of Christ. These postulates form the core of a positive, humanistic political theology. As normative values they can and, more than that, must be brought to bear with greater intensity on modern life if man is, in Kazantzakis' terms, to "save" God, man, the divine, and thereby negate the evil and advance the good in the world. For we have seen that mass technological existence leads to distraction, disillusionment, and to a highly regimented life, an oppressive life in many ways. The individual has quite often been lost sight of, incorporated into the mass by technocratic social planners who initiate overly grandiose schemes for salvation.

Many have lost sight of the fact that seldom is a liberating social order brought about by technocratic innovations or "system adjustments" from above. Nor will this order come, says Kazantzakis, through alliance with an other-worldly dictated order, for there is no directing Being. A constructive liberating order can, in Kazantzakis' view, be wrought only through the spirit of man—action flowing from the individual's sense of injustice and accompanying quest for social justice—joining in pursuit of an ennobling ideal. Kazantzakis had learned from Hellenism that such an ideal must be based on the criteria of East and West, intellect and heart, demonic and divine, community and individuation. Brought back to the lasting power of the Christian myth in search of further criteria, he now found that the ideal order must, like Christianity, be of such inspirational power and richness as to provide a vehicle for man's attentive, unrelenting allegiance. It must be rigorously conducive to the cognizance and fulfillment of the soul's potentiality. It must allow man's choice. Further, this ideal must heed the selfless unifying requirements of love.

Learning these things, Kazantzakis sought the universal theme underlying those all-important three faces of God—Marxism, Hellenism, and Christ—as an answer to Leonidas' query: how does one tell a good ideal from a bad one? The answer is found in his equation of God with freedom in his ultimate interpretation of Christ's message as the attempt "to transcend man's destiny and unite with God, in other words with absolute freedom." (*Report*, 454) The struggle for freedom of God is the universal underlying the movements of Marxism, Hellenism, and Christianity. Therefore, saving God—which can and must occur only within the parameters of Marxist social justice, Hellenism's synthesis, and Christian humanistic criteria—becomes not freedom but the creation of order produced through a quest within these parameters for freedom:

> The greatest virtue on earth is not to become free but to seek freedom in a ruthless, sleepless strife. (*Odyssey*, IV, 478, lines 1172–73)

George Polley has said of Kazantzakis' work: "The primary

contribution in Nikos Kazantzakis' work, as in his life, is struggle, 'the struggle for freedom.' "[48] The recognition of this theme as the culmination of Kazantzakis' thought is shared universally. Blenkinsopp observes of the struggle to save God/freedom:

> The journey is that of Christ from the carpenter's shop to the summit of Golgotha, that of the dispossessed to freedom in *The Greek Passion*, the Neo-Platonic movement from purification to union, and in its uttermost expression, that of the Great Combatant from the lowest forms of life to points beyond man. It is undertaken neither out of blind instinct nor a sure knowledge of the goal. Its reality is experienced as struggle, ascent, suffering; itself its only reward.[49]

Hadgopoulos agrees:

> The true success of Kazantzakis' heroes is that they refuse to yield to human power for its own sake; they maintain ideals by which they live; and if they fail in establishing their ideals, their worth as heroes lies in their struggle and spiritual self-attainment, not in their defeat or victory.[50]

They do not yield to human power "for its own sake" because they are uniformly motivated by the great passion that underlies all liberating political movements—the unquenchable desire for freedom. This struggle allows the release of the spirit from the inhibitions of institutionalized ideology and religion. It presents itself as an unconquerable foe of the technocratic, materialistic ethos. It is conducive to an invigorating theoretical perspective.

The political struggle, while at times necessarily utilizing violent means, leads to a lowering of the total level of violence in the world through its awareness of the demands of brotherhood, unity, love, and respect for the divine in each man. In leading men to shoulder gladly the responsibility of freedom, this quest is irrevocably opposed to the abdication of freedom. This quest, through its fulfillment of these many rich criteria, points to a resolution of the dilemma created by the conflict between, on the one hand, the determinism of necessity, that is, Spinozistic mathematized naturalism, Hegelian absolutized historicism, or both, and on the other hand, the freedom of cosmological limitlessness, that is, Sartrean meaninglessness, Kafkaesque absurdity, or both. This resolution, or concordance, is a higher harmonious truth created in myth that gives birth to a higher man.

ZEUS:	What do you propose to do?
ORESTES:	The folk of Argos are my folk. I must open their eyes.
ZEUS:	Poor people! Your gift to them will be a sad one; of loneliness and shame. You will tear from their eyes the veils I had laid on them, and they will see their lives as they are, foul and futile, a barren boon.
ORESTES:	Why, since it is their lot, should I deny them the despair I have in me?
ZEUS:	What will they make of it?
ORESTES:	What they choose. They're free; and human life begins on the far side of despair.

JEAN-PAUL SARTRE

≡ǁ

5

A Politics of Freedom and Hope

Kazantzakis' was a truly ambitious endeavor to render the insights of his Cretan glance into a comprehensive and saving sociopolitical decalogue. Evaluative criteria were specified from the ethical, theological, artistic, economic, political, and philosophic elements of that perspective which, as a prescriptive theory, are of immense potential value as judgmental standards apropos of politics.

The most enduring characteristic of Kazantzakis' life, art, and political theory was the struggle for freedom. During his lifetime Kazantzakis was bombarded with philosophies, religions, and developments inimical to man's freedom. He was reared as a Christian within a family and society that believed very strongly in God's providential intervention in history. Many of his childhood neighbors, as well as the rulers on Crete during his youth, were Turks who believed firmly in Moslem fatalism. He was aware of the manner in which technological mechanization was structuring men's lives. He knew also that the socialization process had a tremendous affect on the direction of one's life. Two influential intellectual sources were Spengler, who subscribed to a scheme of cultural determinism, and Marx, who subscribed to a scheme of economic determinism. He was cognizant of the manner in which Hegel's scientific historicism linked history, nature, and idea in a cosmic mind that comprehended and ordained past, present, and future. He was equally aware of the manner in which Spinoza's scientific naturalism postulated man as a quantifiable variable in a mathematized universe based on necessity. Kazantzakis was probably versed in Freud's theories concerning the cultural and genetic determinants of life, which replaced will with unconscious motivations. Kazantzakis sought to deliver man from the inhibitions of these many forms of deterministic necessity by offering a new liberating myth-ideal for modern man—the "struggle for freedom."

Seeking to define the worth of this struggle in view of an inhibiting world, Kazantzakis explored the questions of metaphysical versus sociopolitical freedom, unity, and the efficacy of individual action. From this exploration Kazantzakis does not offer freedom qua freedom as a rebuttal to these deterministic forces. This is significant, as is his belief that freedom is the essence of man, and his view, as expressed through his literary characters, of what constitutes the various levels of freedom. Through the Odysseus characterization, Kazantzakis illustrates the important realization that man cannot support full freedom. Kazantzakis portrays Odysseus as one who struggles "beyond freedom," though realizing that absolute freedom is a mythical nonexistent whose attainment would be its negation; therefore, it is through a never-ending and never-fulfilled quest for freedom that we both create our freedom and transcend the hope for freedom. In this erotic stoicism, as Joseph Flay terms it, there is a wedding of fate/necessity and freedom with ontology, history, and nature to form an alternative role for man on a continuum between determinism and meaningless, absolute freedom. This perceptive new decalogue, of man's erotic struggle in harness to the God-rhythm beyond hope and freedom, is of immense utility for modern man in these latter decades of the twentieth century.

Freedom: The Essence of Man

William Stanford says of The Odyssey: "Kazantzakis has singled out the wish to be free as the dominant passion of his hero. In fact, psychologically, his epic is an exploration of the meaning of freedom."[1] One would not overstate Kazantzakis' concern with liberty in saying this is the dominant theme not only of The Odyssey but, indeed, of all his works. There are many dimensions to Kazantzakis' philosophy of freedom, and all his major characters express some element of that philosophy. This is evident not only in The Odyssey but in the Christ novels, in the aptly titled Freedom or Death, and in "The Immortal Free Spirit of Man" as well as in Zorba, whose central theme, along with the clash between action and writing, is the contrast of a free being with one who is not free. Kzantzakis' comprehensive view of freedom includes interrelated personal, political, and metaphysical levels, and both he and his characters express these levels of freedom. It is only with Ulysses' freedom wherein personal, political, and metaphysical freedoms are united and, paradoxically enough, transcended in favor of the struggle for freedom. Central to Kazantzakis' philosophy of freedom is his evaluation of the degree to which modern man does or does not persevere in the maintenance of his liberty.

Liberty on a personal level has, for Kazantzakis, both physical and intellectual dimensions. In discussing the former, Kazantzakis echoes Christian and Platonic teachings of freedom from the dominance of appetitive pleasures of the flesh. With

Plato, Kazantzakis believed that for man's existence to be truly free and just the soul must rule both mind and body. Unlike Plato, however, Kazantzakis, under the influence of Buddhism and Christianity, was at times wont to push this view to an ascetic extreme of extirpation. As a dramatic vehicle for expounding this view, Kazantzakis utilized on several occasions an illness known as "ascetics' disease."

While in Vienna in 1921, Kazantzakis noticed an attractive young woman named Frieda and fantasized an assignation with her the next night in his quarters. Yet when in his fantasy, she was to come to him on that night and others—all of which were postponed by Kazantzakis—Kazantzakis' face became swollen and filled with yellowish-white liquid. Seeking an explanation from Wilhelm Stekel, the leading Freudian in the city, Kazantzakis was reminded of similar outbreaks in the saints' legends and was told:

> Plunged as it is in the Buddhist *weltanschauung,* your soul—or rather what for you goes by the name of soul—believes that sleeping with a woman is a mortal sin. For that reason it refuses to permit its body to commit this sin. Such souls, souls capable of imposing themselves to so great a degree on the flesh, are rare in our age.[2]
> (*Report,* 355–56)

On his leaving Vienna, Kazantzakis' face healed. In a like manner, Manolios, the Christ figure in *The Greek Passion,* contracts ascetics' disease when he is tempted by the immoral widow, *née* Mary Magdalene, of Lycovrissi; yet when he resists the temptation to succumb to the dominance of the bodily appetites, his face becomes healed.

Kazantzakis and Zorba never attained this freedom from the sexual demands of the flesh; and, as Durant indicates, neither seemed to regret this fact. It must be kept in mind that while Kazantzakis believed in the spirit of man he did not reject the flesh—only slavery to lusts—for Kazantzakis was no puritan. In fact, one of his chief complaints against Christianity was that it "soiled the union of man and woman by stigmatizing it as a sin. Whereas formerly it was a holy act, a joyous submission to God's will, in the Christian's terror-shaken soul it degenerated into a transgression." (*Report*, 371) Kazantzakis emphasized the happiness present in the sexual joining of creative, self-actualized men and women, but he knew that the repression of legitimate sexuality brought about by the Christian ethic militates against the ecstatic integrity of the sex act. In a like manner, the hypocritical moralizing inherent in that institutionalized ethic creates, as Nietzsche perceived, profoundly debilitating implications for man's freedom in a related aspect of the personal, physical dimension of liberty that received Kazantzakis' attention—marriage.

Throughout his life Jesus resists marriage, for this would turn him from his God-chosen path. When he faints on the cross, however, Jesus confronts in his imagination the "last temptation" of earthly domesticity. He is led by Satan's angel first to Mary Magdalene and then, after she is slain by Saul, to Lazarus' sisters, Mary and Martha. Castigated by Paul for having abandoned his mission by becoming husband to the sisters, Jesus answers: "Here I lead the life of a man: I eat, drink, work, and have children. The great conflagration subsided, I too became a kind of tranquil fire; I curled up in the fireplace. . . . I set sail to conquer the world but cast anchor in this tiny domestic trough." (*Last Tempt.*, 476) Later, when he attempts to justify his action to the apostles, Judas scorns him: "Your post, deserter, was on the cross and you know it. Others can reclaim barren lands and barren women. Your duty was to mount the cross—that's what I say!" He ridicules Jesus' claim that he has conquered death: "Is that the way to conquer death—by making children, mouthfuls for Charon! You've turned yourself into this meat market and you deliver him morsels to eat. Traitor! Deserter! Coward!" (*Last Tempt.*, 491)

But, as Jesus discovers when he wakes on the cross, his domestic desertion existed only in his subconscious. He had not deserted his post and abandoned the struggle to liberate God; he had fulilled his duty. "A wild, indomitable joy took possession of him. . . . Temptation had captured him for a split second and led him astray. The joys, marriages, and children were lies . . . illusions sent by the Devil. He uttered a triumphant cry: IT IS ACCOMPLISHED."[3] (*Last Tempt.*, 496) In *The Greek Passion*, Manolios is also tempted to marry, but he resists so that he will be free to carry out God's mission.

Kazantzakis' concern with the encumberments of domestic life, no doubt, owes something to Nietzsche, but it is primarily traceable to his first marital experience, which was a very unhappy one. In his marriage with Galetea, from 1911 to 1926, Kazantzakis suffered the torments of the artist ensnared in domestic conflict: "her attitude toward him became ironical and derisive—as reflected in her novel *Men and Supermen*. There is nothing more destructive for a creative genius than to be married to a woman who regards him with a critical and mocking eye."[4] Kazantzakis lived with Eleni Samios, or Helen Kazantzakis, for some eighteen years prior to their marriage in 1945. (An informal though legal ceremony occurred only because Kazantzakis expected, incorrectly as it turned out, to be sent to North America to plead the cause of reconstruction as Greek cabinet minister without portfolio and desired to take Helen with him.) This second marriage, characterized by deep love, understanding, and mutual respect, mitigated to some degree Kazantzakis' view of domestic enslavement, though he never wholly lost his initial uneasiness.

The other dimension of personal liberty, the intellectual realm, involved several things for Kazantzakis, all of which flow from the freedom from the "inner Turks" of ignorance. Though Kazantzakis rejected the over-ambitious claims of intellectualism and scientific-rationalism, he realized that a rigorous intellectual preparation was, for the great majority of men, a vital prerequisite to answering—and perhaps even to formulating—those agonizing questions of the spirit which were his abiding concern. This belief was acted upon in life-long study beginning, as previously noted, on Naxos and Crete, continuing formally from 1902 until 1906 at the University of Athens and from 1907 until 1909 in the school of law at the Sorbonne and the Collége de France, and informally thereafter. As we have also noted, Kazantzakis was well versed in most Occidental and Oriental philosophies and religions. Like Nietzsche, he studied in depth the important roots of Greek art, culture, and thought. In many ways Kazantzakis truly "represents the final justification of the Western man's active search for truth as distinguished from the Easterner's pas-

sivity before truth." Ultimately, Kazantzakis was skeptical of the
"saving power of the intellect of man, though he reaffirms the
Western idea that it is necessary to have an educated and sensitive
mind in order to comprehend its final inadequacy."[5] From his
rigorous and amazing search for truth came intellectual liberation from comforting religious falsehoods as well as from scientific "proofs." With Kazantzakis' continual study and questioning
also came escape from inertia and vegetative satisfaction—as
brought on either by worship of materialistic goals, which received elaboration above, or by intellectual and ideological dogmatism and inflexibility. A consequence of all this was
Kazantzakis' belief that the intellectually liberated man would
scorn, like Nietzsche, the inhibitions of conventional social
strictures—mores, creeds, etc.—and it is with this view that
Kazantzakis moves out of the personal realm of freedom into the
public arena.

Kazantzakis' philosophy of freedom on the political level can
also be discussed in terms of physical and intellectual realms.
Viewing the latter, Kazantzakis emphasized freedom from the
enslavement of ideology, whether of left or right, East or West.
To be a free person—an increasingly difficult spiritual
accomplishment—one must look with a clear eye upon contemporary reality and "must admit the infamy as well as the virtues,
the dark as well as the light, for here on this earth every living
thing—human beings and ideas too—has always been composed
of both." (*England*, 7–8) Kazantzakis was considered "suspect" at
various times by all political and religious factions because of his
resolute effort to maintain his intellectual independence—his
freedom to criticize the deficiencies of all political positions.

> While the Greek Communist could call him decadent, fascist,
> bourgeois, incurably religious, and a warmonger, the Chinese
> Communist could hail him as an apostle of peace, the Orthodox
> could try to prosecute him for atheism, the monarchists could see
> him as a bolshevik rabble-rouser and the communist-controlled
> resistance movement during the occupation could reject him as an
> agent of [English] intelligence.[6]

Kazantzakis was concerned not only with the intellectual dimension of political liberty but also with the physical realm of

political freedom. This latter concern reflected his childhood experience under Turkish rule on Crete. *Freedom or Death,* a fictionalized account of that experience, embodies two views of political freedom. First, there is the traditional quest for liberty—acted out by Captain Michales and his fellow freedom fighters in periodic uprisings—of throwing off the yoke of tyranny and attaining self-rule. Second, there is his ontological view of freedom, expressed in political terms, that the man who has an ideal or myth to believe in is free even though ruled by others. Captain Michales knows the futility of his position after one uprising has been put down and others have returned to their villages, and yet he fights on valiantly under the banner "Freedom or Death." In a similar vein, Prometheus proclaims his freedom even in his chains, for his soul soars beyond tyranny. Like Victor Frankl, Aleksandr Solzhenitsyn, and others in this century, Kazantzakis agrees with Nietzsche that one "who has a why to live can withstand any how." There is, however, no quietist content here—either for Frankl, Solzhenitsyn, or Kazantzakis— for the "why," the guiding belief or idea, will inspire great souls to emulate Captain Michales and never submit willingly to any "how"—of tyranny, injustice, and oppression. The next and highest level of freedom, the metaphysical level, though founded on a personal basis, has important political implications.

Zorba, one of Kazantzakis' most brilliant characterizations, is an attempt to portray, through the powerful contrast between a free being (Zorba) and an unfree being (the Boss) both a description of and a prescription for metaphysical freedom—the immortal free spirit of man. This spirit only fulfills its freedom and immortality so far as man persists in the affirmation of life. It is only through this affirmation of life and the corollary victory over the authority of mortality that humanity in its highest sense is attained. The struggle for freedom of spirit over matter is essential to Kazantzakis' metaphysical level of freedom. He expresses it thus: "Guileful matter has chosen this body . . . slowly to dampen and extinguish the free flame which flickers within me." (*Zorba,* 113)

What is the source of this impetus to the dampening of the flame of freedom, this denial of reality and vitality, this surrender to the void? It comes from the basic dualism that has dominated in one manner or another man's life and philosophy—the inherent mind/rationalism versus body/passion make-up of man. This dualism is of primary importance at the moment when we "reach the edge of the leaf . . . hear the noise of the other leaves of the tremendous tree, feel the sap rising . . . and our hearts swell. . . . From that moment begins" many things. That moment is the ultimate, the most shocking, the most abrasive of our lives; and it, too, is possessed of a dualism, for it can be the most fulfilling, beneficial, enriching, and liberating of all possible moments, or it can be the most fearful, oppressive, sterilizing, and enslaving of all possible moments. At that powerful and potent moment, one can affirm his vital, vivid, rich, free life or can fall into the effete, devitalized mode of existence that is the predicament of those who surrender to the oppression of the metaphysical void.

The mortality of the body, of mundane material existence, can lead man to two equally enslaving outlooks from which he must escape. Bien relates Kazantzakis' view that man must "extricate himself from both hope and fear, the two great millstones which grind Socratic man."[7] It is obvious in what manner fear—arising from the haunting presence of death—can immobilize and destroy the essence of existence—freedom and vitality. Camus found in this fear and consequent abdication of freedom the supreme paradox of the contemporary age. Camus draws attention in the twentieth century, just as Dostoevsky did in the nineteenth century, to the contradiction of men who sing accolades to freedom and yet are unwilling to bear the constant tension that true freedom demands. Camus reveals through Clemence, in *The Fall*, the existential burden that is freedom without God: "Ah, mon cher, for anyone who is alone without God and without a master, the weight of days is dreadful." He describes his contemporaries' reaction to that burden:

> I didn't know that freedom is not a reward or a decoration, nor yet a gift box of dainties. . . . Oh, no! It's a chore, on the contrary, and a long distance race, quite solitary and very exhausting. Alone in a forbidden room, alone in the prisoner's box before the judges, and alone to decide in the face of oneself or in the face of other's judgment. At the end of all freedom is a court sentence; that's why freedom is too heavy to bear.[8]

This being true—and it is true—in what manner do Camus's men, like Kazantzakis', seek to relinquish their burden of freedom? To whom, or for whom, do they look for mastery? Camus argues that although God is dead much of the harsher side of the Christian ethic hangs on, and it is this judgmental morality, this Christian ethic without Christian forgiveness, coupled with the fear of mortality, that leads men to judge their fellows—that leads them to "believe solely in sin, never in grace." Men "don't want freedom or its judgments, they ask to be rapped on the knuckles, they invent dreadful rules, they rush out to build piles of faggots to replace churches."[9]

Modern man has, for both Camus and Kazantzakis, succumbed to this intransigent morality, these absolute judgments and oppressive rule/beliefs, and has built his "piles of faggots to replace churches," primarily by surrendering to ideological comforts through fear. Illusory hope can do the same thing. Hope is capable of channeling men's lives into false and unfulfillable quests, with a postponement of life, as evinced primarily in the hope of other-worldly existence, which can be enslaving. Hope can lead, to quote Bien further, "to optimistic illusion, whether it be the false optimism of Western capitalism or the salvationism of Western religion, or the romantic dreams of non-tragic art."[10] Even Nietzsche, the great destroyer of illusions, falsehoods, and hopes, succumbed in the end and built his pile of faggots: "the superman is just another paradise, another mirage to deceive poor unfortunate man and enable him to endure life and death." (*Report*, 339) Thus the protest against illusion crops up again, the protest against comforting yet emasculating ideas and beliefs that are dangerous to metaphysical freedom. What man must do is mobilize the immense powers and capabilities of his spirituality and combat whatever threatens his humaneness. For Kazantzakis, jut as freedom is the determinant belief of his philosophy, so it is also the determinant essence of humanness: "I think only those people who want to be free are human." (*Zorba*, 151)

What are the implications and meaning of the view of freedom espoused by Kazantzakis for contemporary man? Does his philosophy have any direct relevance for today? It is of the utmost relevance and has many profound contemporary implications. Many of the problems to which Kazantzakis addressed himself are timeless, as testified to by the attention devoted to them by philosophers over the centuries. The principal importance of Kazantzakis' view is in the application of his personal, political, and metaphysical concepts of freedom to the experiential odyssey of twentieth-century man in his Ulysses characterization. Ulysses—like Zorba—is one of Kazantzakis' most important characters and represents the cumulative account of the many contradictory contemporary themes which run through Kazanthzakis' thought. George Scouffas contends that "since Kazantzakis brings to bear on his subject a lifetime of study in philosophy, anthropology, history, religion, and literature, the result is that the basic terms of the exploration become a catalogue of the central motifs and dilemmas of modern Western literature." Furthermore, he believes that it is Kazantzakis' purpose to "expose Odysseus to all the strains and counter-strains that beset modern man, to guide him to a revelatory synthesis that can give him clarity of understanding and ultimate peace, and to do this without depriving him of his status as man."[11]

Odysseus: A Higher Tuth

While some may dispute the "relevance" of Kazantzakis' ambitious sequel to the Homeric epic, few who are familiar with the book deny that it "is the most monumental work of Kazantzakis, and his greatest achievement. In it he comes closest to presenting a unified world view, transcending the antitheses of flesh and spirit."[12] The crucial difference between Kazantzakis' and Homer's Ulysses has to do with freedom. Homer has Ulysses return from his voyage to his wife Penelope, his son Telemachus, his friends and subjects on Ithaca, where he willingly submits to the placidity of that existence. Kazantzakis, on the other hand, begins his epic with Ulysses' dissatisfaction on his return to Ithaca and sends him once more in quest of the elusive invisible cry of freedom, immortality, truth, or both. Kazantzakis begins *The Odyssey* with a paean to freedom:

O Sun, my quick coquetting eye, my red-haired hound, sniff out all
my quarries that I love, give them swift chase, tell me all that you've
seen on earth, all that you've heard, and I shall pass them through
my entrails' secret forge till slowly, with profound caresses, play
and laughter, stones, water, fire, and earth shall be transformed to
spirit, and the mud-winged and heavy soul, freed of its flesh, shall
like a flame serene ascend and fade in sun.[13] ("Prologue," 1, lines
22–30)

Thus Kazantzakis expresses his belief that man has settled for less
from life than it has to offer. Acting out the stages outlined in *The
Saviors of God,* Odysseus seeks the meaning of life and arrives at
the perspective afforded by the Cretan glance—which is freedom. He has "freed himself from everything—religions,
philosophies, political systems—one who has cut away all the
strings. He wants to try all forms of life, feerly, beyond plans and
systems, keeping the thought of death before him as a stimulant."
Odysseus seeks freedom and focuses on his mortality not to
heighten the sensuality of each of life's moments but to make
himself more "capable of embracing and exhausting all things so
that, when death finally came, it would find nothing to take from
him, for it would find an entirely squandered Odysseus."[14]

Odysseus begins his quest for attaining the union of personal,
political, and metaphysical freedom—through abandonment of
wife and family, sexual orgies, revolutions—in a fashion disturbing to many. One who is uneasy about Ulysses' satanic revelries
says: "On several occasions, Odysseus' bestiality and cruelty call in
[to] question his author's wisdom." Stavrou concedes that Odysseus' wanderings are not aimless but represent a quest for the
meaning of life. He doubts, however, whether the participation in
sexual orgies, the angry tirades, and those displays of blood
lust—all evident in Odysseus' initial travels—are the proper way
to learn how to live. Odysseus is happy neither at rest nor play,
and he causes dissatisfaction in those around him. "He is as often
Man Transmogrified as Man Transfigured. . . . He sows discon-
tent like a political agitator, and stirs up dangerous thoughts in
men's minds and forbidden lusts in men's hearts."[15] Kazantzakis'
concern for greatly expanded liberty and his orienting his philosophy in Books I through XII around the individual as the su-

preme value is seen to prove—and if one stops at this point indeed it does prove—that he was an amoral anarchist.

An important aspect of the affirmation of life is the capability of man for both good and evil. When man casts off the phantoms of "Gods, motherlands, ideas," rips away the web of superficial socioreligious agglomerations that enmesh him, and stands as a defiant giant mocking the abyss, then he has transcended the ethical and social institutions that restrict action—he is free. How does Kazantzakis respond to the capacity for evil of this "giant," with his absolute freedom?

While Kazantzakis recognizes in *Zorba* (24) that man is both "a great brute and a God," he does not satisfactorily answer the sociopolitical implications of his philosophy of absolute freedom. In keeping with his philosophy, which at this point is concerned with the divine element of those great souls in the world, he is not required to go into the ethical and social implications. For Kazantzakis' concept of freedom is primarily an ontological one that transcends sociopolitical concepts. It is concerned with the very being of freedom, with the primordial and eternal infinitude of that freedom. Thus Bien could correctly deal with the issue of Kazantzakis' freeing the beast as well as the angel in man in the following manner: Zorba is "an incarnation of dissonance. And in all this he directly mimics the contradictory nature of life itself." Kazantzakis confesses that he "had never seen such a friendly accord between a man and the universe!" Zorba mirrors the universe; thus he is the thing-in-itself, who in doing as he pleases embodies the universal will. Kazantzakis tells Zorba: even if you would go wrong "you couldn't. You're like a lion, shall we say, or a wolf. That kind of beast never behaves as if it were a sheep or a donkey; it is never untrue to its nature."[16] The capacity for greatness lies in this defiance of evil, in the overcoming of evil. This is man truly freed.

Therefore, while there is certainly room for valid criticism of Kazantzakis' excesses (which constitute one of his most serious problems in the area of political philosophy), perhaps such criticis take only a superficial view. Reading further in *The Odyssey,* one gains a fuller picture of the issue as Kazantzakis qualifies his position in such a manner as to negate the immediate and political

import of Odysseus' more undesirable behavior. Thus, in Books
XIII, XIV, and XV Odysseus overcomes and surpasses, in
Nietzschean fashion,[17] his baser, evil drives, and he accepts responsibility and a measure of discipline. Odysseus matures and
leads his fellows as a political prophet in founding the ideal city.
When this is coupled with the importance of the concepts of unity,
brotherhood, and man's duty in Kazantzakis' mature thought,
and with the recognition that although Kazantzakis and Odysseus
sought in Marxist fashion to destroy outmoded dogmas and political forms, they fought not merely to destroy but also to rebuild,
one comes to the conclusion that it "is no longer possible to dismiss
The Odyssey as a glorification of total 'freedom'—that is, of
immorality—a kind of belated echo of Schiller's *Robbers*. There is
something far greater at stake here."[18] This greater, more profound theme underlying Odysseus' adventures is that total freedom is its own negation.

Colin Wilson, who sees Kazantzakis as an "outsider" (one who
detests and fears the will-destroying power of contentment),
states our thesis:

> There is a strange and absurd paradox about human nature,
> which is expressed in Fichte's comment: "To be free is nothing; to
> *become* free is very heaven." In the moment when a human being
> experiences freedom, inner doors open; he sees over endless
> plains; his freedom stretches around him like the vast spaces of a
> cathedral. But within days or hours he has become accustomed to
> freedom; the mind closes; it yawns and falls asleep. This sleep is the
> greatest enemy of human beings. The cathedral turns into a nar-
> row room with all the windows closed. Freedom ceases to be free-
> dom. But how absurd! The freedom is still there, just as a window is
> still there, even when you have drawn the curtains across it.
> This is still the greatest problem of modern man, the problem
> that blocks his evolution. . . . A few major writers have recognised
> it, indeed—Sartre, Camus, Thomas Mann—but have decided it is
> insoluble. "It is meaningless that we live and meaningless that we
> die," says Sartre; "Man is a useless passion."
> Kazantzakis is the only contemporary writer who saw the prob-
> lem, faced it, and spent his life fighting like a demon to solve it. The
> greatness of his work lies in this demonic quality. It is also heroic;

Kazantzakis is the only modern writer of whom one could use the word "Promethean."[19]

Odysseus' journey is an agonizing portrayal of Kazantzakis' effort to solve this problem and provide meaning to human life while at the same time preserving freedom.

After his ideal city is destroyed (Book XVI), the quest for freedom "dominates every stage of Odysseus' pilgrimage. . . . [and] his chief concern is to search his own mind and the mind of other freedom-loving persons for the essence of liberty."[20] This is most evident in Book XVII (which Prevelakis calls Absolute Freedom[21]), where in his mind Odysseus plays as the God-Creator of life. He calls to existence an old king, prince, slave, warrior-king, and maiden, and they perform the despairing drama of man's existence under his sentence of death. In Books XVIII through XXI, Odysseus resumes his southward journey through life, meeting and rejecting representative types: Buddha, a nihilist, Don Quixote, and Jesus, all of whom falsely proclaim a unique escape from the death sentence. He arrives at a polar village (Book XXII) and there, preparing to meet death, recalls his exhaustive, much-experienced journey through life. In Book XXIV, the last, his former companions, both living and dead, join him for the final reunion at the moment of his death:

Then flesh dissolved, glances congealed, the heart's pulse stopped,
and the great mind leapt to the peak of its holy freedom,
fluttered with empty wings, then upright through the air
soared high and freed itself from its last cage, its freedom.
(lines 1390–94)

There are both positive and negative lessons to be derived from this magnificent pilgrimage.

The positive value lies in the dynamic example of one who rejects every false hope; who will not succumb to the void awaiting; who will not abdicate his freedom; who will not exchange his liberty for any Grand Inquisitor's mastery, mystery, and miracle. It is at the same time a profound exploration, by one of tremendous learning and intellect, of the major worldviews confronting modern man. Yet, as with Odysseus' excesses before the ideal city,

there is something disturbing about the excessiveness of his absolute freedom in the latter stages of his life. In this excessiveness
lies the negative lesson of *The Odyssey;* "It is not that Kazantzakis
has dared too much in his complete exploration of the meaning of
freedom, but that, in a sense, he has exposed the subject beyond
most profitable return in terms of meaning." The freedom that
Odysseus seeks so rigorously eventually reveals itself as the negation of itself, as nothingness, as that which is not, as the nonexistent,
as nonbeing.

One is ultimately led to realize, on this deepest and most profound level of *The Odyssey,* that, rather than emulate Odysseus
(after the fashion of Book XVI) and *never* commit ourselves, we
must learn from him *how* to commit ourselves. In the sentiment
that both life and art must have limits (for absolute freedom is a
contradiction in terms) is found the "greatest irony of all in *The
Odyssey.*" In his synopsis Friar "touches on it when he describes
Odysseus' death as freeing his mind from its 'last cage, that of its
freedom.' Odysseus has been imprisoned in an abstraction and a
category."[23] The true road for man lies neither in contentless,
self-destroying absolute freedom nor in such dogmatic,
foredoomed commitments as those exemplified by the tightly-
structured scientific-naturalism of Odysseus' ideal city.

Realizing that "freedom without virtue or goodness is of the
devil" (*Frat.,* 173), Kazantzakis knows that the egoistic path of
Odysseus is in many ways as politically undesirable as the ideological paths of the bourgeoisie and the Marxists. In *Report,* therefore,
in the section "When the Germ of 'The Odyssey' Formed Fruit
Within Me," he says: "The human being cannot support absolute
freedom; such freedom leads him to chaos. If it were possible for
a man to be born with absolute freedom, his first duty if he wished
to be of some use on earth, would be to circumscribe that freedom." (*Report,* 469) The only way to surpass this inhibiting truth is
to submit to it—as Kazantzakis discovered in his own life. The
circle is closed and man goes beyond freedom to come back to the
struggle toward freedom. Thus, limitation of absolute freedom
leads to an unending quest for affirmation in the face of negativ-
ity. This gives purpose and therefore a measure of harmony and
satisfaction to our lives.

This powerful dialectic operates on only the highest level of existence once man has passed like Odysseus through the stages of *The Saviors of God* and joined with man, God, and nature in the cosmogenic struggle of life on earth. The cosmogenic harmony revolves around the insight that, just as "the highest art is passion that is controlled; order in the midst of chaos; serenity both in joy and pain" (*Spain*, p. 46), so in like manner the "highest politics" lies in the proper tension between liberty and unity, individualism and community, spontaneity and order, change and constancy. Neither absolute freedom nor absolute necessity is offered here. Kazantzakis' compassionate criteria of love, free choice, social justice, and human dignity mark a roadway between and beyond the two that answers in a positive manner the central issues of anxiety, alienation, and the anomic condition of our time.

Joseph Flay, in what is undeniably the most perceptive analysis of Kazantzakis' thought, goes directly to the heart of this theme. He sees the overriding question confronting twentieth-century Western civilization as "the fate of the individual in a cosmos which is seen as Godless and yet overwhelming in its power over the individual." Compounding the difficulty of arriving at an answer to this question are two contesting views: (1) the individual is only a function of a quantifiable whole as professed under the impetus of the scientific, industrial, and cybernetic revolutions; (2) the individual, with his desires, projects, and hopes, is irrevocably separate from historical necessity. In Flay's opinion this confrontation of views has given rise to a question of meaning "which has left us with the present existential theme, at once struggling against both the mathematized universe and the inexorableness of history." Hegel resolved this question of meaning in favor of historicity by saying that the individual must stoically submit to historical destiny. Nietzsche, Kierkegaard, and Marx each resolved (in Flay's interpretation) to take the opposite course from Hegel and forever fight the agonizing battle against this absolute necessity. Flay contends that Kazantzakis accepts and rejects both views in taking a third course: "Beyond both the bland stoicism of Hegel and the agonizing eroticism of the existentialist, Kazantzakis finds a credo which I suggest might best be described as 'erotic stoicism.' "[24]

Whether Kazantzakis does truly find another course or whether he merely rephrases in his own way the existentialist perspective is open to dispute. Nevertheless, Flay's felicitous term "erotic stoicism" embodies very well Kazantzakis' hard-won knowledge that Spinoza's and Hegel's insights into the forces of natural and historical necessity cannot be so easily dismissed as many existentialists and Marxists have imagined. It incorporates the lesson that the ennobling yet futile battle against necessity does, however, call forth the qualities of the higher man. Therefore, Kazantzakis argues, the correct path lies neither in completely accepting nor completely rejecting necessity, but in choosing how to battle for and with it and thereby to overcome it: "Indeed," Friar says, "it is the greatest glory of man that he can set himself his own purpose, and in this manner not only control but also direct the mysterious forces which create him and which might one day destroy him as a species."[25]

Kazantzakis discusses the importance of setting a purpose in life that becomes the essence of life. This central passion of every integral man, which may be love, beauty, knowledge, etc., "lends unity to his thoughts and actions; it helps him find or invent the cosmic harmony. . . . Alas for the man who does not feel himself governed inside by an absolute monarch. His ungoverned, incoherent life is scattered to the four winds." He reports to his "grandfather" El Greco, in a continuation of the above passage, on their essence:

> Our center, grandfather, the center which swept the visible world into its whirl and fought to elevate it to the upper level of valor and responsibility, was the battle with God. Which God? The fierce summit of man's soul, the summit which we are ceaselessly about to attain and which ceaselessly jumps to its feet and climbs still higher. 'Does man battle with God?' some acquaintances asked me sarcastically one day. I answered them, 'With whom else do you expect him to battle?' Truly, with whom else?
>
> That was why the whole of our lives was an ascent, grandfather—ascent, precipice, solitude. We set out with many fellow strugglers, many ideas, a great escort. But as we ascended and as the summit shifted and became more remote, fellow strugglers, ideas, and hopes kept bidding us farewell; out of

breath, they were neither willing nor able to mount higher. We remained alone, our eyes riveted upon the Moving Monad, the shifting summit. We were swayed neither by arrogance nor by the naive certainty that one day the summit would stand still and we would reach it; nor yet, even if we should reach it, by the belief that there on high we would find happiness, salvation, and paradise. We ascended because the very act of ascending for us, was happiness, salvation, and paradise. (*Report,* 494–95)

In setting our purpose, in not only realizing that we are determined but choosing by what we are determined, we become cocreators of our fate, cocontrollers of history and nature, collaboraters with destiny. We are no longer Beckett's and Kafka's apathetic visions of immobilizing fate. By "loving fate" in the Nietzschean sense, we are free and transcend fate's terrors. Thus, Kazantzakis could consistently hold to an apparent contradiction: "Of my own free will I accept necessity"; and "But an exacting soul . . . was born precisely to declare war against this law of necessity." (*Report,* 423, 436)

Kazantzakis knows, of course, that ultimately we are all doomed to defeat by the death sentence under which we all labor; therefore, ours is an absurd existence. This very absurdity, however, rather than negating the importance of the struggle, enhances it. It is not victory over death that defines man's worth. Rather, life's merit is conferred by a threefold defiance of the unconquerable: first, "the struggle for victory"; second, to "live and die bravely, without condescending to accept any recompense"; and third, "the certainty that no recompense exists must not make our blood run cold, but must fill us with joy, pride, and manly courage." (*Report,* 482)

This difficult process of self-salvation is never easy, never comfortable; it is always marked by strife, suffering, and defeats. It is couched in despair. "Only beyond absolute despair is the door to absolute hope found. Alas to that man who cannot mount the final dreadful step which rises above absolute despair; such a man is necessarily incurably despairing."[26] But the one who *does* mount the final step discovers a joyous immortality unknowable by those who are weak of spirit and are attracted to lesser, materialistic goals.

Kazantzakis would say to despairing twentieth-century man that he must revise the Cartesian *cogito*, "I think, therefore I am," to "I strive, therefore I am." He must strive even though he knows the inevitability of eventual defeat; he must strive within the parameters of human unity, virtue, reciprocity; he must strive for the higher existence beyond hope and freedom—this is Kazantzakis' solution to the anxiety, meaninglessness, anomie, ideological dogma, and atomic terror of modern life.[27] (Flay concludes, in regard to this solution: "Nothing is guaranteed, nothing is certain, neither victory nor defeat!") It is crucial, Kazantzakis teaches, that we "accept and fight fate with all our energy, not in order to subdue it, but because it is *our* fate and *our* destiny and a worthy opponent"; that we "accept the truth that we cannot force our eroticism on others, but that they themselves must either make that act of will which unleashes it, or remain submerged in their fantasies and their repression"; and that we "must hear the cry of mankind for salvation, but must not save them by giving them false hopes for certainty."[28]

As political theorists look back upon Kazantzakis' life and thought, they will find, in addition to his intense concern with freedom, a more subtle and in many ways equally pervasive idea that seems to stand out above all others. This is Kazantzakis' profound recognition of the irrevocable link between hope and politics. Kazantzakis' political thought is a stinging rebuttal to the false, ideological offerings of illusory "hope for certainty" of right and left. He offers an important, affirmative, affectionate, and stimulating politics for the spirit of hope and freedom.

Political Theory and the Hope of the Present

The implications of hope and despair have long been debated apropos of politics by political theorists. Machiavelli once identified a major error of men as their not knowing how and when to limit their hopes. Kazantzakis believed hope is extremely relevant to politics, particularly for Western man, primarily because of the manner in which the two central themes of Western culture—scientific rationalism and Christianity—have influenced both hope and politics.[29] If an observer proceeds on this belief, as an analytical approach to the study of contemporary political thought in the West, he arrives at a particular "angle of vision": "each theorist has viewed the problem of political philosophy from a different perspective. This suggests that political philosophy constitutes a form of 'seeing' political phenomena and that the way in which a phenomenon will be visualized depends in large measure on where the viewer 'stands.' "[30]

Kazantzakis' "angle of vision" or perspective enables an observer to stand in the midst of the complexities and apparently insoluble ideological contradictions of late nineteenth- and twentieth-century political thought and unravel and distinguish the intricate and shifting morass of modern politics. The ideologies that dominate these politics were born in the important crucible of the latter half of the nineteenth century—during the time of Kazantzakis' birth. Midwifery duties, so to speak, were performed by the central and unique role in men's lives of hope and despair, occasioned at that particular juncture in the West by both the increasing impetus of scientism and the accelerating loss of faith. Valuable insight into this relationship of hope and despair and contemporary world politics is afforded by Kazantzakis' perspective. This is due to his creativeness and integrity. It is also due to his independence. As one analyst remarks, "an intellectual position independent both of the Soviet creed and of the conventional assumptions dominant in Western society, can . . . point beyond accepted thought patterns to a new synthesis."[31] If the anxious lot of man is to be bettered, we must go beyond the accepted thought patterns that have plunged our age into a muck of ideological confusion. Wolin, in his immensely important work, assigns to political theory the task of pointing the way out for man from his despair and hopelessness:

> political theory must once again be viewed as that form of knowledge which deals with what is general and integrative to man, a life of common involvements. The urgency of these tasks is obvious, for human existence is not going to be decided at the lesser level of small associations: it is the political order that is making fateful decisions about man's survival in an age haunted by the possibility of unlimited destruction.[32]

An exit can be found only through the compassionate, intelligent use of a political philosophy that draws from all fruitful areas of political inquiry and, like Kazantzakis, "hears mankind's cry for salvation but does not save them by giving false hopes for certainty."

In his inimitable way, Bertrand Russell captured the tragic, hopeless essence of the contemporary predicament:

> That man is the product of causes which had no prevision of the end they were achieving; that his origin, his growth, his hopes and fears, his loves, and his beliefs, are but the outcome of accidental collocations of atoms; that no fire, no heroism, no intensity of thought and feeling, can preserve an individual life beyond the grave; that all the labors of the ages, all the devotion, all the inspiration, all the noon-day brightness of human genius, are destined to extinction in the vast death of the solar system, and that the whole temple of man's achievements must inevitably be buried beneath the debris of a universe in ruins—all these things, if not quite beyond dispute, are yet so nearly certain, that no philosophy which rejects them can hope to stand. Only within the scaffolding of these truths, only on the firm foundation of unyielding despair, can the soul's habitation be safely built.[33]

Both East and West have sought, for various reasons and in various ways, to escape the strictures of these basic truths, and thus neither East nor West has built a firm philosophical foundation that "can hope to stand." Rather, they have eroded the creative potentiality described in Russell's apt analysis and now find that not only no philosophy but also no political system that neglects that assessment "can hope to stand."

Their evasion has taken two main forms. One is through attempts to replace teleological purposelessness with new artificial, homogeneous ethical-moral systems that, to recall Flay's comment, strive to "force their eroticism on others." This has resulted in a horrifying new political form—totalitarianism. The other, more subtle evasion, evinced in the serene overlooking of the realities that Russell speaks of, arises out of a misguided faith or belief in comatose, outmoded ideals and progressivistic illusions. This evasion is most evident in capitalist democracies. Both evasions exemplify a fatal sin, in terms of Kazantzakis' political thought, that of abandoning the struggle. Speaking for a wide segment of humanity within the United States, James Baldwin writes to his nephew: "You know, and I know, that the country is celebrating one hundred years of freedom one hundred years too soon. We cannot be free until they are free."[34] They have learned as we all must learn the rightness of Kazantzakis' insight that "none are saved until all are saved . . . none are free until all are free."

Camus, in a moving defense of this belief, held by Baldwin and Kazantzakis, that all must be saved if life is to be made worthy, wrote to his German friend: "With your scornful smile you will ask me: What do you mean by saving man? And with all my being I shout to you that I mean not mutilating him and yet giving him a chance to that justice that man alone can conceive."[35] This sentiment is particularly apt in the late twentieth century as the United States celebrates its revolutionary and constitutional periods with grandiose rites organized by those in power to glorify two hundred years of "freedom." What is this freedom to the poor, the illiterate, the powerless, the unspoken for, the ones left behind by the mad onrushing, uncaring, directionless "progress" of our technological society? For these many segments of the citizenry of the supposedly enlightened, liberated West, as well as for many people of the authoritarian East, mere existence is truly a bitter ordeal.

In their oppression, bitter isolation, and hopelessness there is a fusion of the results of both capitalist democracy and totalitarianism. The bankruptcy of both theories arises from the ethical hiatus implicit in them, by their arbitrary basis for policy, and by the failure of both to address the "essence" of man—his liberated humanness. Neither has built on the firm foundation of unyielding despair. Their parallel failings attest to the truth of Walker Percy's observation, "Losing hope is not so bad. There's something worse: losing hope and hiding it from yourself."[36]

Kazantzakis' political philosophy is invaluable in the endeavor to rectify these mistakes and to inculcate some common humanitarian values into a political ethic. His humanism and brilliance have become beacons for some at a time when more and more people are awakening to the dangers of technocratic society and to the possibilities of man for great good and great evil. His counsel to confront and thereby to surpass the inhibitions of mortality is extremely relevant in this nuclear age, when we live with the fearful capability of self-destruction. His concern with individual greatness through self-realization, his attack on ideological heresies of left and right, East and West, and his strong support of the demands of love, unity, will, and brotherhood, are much needed in this fratricidal era, with its racial, national, ideological, economic, and religious Vietnams, Middle Easts, Africas, and North Irelands. The strength, consistency, and integrity with which Kazantzakis stated his themes have placed him in the forefront of those who have attempted, like his hallowed precursor saviors, to carve a new riverbed of the spirit leading out of the transitional *angst*-ridden age. The forcefulness and uncompromising tone of Kazantzakis' explication of his beliefs is why Kazantzakis offers a basis for a politics beyond illusory scientific faith, destructive nihilistic despair, and ideology—hope for the future. The overwhelming significance of such a path for human existence is obvious, for, as the doomed existential poet Hölderlin explained: "What would life be without hope? A spark that leaps from a coal and goes out, a blast of wind in the dreary time of the year, heard for a moment and then still forever. . . . Nothing would live if it did not hope."[37]

But as is eminently clear by now, many governments, leaders, movements, and thinkers rush to offer false hopes. Why is Kazantzakis any different? He is unique in offering a standard, a "Realometer" to borrow a term from Thoreau, by which to measure such hopes. Such an instrument is critical. Percy's "moviegoer" Binx Bolling is atypical in his ability to smell out tainted offerings because he inherited from his father

a good nose for merde, for every species of shit that flies—my only talent—smelling merde from every quarter, living in fact in the very century of merde, the great shithouse of scientific humanism, where needs are satisfied, everyone becomes an anyone, a warm and creative person, and prospers like a dung beetle, and one hundred percent of people are humanists and ninety-eight percent believe in God, and men are dead, dead, dead.[38]

For those who, unlike Binx, do not live in books and failed to inherit such a convenient olfactory organ, Kazantzakis' political philosophy serves as an invaluable crap-detector. In Kazantzakis' politics of struggle there is an operational ethic, a meaningful morality, an answer for modern man. It is not merely a beautiful and haunting abstraction, a powerful literary delusion as bankrupt in an empirical sense as so many other proposals have proven to be.

Kazantzakis' heroic "cry" is enjoying ever-increasing attention, particularly among young people.[39] Many today are seeking freedom and hope in Kazantzakis' terms—new levels of consciousness, of salvation, of deliverance. His popularity and staying power is exhibiting greater potential than that of many of his contemporaries. As Kazantzakis' thought on theology, literature, etc., comes under increasing scrutiny, he is gaining recognition as one of the seminal figures of the twentieth century. I submit that Kazantzakis, who is primarily a literatist, will be increasingly viewed from the angle of political philosophy.

There are many justifications for this belief, three of the most important being the nature of his imaginative genius, the nature of the times, and the nature of his infusion of Eastern thought into the West. On the first point, one commentator on the relation of literature and sociopolitical theory contends that the concern with an individual creative consciousness suggests a "link between social thought and literature: 'consciousness,' 'construction'—the fabrication of a personal world in which the individual self can find existence bearable—these are the key terms that social theory and imaginative literature hold in common." These are also the terms that characterize the nature of Kazantzakis' genius and thus render his imaginative literature pertinent to sociopolitical theory. The same individual explains the turn of the immediate preWorld War I novelists to political themes: [they were] "living under high tension . . . striving to hold together the contradictions that were tearing them asunder . . . living in historical circumstances in which all fixed norms were lacking: the old ethic had collapsed—and it was far from clear where the new one was to be found."[40] Again, an apt description of Kazantzakis, the nature of his times, his thought, his complexity, and an equally valid description of our chaotic time. Kazantzakis is a true compatriot of Gide, Mann, Hesse, and others in embodying the moving creative spirit of the literatist involved in sociopolitical themes and offers much sustenance for our age.

In regard to the last point, Kazantzakis incorporates Eastern thought to bring a true universalistic view to political questions: "Kazantzakis escapes simplifying definitions as a continent rejects them. Kazantzakis is Christian and heathen, anarchist, humanist and stoic sage, alternately and sometimes simultaneously." He is a member of no "school." He is not essentially European but Cretan, and Crete lies equidistant from Europe, Africa, and Asia. "As Africa's flame scorches Crete in summer, so it burns in the blood of this man who strove for many long years, to build a synthesis from Greek and Oriental thought."[41] Historically, there has been a dangerous overlooking of the contributions of thinkers not in the main channel of Anglo-American/European political thought. Whatever the reason for this, with the growing volume of translation today, with the inspiring move to more mutual understanding and cooperation between East and West, and with the welcome awareness of the timeless value of Eastern thought, it is only logical to expect that thinkers like Kazantzakis, who have attempted a synthesis as a way out of the transitional age, will attract increasing attention. In addition to these reasons pointing to an increased awareness of an interest in Kazantzakis' political thought, he will be studied for his uniquely provocative offering of hope.

Kazantzakis resolutely condemned false hope and resoundingly counseled man to fight forever the battle for the ascent. Modern man must learn, as did Kazantzakis, that in questing for the summit of men's souls the casting off of mundane hope and illusory freedom is an occasion not for despair and anxiety but for joy and celebration.

At the zenith of human capabilities which, following Kazantzakis, we must seek, one passes from those debasing limits so despised by Kazantzakis to link with God. This is done individually by man and collectively, or politically, by mankind through operationalizing those ennobling, liberating, and eminently applicable criteria of free choice, respect for man, love, social justice, communitarian needs, individuation, integration of the daimonic, and by heeding the counsel of both intellect and heart. In this manner is discovered a multitiered political theory that reveals in their falsity those twentieth-century masks of nihilism-escapism of Nietzsche or Buddha, the otherworldliness of the institutionalized church, and the materialism of both Marxist-Leninist revolution and Western scientific democracy.

By following Kazantzakis' politics of salvation, mankind successfully traverses the epoch of nihilism Nietzsche foresaw and achieves the vital transvaluation of an outmoded morality. They learn with Zorba, Odysseus, and El Greco how to link with the cosmological *élan vital* in a truly aspirational existence that defies the abyss and all debilitating doctrines founded on its terror. They reject the eschatologically justified ethic of homicide in fulfilling the extremely difficult demands of true rebellion, realizing that every moment is eternity and all men are brothers. They willingly uphold the cost of discipleship in rejecting the politics of secular messiahs. They utilize the benefits of science, yet do not make a new faith of science, knowing that science is but one aspect of a truly well-rounded existence. They listen closely to those men of the spirit within their midst, always seeking as their leaders ones who understand not only outer but, more importantly, inner life. They strive to emulate the religious individual who lives on only the highest level beyond the confines of the present. They emphasize not technique but content, not organization but spirit, not the few but the many. These are the true indices of hope that lead to the highest degree of beatitude attainable in political life.

Notes

Chapter 1

1. Friedrich Nietzsche, *The Portable Nietzsche,* ed. Walter Kaufmann (New York: The Viking Press, 1954), p. 1.

2. Until two years before his death, Kazantzakis mistakenly thought he was born in 1885. His wife Helen Kazantzakis, in *Nikos Kazantzakis: A Biography based on his Letters,* trans. Amy Mims (New York: Simon and Schuster, Inc., 1968), p. 532, relates that on "February 18, 1955, we celebrated Nikos' seventieth birthday—at least, so we thought. In reality he was already seventy-two years old. After his death, we discovered by chance the exact date of his birth, inscribed in his own hand, in a schoolbook. 'I was born on February 18, 1883, on a Friday.' A great joy, for me at least. We had won two years from Death."

For a chronological account of Kazantzakis' life and work, see Saralyn Poole Hadgopoulos, "Odysseus' Choice: A Comparison and Contrast of Works by Albert Camus and Nikos Kazantzakis" (unpublished Ph.D. dissertation, Emory University, 1965), pp. 164–70. As indicated in the Introduction, the most extensive factual material is to be found in these and the works cited immediately below. All works are noted, unless otherwise indicated, by the date of their translation into English.

Nikos Kazantzakis, *Report To Greco,* trans. P. A. Bien with Introduction by Helen Kazantzakis (New York: Simon and Schuster, Inc., 1965).

Pandelis Prevelakis, *Nikos Kazantzakis And His Odyssey,* trans. Philip Sherrard with Preface by Kimon Friar (New York: Simon and Schuster, Inc., 1961).

3. As great a literary talent as Kazantzakis is and as empathetic as his views are to many segments of the worldwide counterculture movement, one is compelled to conclude he would receive little sympathy from the Women's Liberation arm of the movement, owing to his ambivalence on the potentiality and role of women. Will Durant describes one side of Kazantzakis' views on the subject in "Nikos Kazantzakis," in his and Ariel Durant's *Interpretations of Life: A Survey of Contemporary Literature* (New York: Simon and Schuster, Inc., 1970), pp. 279, 280–81. Kazantzakis "had many intimacies, but he resented their permanence. He felt that women checked his grand designs. 'They're a pest. "Forward!" you say, and they say, "Stop!" ' (Some pundits have thought the opposite.) 'The age-old heart inside me . . . repulses women and refuses to trust them or permit them to penetrate deeply within me and take possession. Women are simply ornaments for men, and more often a sickness and a neces-

sity.' In healthier moments he listed four gifts as basic to a man's life: 'earth, water, bread, and woman'; or, again, 'food, drink, woman, and the dance' ". . . . "Zorba says, 'You keep teasing me and saying I'm fond of the women. Why shouldn't I be fond of them, when they're all weak creatures who . . . surrender on the spot if you just catch hold of their breasts?' " The other side of his nature is explained by Mrs. Kazantzakis in a letter on the manuscript from her home in Geneva, November 19, 1976. "Yes! Nikos was afraid of passion, that is the perils of Circe and Calypso. . . . Afraid he was and yet in love a great part of his life. He was so very tender and passionate and respectful. I am sure that no one has ever heard Nikos Kazantzakis say a harsh word against a woman in whom he has once been interested, even one or two who made him suffer. Remember also in his confession to Greco, 'women I loved'."

4. Kazantzakis, letter to Eleni Samios, 1933, in H. Kazantzakis, *Nikos Kazantzakis*, p. 267.

5. Kazantzakis, letter to P. Prevelakis, 1932, in Prevelakis, *Nikos Kazantzakis and his Odyssey*, pp. 147–48.

6. While *Report* is invaluable as a guidebook to the development of Kazantzakis' thought, it is not a precise, detailed work but an artistic, novelistic effort characterized by many factual inaccuracies. Prevelakis, *Nikos Kazantzakis and his Odyssey*, p. 167, notes that "Kazantzakis has here made a myth of his life. 'Poetry and Truth.' He has confused the dates, put ideal order into his struggles, given harmony to his life. Imagination has given him whatever life denied him." As Kazantzakis, *Report*, p. 15, concedes, "My *Report To Greco* is not an autobiography." He is "mixing truth with fantasy." This obviously creates problems for the reader. Rather than quibble over details, we have chosen to do as Kazantzakis did and simply pass "over many ephemeral things" (letter to Iannis Kakridis, 1956, in H. Kazantzakis, *Nikos Kazantzakis*, p. 547), in hopes of grasping the more important personalities and issues that shaped his development. Thus, if there are some modifications on his part, we take our stand with Alexander Eliot, who reviewed *Report*, "The Widening Gyre," *Bookweek*, XI (August 8, 1965), p. 13: "Well, why not? The warm breath of life itself is bound to cast a mist over cold facts. And memory is a living thing. Therefore anybody's autobiography will contain 'some small modifications.' " Equally important as facts for our purpose is Kazantzakis' interpretation of them!

7. In the translator's note to Kazantzakis, *Report*, p. 13, Bien gives this definition: "A true man, i.e., brave and strong, able to resist pain, etc. The term was originally applied to the foot soldiers accompanying mounted knights, later to any soldier, now to any young man who has soldier-like qualities. In Greece today it is an unqualified term of praise."

8. Prevelakis, *Nikos Kazantzakis and his Odyssey*, p. 150. *Thério* or *thirío* in Greek does not really mean beast. When one speaks of a man, a child, or even a woman as *thirío*, it means that he or she is a very strong person.

9. Kazantzakis, letter to Eleni Samios, 1933, in H. Kazantzakis, *Nikos Kazantzakis*, pp. 266–67. Many years later Kazantzakis would say in *Report*, p. 30, "the secret hatred I felt for my father was able, after his death, to turn to love."

10. Peter Bien, "Nikos Kazantzakis," *The Politics of Twentieth-Century Novelists*, ed. George A. Panichas with Foreword by John A. Aldridge (New York: Hawthorn Books, Inc., 1971), p. 144. Another commentator, Adreas K. Poulakidas, "The Novels of Kazantzakis and Their Existential Sources" (unpublished Ph.D. dissertation, Indiana University, 1967), p. 148, agrees that "by 1909 the basic philosophical tenets which are to guide and determine Kazantzakis' future outlook have been firmly implanted in his twenty-six-year-old mind."

11. See also pp. 44–46.

12. Will Durant, "Nikos Kazantzakis," in his and Ariel Durant's *Interpretations of Life*, p. 270. Morton P. Levitt, "The Cretan Glance: The World and Art of Nikos Kazantzakis," *Journal of Modern Literature*, II (November 1971), pp. 165–66, finds the intriguing history of Crete in many ways "unlike that of any other Western nation, a long and virtually unbroken succession of foreign domination and unsuccessful revolts." He recounts a local saying that for the past several hundred years "each generation of Cretan men married, raised a son to continue the line, and went off to the mountains to fight the invaders." The most recent invasion was the German landing of 1941, which the Cretans resisted fiercely with knives and old guns. They inflicted heavy casualties and suffered bloody reprisals. Levitt finds further testimony to the Cretan love of freedom in that "it was only on Crete that the recent military coup was resisted with armed force: it was not for monarchy that the islanders fought, but for the principles of freedom which underlay their entire history. The new military government responded by preventing the planned celebration of the tenth anniversary of the death of Nikos Kazantzakis: the dictatorship recognized its enemy even in death."

13. See also pp. 73–79.

14. This dramatic anecdote is, by all accounts, a true tale that sheds light on one of Kazantzakis' abiding concerns.

15. See also pp. 38, 50, 66.

16. Prevelakis, *Nikos Kazantzakis and his Odyssey*, p. 15.

17. Kazantzakis, letter to Stamos Diamantaras, 1951, in H. Kazantzakis, *Nikos Kazantzakis*, p. 494.

18. T. Walter Wallbank, et al., *Civilization Past and Present*, 6th ed. (Glenview, Ill.: Scott, Foresman, & Company, 1969), II. The immediately ensuing information comes largely from Part Four, "Realism and Realpolitik," which provides a simple, clear discussion of the sociopolitical and intellectual milieu of the period.

19. *Ibid.*, p. 363.

20. Kazantzakis, in *Report*, lists in two places these "steps": p. 15, "Christ, Buddha, Lenin, Odysseus"; p. 445, "Homer, Buddha, Nietzsche, Bergson, and Zorba. The first, for me, was the peaceful, brilliantly luminous eye, like the sun's disk, which illuminated the entire universe with its redemptive splendor; Buddha, the bottomless jet-dark eye in which the world drowned and was delivered. Bergson relieved me of various unsolved philosophical problems which tormented me in my early youth; Nietzsche enriched me with new anguishes and instructed me how to transform misfortune, bitterness, and uncertainty into pride; Zorba taught me to love life and have no fear of death." Friar, in an editorial comment on the manuscript, Athens, March, 1977, notes: "He was always adding and changing this list. His Cantos *(Terza Rima)* contain twenty poems to various persons who deeply influenced him, the 'bodyguards to the *Odyssey!*' "

21. Kimon Friar, "Introduction" to Nikos Kazantzakis, *The Odyssey: A Modern Sequel*, trans. Kimon Friar (New York: Simon and Schuster, Inc. 1958), xiv; see also pp. 12–13 above. For those interested in more extensive treatments of Kazantzakis' intellectual debts, see: "Nikos Kazantzakis Special Number," *Journal of Modern Literature*, II (November 1971); Poulakidas, "The Novels of Kazantzakis and Their Existential Sources" (unpublished Ph.D. dissertation); Ralph N. Oyer, "Progress Variations: A Treatise on Alfred North Whitehead and Nikos Kazantzakis" (unpublished M.A. thesis); Kathleen Fuller, "Nietzsche and Kazantzakis: The Will to Power and Struggle for Freedom in *The Odyssey*" (unpublished A.B. thesis); and most important, Kimon Friar, "Nikos Kazantzakis in the United States" *Literary Review*, XVIII (Summer 1975).

22. Minas Savvas, "Kazantzakis And Marxism," *Journal of Modern Literature*, II (November 1971), p. 284.

23. Andreas K. Poulakidas, "Kazantzakis' *Zorba the Greek* and Nietzsche's *Thus Spake Zarathustra*," *Philological Quarterly*, XXXXIX (1970), pp. 234–35. Poulakidas points out that in Paris in 1907 and 1908 Kazantzakis chose as his dissertation subject, "Friedrich Nietzsche and His Philosophy of Right"; that around 1915 he translated Nietzsche's *Thus Spake Zarathustra* into modern Greek; and that he titled one of the most revealing chapters of *Report*, "Paris. Nietzsche the Great Martyr."

24. Kazantzakis, *Report,* p. 318, tells of how he was first introduced to Nietzsche's philosophy in Paris by a young girl in the Bibliotheque Sainte-Genevieve who showed a man's photograph in a large book to him with the person's name covered and said "it's you—the very image. . . . Don't you recognize him? Is it the first time you've seen him? It's Nietzsche!"

"Nietzsche! I had heard of him, but still had not read any of his books."

However, according to Peter Bien, "Kazantzakis' Nietzscheanism," *Journal of Modern Literature,* II (November 1971), p. 248, he actually was "aware of Nietzsche before he went to Paris. His first wife claims in her fictionalized biography of him that he first read Nietzsche in high school. We should remember that in these years (1899–1902) Nietzsche's thought was well known in Greece and was already exerting an influence on writers . . . thus it would have been natural for Kazantzakis' curiosity to have been aroused at this early age, and if not then, certainly during his years as a university student in Athens (1902–1906)."

25. Kazantzakis, letter to Iannis Angelakis, 1917, in H. Kazantzakis, *Nikos Kazantzakis,* p. 66. Bien, "Kazantzakis' Nietzscheanism," *Journal of Modern Literature,* cites from *Letters to Galetea* (Athens 1959), two instances, pp. 247 and 250 respectively, of this identification as related by Kazantzakis to his first wife in a letter from Berlin in 1922: "The other day a German I know ran up to me as I was returning some books to the library and told me with emotion that seeing me he had suddenly thought he had seen Nietzsche"; and, recalling a visit to Nietzsche's birthplace in Naumburg, he was shaken by "the tragic face of that man who bears such affinity to my spiritual and corporeal constitution."

26. Nietzsche, *Thus Spake Zarathustra, The Portable Nietzsche,* p. 124.

27. Friedrich Nietzsche, *The Will To Power,* trans. Walter Kaufmann and R. J. Hollingdale with Commentary by Kaufmann (New York: The Viking Press, 1954), pp. 9–10.

28. Nietzsche, quoted in José Ortega y Gasset, *The Revolt of the Masses,* trans. anon. (New York: W. W. Norton and Company, Inc., 1932), p. 59.

29. Peter Bien, "*Zorba the Greek,* Nietzsche, and the Perennial Greek Predicament," *Antioch Review,* XXV (Spring 1965), pp. 155, 151.

30. Poulakidas, *Philological Quarterly,* XXXXIX (1970), pp. 243–44. It should be noted that Mrs. Kazantzakis, while agreeing that Nikos "*was* influenced by Bergson and Nietzsche," stresses that he was also influenced "by Buddha, Lenin, and Zorba." Thus, to her it seems "very funny to pretend that *Zorba* was solely modeled on *The Birth of Tragedy* or *Thus Spake Zarathrusta.*" Letter, Geneva, November 19, 1976.

31. Friar, "Introduction," Kazantzakis' *The Odyssey,* pp. xiv–xv. For

similar lists of Nietzsche's contributions to Kazantzakis' art and philoso-
phy, see: Poulakidas, "The Novels of Kazantzakis and Their Existential
Sources" (unpublished Ph.D. dissertation), p. 240; and Bien, *Journal of
Modern Literature*, II (November 1971), p. 264.

32. Andreas K. Poulakidas, "Kazantzakis and Bergson: Metaphysic
Aestheticians," *Journal of Modern Literature*, II (November 1971), p. 267.

33. Robert S. Brumbaugh and Newton P. Stallknecht, *The Spirit of
Western Philosophy*, (New York: David McKay Company, Inc., 1964), p.
421. The present discussion owes much to this work.

34. Kazantzakis, cited by Friar, "Introduction," Kazantzakis', *The
Odyssey*, p. xvi.

35. Henri Bergson, *Creative Evolution*, quoted in Brumbaugh and
Stallknecht, *The Spirit of Western Philosophy*, p. 439.

36. H. Stuart Hughes, *Consciousness and Society: The Reorientation of
European Social Thought*, 1890–1930 (New York: Alfred A. Knopf, 1958),
p. 121.

37. Bergson, *Creative Evolution*, quoted in Brumbaugh and
Stallknecht, *The Spirit of Western Philosophy*, p. 440. Maurice Friedman,
"The Modern Vitalist: Bergson and Kazantzakis," in his *To Deny Our
Nothingness: Contemporary Images of Man* (New York: Delacorte Press,
1967), p. 65, discusses the importance for Bergson's thought of the
concept of lived time: "To recover authentic existence we must move
from the world of spatialized, quantitative, successive time to the organic
flow of time. Like Kierkegaard, Bergson distinguished between the
becoming, or process of the inner soul and the tendency to fix these
processes into objects, categories, and words in the outer world."

38. Adele Bloch, "The Dual Masks of Nikos Kazantzakis," *Journal of
Modern Literature*, II (November 1971), p. 189.

39. Bien, *Antioch Review*, XXV (1965), p. 155.

40. Tom Doulis, "Kazantzakis and The Meaning of Suffering,"
Northwest Review, VI (Winter 1963), p. 57.

41. We have borrowed from Spinoza and chosen to designate the
ascendant process of attaining Zorbaic perspective emendation of our
existence, rather than improvement or amendment or purgation or
cultivation or other possible descriptive terms, as this best connotes the
act of following our inherent desires, i.e., the divine in man, to an
unhindered, uninhibited, self-willed conscious celebration of life and
infinity. Even though Kazantzakis' and Spinoza's methods were quite
different in many ways, interestingly enough, their point of departure
and to a lesser extent their destination were the same. We have labeled
Kazantzakis' triadic stages to deliverance, spelled out in *The Saviors of God*

and followed by Odysseus, epistemological emendation, ethico-existent emendation, and metaphysical emendation, drawing support for our designations from the following interpretations: Peter Bien, *Nikos Kazantzakis* (New York: Columbia University Press, 1972), pp. 23–24, labels the preparatory stage the "epistemological section," and discusses the following stages in ethico-religious and metaphysical terms respectively. Friar, "Introduction," Kazantzakis' *The Odyssey*, p. xiii, without using our specific terms, analyzes the steps in the fashion we have followed. W. B. Stanford, *The Ulysses Theme: A Study in the Adaptability of a Traditional Hero* (New York: Barnes & Noble, Inc., 1964), p. 236, describes Odysseus as passing through the phases of doing, being, and becoming, which correspond roughly to our labels.

42. Bien, *Nikos Kazantzakis*, p. 24.

43. Plato, *The Republic*, trans. B. Jowett (New York: Vintage Books, A Division of Random House, n.d.), pp. 258 and 232.

44. Friar, "Introduction" to Kazantzakis' *The Odyssey*, pp. xiii–xiv.

45. Hermann Hesse, *Demian*, trans. M. Roloff and M. Lebeck (New York: Harper & Row, Publishers, 1965), pp. 108–110.

Chapter 2

1. Bien, *Journal of Modern Literature*, II (November, 1972), p. 265.

2. Kazantzakis, quoted in H. Kazantzakis, *Nikos Kazantzakis*, pp. 89–90.

3. Kazantzakis, *ibid.*, p. 343.

4. Kazantzakis, letter to E. Samios, *ibid.*, p. 168.

5. Nikos Kazantzakis, "Apology," *ibid.*, pp. 568–69.

6. Kazantzakis, quoted in Prevelakis, *Nikos Kazantzakis and his Odyssey*, p. 130. Kazantzakis in *Report*, p. 420, in the section devoted to the Russian period, writes: "The entire world is a Pompeii shortly before the eruption! What is the use of such a world with its brazen women, faithless men, with its villainy, injustice, and disease? All these sharp merchants, anthropophagic triggermen, these priests trading god in retail, these panders and eunuchs—why would they live? Why should all these children grow up to occupy the places their parents occupied in the taverns, factories, and brothels? . . . Let the barbarians come to clear the unobstructed road and open a new riverbed for the spirit."

7. Prevelakis, *Nikos Kazantzakis and his Odyssey*, p. 137.

8. *Ibid.*, p. 137; and H. Kazantzakis, *Nikos Kazantzakis*, pp. 199 and 222. In her letter, Geneva, November 29, 1976, Mrs. Kazantzakis emphasizes

that, in her view "it is unfair to say that Kazantzakis remained indifferent" to the Serge family's difficulties. Indeed, she considers it possible that Serge, "well known by Stalin as an active Trotskyite," and his family may have "suffered increased persecution because of the publication of Istrati's three volume work, which appeared in France under his signature, but which was written partly (the last two volumes) by Serge and another Trotskyite friend of his." She and Kazantzakis "tried and in some ways helped Serge when he was later in Paris."

Also, the dispute with Istrati was only temporary. They would reaffirm their friendship. In a letter in 1932 Panait would write: "What's become of you, my dear Nikos? I miss you. I'm seriously ill and still cannot forget your great unique face. If you're still angry forgive me. And give me a sign of life. Your Panait." Mrs. Kazantzakis says, "Nikos always loved Panait. He only disagreed with him for this one book, because Panait mentioned only the bad side of things in the U.S.S.R. without a word about the good things the Communists under Stalin achieved or were accomplishing at the time." The two old friends were discussing a joint effort just prior to Istrati's death. "A few months before his death, Panait wrote a very warm letter to Nikos asking permission to come to Aegina in order to write a book together on the U.S.S.R. Unfortunately, his end was to come too soon."

9. Poulakidas, "The Novels of Kazantzakis And Their Existential Sources" (unpublished Ph.D. dissertation), p. 112. There may be a great deal of what the psychoanalysts call "transference" in this identification; for Kazantzakis' father had, by his larger-than-life call to action, intimidated Nikos (*Report*, p. 475): "He it was who reduced my blood to ink." And Lenin provided a panoramic fulfillment of the quest for action on a gigantic scale. Kazantzakis probably realized this, for he was most likely familiar with Freud's works, claiming in *Report* to have read them during his confinement for a skin ailment in Vienna in 1921. It's unclear whether he actually did so. Friar writes that "Kazantzakis told him he had never read Freud, but he, Friar, never believed him." Editorial comment, Athens, March, 1977.

10. Kazantzakis, *Nikos Kazantzakis*, pp. 437, 485.

11. Prevelakis, *Nikos Kazantzakis and his Odyssey*, p. 127. Helen, in "An Afterword to Kazantzakis," *Toda Raba*, p. 204, gives her impression of Kazantzakis during this time in a strikingly similar manner: "In that delicate, slender, disciplined body of his, in those burning eyes, in that dialectical talent which could bring order out of chaos, these young people [reference to Berlin associates] put their trust; it was from him so they thought, that salvation was to come. . . . Certainly he thought so

himself for a brief period of time. He would abandon art . . . deny his most recent love, Buddha. He would learn a manual trade to earn his living. Then he would expand his field of action, and go to the U.S.S.R."

12. Kazantzakis, letter to E. Samios, 1927, in H. Kazantzakis, *Nikos Kazantzakis*, p. 159.

13. Alfred Kazin, "Thoreau and American Power," *Atlantic Monthly*, CCXXLLL (May 1969), pp. 60–62.

14. Richard W. Chilson, "The Christ of Nikos Kazantzakis," *Thought*, XLVII (April 1972), p. 70. Mrs. Kazantzakis (letter, Geneva, November 29, 1976) agrees that Nikos "spent thousands of hours writing," but she dissents from the view that this was devitalizing. "In the time he gave to life I can swear he lived ten times more intensely than any other human being I have met! You should have seen him when he traveled, or when walking in the country, or when tasting a fruit—grapes, watermelons, or figs—or with a man or woman in whom he was interested. You simply cannot measure Nikos Kazantzakis with the common measures."

15. Kazin, *Atlantic Monthly*, CCXXXLLL (May, 1970), p. 68.

16. Prevelakis, *Nikos Kazantzakis and his Odyssey*, p. 127.

17. Prevelakis, *Nikos Kazantzakis and his Odyssey*, footnote 133, pp. 181–82, suggests in an interesting passage that Buddha, Christ, and Lenin all personify for Kazantzakis "the universal power of the human word. . . . From statistics issued by UNESCO we learn, moreover, that from 1948 to 1955 Lenin had been translated 968 times; the Bible is second."

18. The material to p. 76 on Camus is based upon my "The Politics of H. D. Thoreau" (unpublished M.A. thesis, Baton Rouge, Louisiana State University, 1969), pp. 88–94.

19. Albert Camus, *The Rebel*, trans., Anthony Bower (New York: Alfred A. Knopf, 1957), p. 297.

20. Camus, *The Rebel*, p. 292.

21. Fred Wilhoite, *Beyond Nihilism: Albert Camus's Contribution to Political Thought* (Baton Rouge, La.: Louisiana State University Press, 1968), p. 152.

22. Camus, quoted in *ibid.*, pp. 110–11.

23. Fred Wilhoite, "Albert Camus's Politics of Rebellion," *Western Political Quarterly*, XIV (June 1961), p. 411.

24. Camus, *The Rebel*, p. 306.

25. Hadgopoulos, "Odysseus' Choice: A Comparison and Contrast of Works by Albert Camus and Nikos Kazantzakis" (unpublished Ph.D. dissertation), pp. 63–64.

26. Kazantzakis, quoted in Bien, *The Politics of Twentieth Century*

Novelists, ed. Panichas, p. 142.

27. Ibid., p. 143. Kazantzakis (*Report,* p. 470) came to understand the creative course of his journey: "Had nothing gone to waste, then? Considered separately, each of my intellectual ramblings and sidewise tacks seemed wasted time, the product of an unjelled, disordered mind. But now I saw that considered all together they constituted a straight and unerring line which knew full well that only by sidewise tacks could it advance over this uneven earth. And my infidelities toward the great ideas—I had abandoned them after being successively fascinated and disillusioned—taken all together these infidelities constituted an unshakable faith in the essence. It seemed that luck (How shall we call it? Not luck, but destiny) had eyes and compassion; it had taken me by the hand and guided me to do. It expected me to hear the Cry of the future, and to exert every effort to divine what that Cry wanted, why it was calling, and where it invited us to go."

28. Kazantzakis, letter to Borje Knos, 1948, in H. Kazantzakis, *Nikos Kazantzakis,* p. 474.

29. Kazantzakis, *ibid.,* p. 535.

30. Bien, *Nikos Kazantzakis,* pp. 35, 39.

31. Poulakidas, *Philological Quarterly,* XLOX (April 1970), pp. 234–35. Other commentators have discovered this surgeon-like portrayal of the intellectual-literatist and the passionate luxuriate in Kazantzakis' make-up as the central theme of *Zorba.* C. N. Stavrou, "The Limits of the Possible: Nikos Kazantzakis' Arduous Odyssey," *Southwest Review,* LCII (Winter 1972), p. 63, states that in *"Zorba the Greek,* the author-narrator constantly berates himself for his inability to espouse a life of the senses." Joseph Blenkinsopp, "My Entire Soul Is A Cry," *Commonweal,* XCI (February 26, 1971), p. 515, wonders while reading *Zorba* whether the Boss will complete his manuscript, learn to dance, learn to love, and sever the strings to be drawn into Zorba's world? "The dramatic climax ought to come (it does in the movie) with the Nietzschean moment of the collapse of the cableline and ensuing dance on the shore. Only at this point the author is defeated by his own autobiographical honesty. He was too much convinced that writing was a second-order activity, a *faute de mieux;* he tells us elsewhere that when he came to know Zorba at the age of thirty-four it was already too late; he had degenerated into an incurable pen-pusher. And so the Boss, though turned on by Zorba, was not driven out of his wretched mind." Colin Wilson, *The Strength To Dream* (Boston: Little, Brown & Company, 1960), p. 208, believes that Kazantzakis was all his life ashamed of "being a 'pen-pusher,' and hankered after the life of action. . . . This same self-division is apparent in . . . *Zorba the Greek.* . . .

Most of the book is taken up with the adventures of Zorba, a kind of lesser Ulysses, healthy, happy, roguish, loving women, wine and food, completely lacking in self-division, while Kazantzakis struggles with an epic about the Buddha and renunciation. . . . Kazantzakis . . . is the unhappy intellectual, who never makes the effort to heal his own self-division and become reconciled to the 'original sin' that makes him at once greater and less happy than Zorba."

32. Colin Wilson, "The Greatness of Nikos Kazantzakis," *Minnesota Review*, VIII (1968), pp. 179–80. This enormous will to expression is why what Thomas L. King, in "Kazantzakis' Prometheus Trilogy: The Ideas And Their Dramatic Rendering" (unpublished Ph.D. dissertation, Indian University, 1970), pp. 157–60, says of Kazantzakis is perceptive. He "sought to use all the devices available both to the writer and to the theatre to express his thought. He has not limited himself to the conventional dramatic style of the late nineteenth and early twentieth centuries, nor has he limited himself to the devices of the poet and the novelist. Instead he has embodied his ideas in drama by producing a complex mixture of as many of those devices available to the creative artist as he could include. He uses poetry, prose, narrative, description, choral utterance, film, the sounds of nature (particularly of birds and the sea), dialogue, lengthy single-character exposition and soliloquy, masks, interaction of characters, and all the lights and sounds of the theatre to produce a drama that cares little for the niceties of logical construction or the separation of artistic media. He does not limit himself to what is, in the strictest sense, purely dramatic. He piles effect on top of effect, sometimes simultaneously, to produce a rush of effects all designed to create both an arresting spectacle and a vehicle for his ideas. The drama of Kazantzakis is a drama in which the novelist and poet strain at the bonds of the dramatic and the dramatist utilizes all the devices of the theatre to make the vision of the novel and poem come alive."

Chapter 3

1. Nikos Kazantzakis, "The Immortal Free Spirit of Man," *Life And Letters*, L (September 1946), p. 126.

2. Kazantzakis, *Report*, p. 369, recounts Itka's rabid scorn of Buddha when he told her: "I know another Messiah who delivers man from hunger and also from satiety, from injustice and also from justice. And what is most important, from all Messiahs."

"And his name is . . ."

"Buddha!"

She smiled disdainfully, then said in an angry voice, "I've heard of him. He's a ghost. My messiah is made of flesh and blood."

3. Robert Tucker, *Philosophy and Myth in Karl Marx* (Cambridge: Cambridge University Press, 1961), p. 81.

4. Tucker, *Philosophy and Myth in Karl Marx*, p. 100.

5. Raymond Aron, *Main Currents in Sociological Thought*, trans. Richard Howard and Helen Weaver (New York: Basic Books, Inc., 1965), I, p. 112.

6. Karl Marx, *Economic and Philosophic Manuscripts of 1844*, trans. Martin Milligan (Moscow: Foreign Language Publishing House, 1959), pp. 75, 102.

7. *Letters to Galetea*, cited by Savvas, *Journal of Modern Literature*, II (November 1971), p. 286.

8. Prevelakis, *Nikos Kazantzakis and his Odyssey*, p. 61.

9. Oswald Spengler, *The Decline of the West* (German edition, I, pp. 144–45), quoted in Prevelakis, *Nikos* etc., p. 60.

10. Talcott Parsons, *The Structure of Social Action* (2d ed.: Glencoe, Illinois, 1949), p. 179, quoted in Hughes, *Consciousness and Society*, p. 378.

11. Hughes, *Consciousness and Society*, p. 378.

12. Ortega, in *The Revolt of the Masses*, p. 196, sees this world crisis as the "demoralization" of Europe deriving from the fact that "life to-day is the fruit of an interregnum of an empty space between two organizations of historical rule—that which was, that which is to be." The provisional nature of Ortega's world has many implications for man. Since such provisionalism leads to an unguided, rudderless, public life, men are uncertain what to think, what to do, how to act. There is no "programme," to use one of Ortega's favorite words, which lends credence to actions, gives expectations to the future, and gives connectedness to the past. In such a situation "men do not know what institutions to serve in truth; women do not know what type of men they in truth prefer."

13. Kazantzakis, *Life and Letters*, L (September 1946), p. 124.

14. Hadgopoulous, "Odysseus' Choice: A Comparison and Contrast of Works by Albert Camus and Nikos Kazantzakis" (unpublished Ph.D. dissertation), pp. 35–36.

15. Kazantzakis, *Life And Letters*, L (September 1946), p. 124.

16. Kazantzakis, "Apology," H. Kazantzakis, *Nikos Kazantzakis*, pp. 565–66.

17. Kazantzakis, in *Toda Raba*, pp. 39–40, has Mikhailovich say, "I also know what you Communists do not know and do not dare to know; that as soon as the attackers get the power—the table—they too will start to get fat and paralyzed. And other hungry, suffering masses will rise on earth

again. So will waves of human beings rise and fall in an unceasing rhythm until the end of time. That's what I know, oh, you little practical souls."

18. Kazantzakis, in H. Kazantzakis, *Nikos Kazantzakis*, p. 342.

19. Kazantzakis, "Friedrich Nietzsche's Philosophy of Law and the State," cited by Bien, *Journal of Modern Literature*, II (November 1971), pp. 253–54.

20. Dietrich Bonhoeffer, *The Cost of Discipleship*, trans. R. H. Fuller with Foreword by G. K. A. Bell and a Memoir by G. Leibholz. (rev. ed.; New York: The MacMillan Company, 1949), p. 121.

21. Kazantzakis, Letter to Borje Knos, 1950, in H. Kazantzakis, *Nikos Kazantzakis*, p. 491.

22. Kazantzakis, Acceptance Address to the International Peace Committee in Vienna, 1956, in H. Kazantzakis, *Nikos* etc., pp. 544–45.

23. Kazantzakis, letter to Pierre Sipriot, 1954, in H. Kazantzakis, *Nikos Kazantzakis*, p. 529. In *England* (New York: Simon and Schuster, Inc., 1965), p. 111, Kazantzakis observes that attempts to turn back from the present and future are "vain romanticizing and nostalgia."

24. Kazantzakis, "Prometheus Trilogy," quoted in King, "Kazantzakis' Prometheus Trilogy: The Ideas and Their Dramatic Rendering" (unpublished Ph.D. dissertation), p. 84.

25. Kazantzakis, letter to Pierre Sipriot, 1954, in H. Kazantzakis, *Nikos Kazantzakis*, p. 529.

26. Kazantzakis, Letter to Tea Anemoyanni, 1946, in ibid., p. 449.

27. Herbert Marcuse, *One Dimensional Man: Studies in the Ideology of Advanced Industrial Society* (London: Routledge & Kegan Paul, Ltd, 1964), pp. 243 & 10.

28. Kazantzakis, *Life and Letters*, L (September 1946), p. 124.

29. See Bien, *Journal of Modern Literature*, II (November 1971) p. 253.

30. John Dewey, *Liberalism And Social Action* (New York: G. P. Putnam's Sons, 1935), p. 79.

31. Kazantzakis, Letter to Iannis Kakridis, 1946, in H. Kazantzakis, *Nikos Kazantzakis*, p. 456.

32. The discussion of Tillich's thought comes directly from a seminar lecture, Philosophy 203, Metaphysics, Fall, 1970, by Dr. James F. Anderson of the Louisiana State University department of philosophy. See his *Paul Tillich: Basics In His Thought* (Albany, New York: Magi Books, Inc., 1972). Karl Mannheim, *Ideology And Utopia: An Introduction To The Sociology of Knowledge*, trans. Louis Wirth and Edward Shils (New York: Harcourt, Brace & World, Inc., 1936), sees this as functional rationality whereby rationality is transubstantiated into irrationality. Mannheim recognizes the destructive effect which functional rationality has upon

human capacity for rational, reflective judgment. He brings up the possibility of the technique or organizational process becoming both the means and end as it replaces the value or true goal for which it is supposed to be utilized. This critique is paralleled by Marcuse's in *One Dimensional Man*. The major specific development that Marcuse feels to be the greatest contributor to both the rise and the maintenance of modern society's technological totalitarianism is the abandonment of theory in favor of positivisitic philosophy. Positivism, rational scientism, and behaviorism are viewed by Marcuse as corruptions of philosophy and he attacks the embodiment of these methodologically oriented developments as perverting modern thought, modern philosophy, and modern sociology. The addiction to scientism, i.e., to fact, has led to a loss of: (1) an historical perspective; (2) a comprehensive world view; (3) any concept of transcendence. He argues that the emphasis on fact, on what is, with no regard to what ought to be, has a static bias which reinforces the repressiveness of the status quo and further flattens both the philosophical and personal horizon to its one-dimensional perspective. Marcuse states, correctly it seems, that this scientism is not a party matter but is found throughout the spectrum of political philosophy—liberal and conservative. Social philosophers have, under the weight of scientific-positivism, come to view their role, according to Marcuse (p. 211) as a "descriptive analysis of facts that blocks the apprehension of facts, and becomes an element of the ideology which sustains the facts. . . . Nothing remains of ideology but the recognition of that which is. . . . The world tends to become the stuff of total administration, which absorbs even the administrators." This has resulted, Marcuse believes, in the intellectuals' losing their ability to synthesize in the traditional Western manner; to criticize, which is their proper role as the forerunners of social change; and to postulate and inculcate value into both their endeavors and those of the society as a whole. Marcuse is particularly sincere and intense when he criticizes the many sociopolitical adherents of behaviorism for their addiction to quantification, their narrow specialization, and their involvement with the overworked distinction between fact and value. The new intellectuals, in Marcuse's analysis, have abdicated their role of criticism and have become part of the establishment—supporters of, participants in, and subject to the repression of technological civilization.

33. This is brilliantly illuminated in two of the most important works of recent years. David Halberstam, *The Best and the Brightest* (New York: Random House, Inc., 1969), explores how the technically superior minds of the post-World War II generation led the United States into the most ghastly blunder of American foreign policy since World War I. In a

broader study, *Where the Wasteland Ends* (Garden City, New York: Doubleday & Company, Inc., 1972), Theodore Roszak makes eminently clear the multifold ramifications of this "psychic rift" upon which Western civilization is constructed. See especially chapters V & VI.

34. Kazantzakis, conversation with E. Samios, in H. Kazantzakis, *Nikos Kazantzakis*, p. 150.

35. Ortega, *The Revolt of the Masses*, pp. 120–21.

36. Kazantzakis, cited by Friar, "Introduction," Kazantzakis', *The Odyssey*, p. xxii.

37. Wilson, *Minnesota Review*, VIII (1968), pp. 177–78. Wilson goes further to scold Kazantzakis for not systematically developing this insight; this "should lead to the recognition that if the mind possesses this freedom, then the immediate problem is to find methods for increasing the recognition. Not mystical flashes: they are too brief and unreliable; nor drug-inspired ecstasies of oneness with the universe. A scientific method, an extension of what we at present call science and philosophy.

"I feel that it is at this point that Kazantzakis' mind refused to take the final leap; it falls back. His admirers—although I count myself among them—may dispute this. I can only state my own opinion for what it is worth."

Wilson demands far too much here. The greatest art is never so radically divorced from physical stimuli as to be solely of the mind. Kazantzakis gloried both in the mind's creative capability and the body's physical earthbound existence. Thus he knew that for the artist's mind to make Wilson's "final leap" would be a betrayal of the vital polarity of mind and body.

38. Kazantzakis, quoted in Friar, "Introduction" to Kazantzakis' *The Odyssey*, p. xii.

39. Kazantzakis, conversation with Pierre Sipriot, in H. Kazantzakis, *Nikos Kazantzakis*, p. 529.

40. William Barrett, *Irrational Man: A Study in Existential Philosophy* (Garden City, New York: Doubleday & Company, Inc., 1958), pp. 146–47, describes this process: "Thus the three 'stages on life's way,' as Kierkegaard called them, are not to be taken as different floors of a building; if I rise from the aesthetic to the ethical it does not mean that I have left the lower floor entirely behind me. Rather, both attitudes are stages on the way from the periphery to the center of the self, and the periphery is still preserved when we have learned to dwell a little closer to our center."

41. Søren Kierkegaard, "The Aesthetic, The Ethical, and The Religious," in *The Living Thoughts of Kierkegaard*, presented by W. H. Auden,

ed. with an Introduction by Alfred O. Mendel (New York: David McKay Company, Inc., 1952), pp. 87, 70–71, 74, 95, 113.

42. Barrett, *Irrational Man,* pp. 148–49.

43. Kierkegaard, *The Living Thoughts of Kierkegaard,* presented by Auden, p. 102.

44. Kazantzakis, *Life and Letters,* L (September 1946), pp. 124–25.

45. Kazantzakis, letter to Prevelakis, 1932, in H. Kazantzakis, *Nikos Kazantzakis,* p. 256.

46. Bien, *The Politics of Twentieth Century Novelists,* ed. Panichas, p. 137.

47. Kazantzakis, conversation with Marinetti, in H. Kazantzakis, *Nikos Kazantzakis,* p. 110.

48. Bien, *The Politics of Twentieth Century Novelists,* ed. Panichas, pp. 156–57.

49. T. S. Eliot, *Notes Toward a Definition of Culture* (London: Faber & Faber, Limited, 1948), p. 117.

50. *Ibid.,* pp. 86, 87, 94, 116.

51. *Ibid.,* pp. 84, 113, 57.

52. Kazantzakis, letter to E. Samios, 1929, in H. Kazantzakis, *Nikos Kazantzakis,* p. 203.

53. Kazantzakis, letter to Borje Knos, 1952, in H. Kazantzakis, *Nikos* etc., p. 507.

54. Quoted in Friar, "Introduction" to Kazantzakis' *The Odyssey,* p. xxix. Adonis Decavelles, "The Torrent and the Sun," *Poetry,* XCV (December 1959), p. 178, assesses *The Odyssey* in terms of this theme: "He has gone for his major source to the demotic language which in its numerous dialects preserves roots and elements from all periods, from Homer to the present day. To this he added what he has borrowed from written records of folk literature, and from all this he has produced a homogeneous and powerfully expressive medium, peculiarly his own, and the perfect tool for his cosmic, burning message. The language he has used is itself another Odyssey in its explorations and achievements. His words are like wild plants pulled from the deep bosom of the earth, roots and all. They smell of their passionate and lusty earthiness, of their newborn freshness. And yet in the old soil their roots have fed upon the ages of the long tradition, the centuries of human blood and wisdom. There is this duality-in-one in Kazantzakis himself and in his Odysseus. This only reflects the endless dualities synthesized and reconciled in Kazantzakis and his Odysseus in the warmth of life and art."

The contest between supporters of purist Greek and supporters of the demotic is not waged merely on an academic or literary level as Friar, "Introduction" to Kazantzakis' *The Odyssey,* p. xxviii, explains: "Since the birth of the modern Greek nation, a passionate battle has raged between scholars and academicians on the one hand, who have tried to impose the purist tongue from above, and most authors—poets, novelists, dramatists—who, equally proud of their long tradition, have found themselves unable to express their emotions in an artificial and bloodless tongue whose textual roots go so deep as to evolve into no living blossom. Fifty years ago Athenians rioted in the streets when a troupe tried to stage *The Oresteia* in modern translation, and several students were killed in an attempt to keep The New Testament from being translated into the demotic tongue."

55. Kazantzakis, cited by Levitt, *Journal of Modern Literature*, II (November 1971), p. 163.

Chapter 4

1. Bien, *The Politics of Twentieth Century Novelists*, ed. Panichas, p. 139.

2. Benedict de Spinoza, *Ethics*, based on trans. of William H. White, as revised by Amelia Hutchinson, ed. with Introduction by James Gutmann (New York: Hafner Publishing Company, Inc., 1949), pp. 55, 275, 125.

3. Durant, *Interpretations of Life*, p. 290.

4. Those who believe in Kazantzakis' atheism state their views as follows:

Bloch, *Journal of Modern Literature*, II (November 1971), p. 190: "To Kazantzakis death is the only certainty, and even death may be a dream. Yet the Greek poet's nature is permeated with extreme religiosity and a thirst for sainthood. . . . The Divine Being who is neither the Biblical nor the Christian God, bears the innumerable masks of nature and is a pure projection of the human mind who conceives It. To Kazantzakis God is merely a human creation."

Prevelakis, *Nikos Kazantzakis and his Odyssey*, p. 135: "But behind appearances does there exist a metaphysical unity, a real Being? The conclusions of *The Saviors of God* had given the answer. Is there at least an ethical world? Moralists sell the temporal as eternal. Nothing exists except an inconceivable and continually renewed energy. Man out of conceit identifies himself with it, rides with tragic joy the cataract bearing him towards the abyss."

H. Kazantzakis, *Nikos Kazantzakis*, p. 433, relates how their marriage ceremony was moving "even for atheists like ourselves."

Those who deny the atheism of Kazantzakis' later years say:

C. N. Stavrou, "Some Notes on Nikos Kazantzakis," *Colorado Quarterly*, XII (Winter 1964), p. 321: "Kazantzakis, like Joyce, made some bold

Icarian passes at the sun, but the wax on his wings never melted to the point of danger. Kazantzakis' Odysseus conceives of himself as a species of Nietzschean Superman and may be called an atheist. But the Kazantzakis of *The Last Temptation of Christ* accomplished a prodigal's return home in exemplary fashion—doubly secure, be it added, in the knowledge that he was saved and that his safety could not be attributed to a cloistered virtue. The godlessness of a James Joyce was completely antithetical to Kazantzakis' perception and response to life although he himself was not completely aware of it until relatively late in life. However, *The Poor Man of God,* a work about St. Francis, reveals the ancient mariner Kazantzakis returning to the belief of the young boy raised by the Franciscan monks and to the devoutness of the young man seeking enlightenment in the monasteries of Macedonia. Neither his exile from country nor his apostasy from Church was as final or as irrevocable as Joyce's."

Poulakidas, "The Novels of Kazantzakis And Their Existential Sources" (unpublished Ph.D. dissertation), pp. 147–48, contends that while on the one hand Odysseus, Zorba, and Captain Michales reject religious comfort and do not really belong to the Christian community "on the other hand, Kazantzakis does not refuse to acknowledge the power and values of Christ's message. *The Last Temptation of Christ, The Greek Passion, Saint Francis,* and *The Fratricides* are Kazantzakis' testimony in behalf of a positive theology: 'only this final One still lives and reigns as God.' To ignore this side of Kazantzakis is very misleading, because one is then tempted to align him with the French existentialists, Sartre and Camus. One can say that *The Fratricides,* published posthumously, was written so that Kazantzakis could assure for himself a mansion in heaven and that it is his repentance and confession, his repudiation and nullification of his great 'Silence' and *Sequel* written at the prime of his life. This, of course, is stretching the point. One must consider all of Kazantzakis' works and not only part of it in understanding Odysseus and the other characters."

5. H. Kazantzakis, *Nikos Kazantzakis,* pp. 561–62.

6. Blenkinsopp, *Commonweal,* XCIII (February 26, 1971), p. 518, has recognized that "in Kazantzakis' thinking there are unresolved antinomies, ambiguities, unreconciled polarities of expression." This has led to many philosophical contradictions and differing interpretations of his major views—including nihilism.

One school, to which the following belong, contends Kazantzakis was a nihilist:

Prevelakis, *Nikos Kazantzakis and his Odyssey,* p. 134, finds Kazantzakis in the mid-1920's turning toward total nihilism."

Owen A. Aldridge, "The Modern Spirit: Kazantzakis and Some of his Contemporaries," *Journal of Modern Literature*, II (November 1971), p. 305, specifies a "most important philosophic theme underlying Kazantzakis' major works—the concept of heroic nihilism."

Will Durant, *Interpretations of Life*, p. 289, believes *The Odyssey* to be possibly the outstanding poem of the century "despite the nihilism of its philosophy."

Another school holds that Kazantzakis was not a nihilist:

Hadgopoulos, "Odysseus' Choice: A Comparison and Contrast of Works by Albert Camus and Nikos Kazantzakis" (unpublished Ph.D. dissertation), p. 150; "both Camus and Kazantzakis attempted to chart a way out of nihilism, the contemporary anguish and misery which has led to a sense of human indifference and spiritual apathy."

Stanford, *The Ulysses Theme*, p. 233, discusses how Odysseus and the beautiful courtesan, Margaro, realize the insubstantiality of the world. The young prince, who has learned this from them, "decides to cast away all his earthly possessions. He has chose the via negativa. But Margaro and Odysseus choose the way of acceptance; they will endeavor to fill the vacuum of life with joy. In this episode the Odysseus of Kazantzakis rejects the ultimate nihilism of Pascoli's Ulysses, just as he has earlier rejected the hollow heroics of d'Annunzio's Navigator Hero."

Friar, "Preface," to Prevelakis', *Nikos Kazantzakis and his Odyssey*, p. 10, expresses his only objection to Prevelakis' interpretation of Kazantzakis is that he, Friar, unlike Prevelakis, does not believe Kazantzakis to be a nihilist; "what impressed me most, what I found exhilarating and tonic, was the heroic affirmation of life which he shouted into the maw of the obliterating void. What I recall most is the great Yes, and not the great No. . . . I am certain that what a reader ultimately derives from *The Odyssey*, as from *The Saviors of God*, is not nihilistic despair but the exaltation of life and man's fate."

7. Frederick J. Hoffman, "The Friends of God: Dostoevsky and Kazantzakis," in his *The Imagination's New Beginning* (South Bend, Ind.: University of Notre Dame Press, 1967), p. 49. Bonhoeffer is another who made the compelling demand that we must save God. In the second verse of "Christian and Unbeliever," *Letters and Papers from Prison*, ed. Eberhard Bethge (New York: The MacMillan Co., 1963), p. 25:

Men go to God when he is sore bested;
find him poor and scorned, without shelter or
    bread,

whelmed under weight of the wicked, the weak,
    the dead:
Christians stand by God in his hour of grieving.
We will explore in a later section the manner in which Bonhoeffer's
concept, written above a few months prior to his execution, parallels
Kazantzakis' in fulfilling the logic of Hoffman's analysis.

8. Kazantzakis, letter to Borje Knos, 1952, in H. Kazantzakis, *Nikos Kazantzakis*, p. 507.

9. Bien, *Nikos Kazantzakis*, p. 18.

10. Wilson, *Minnesota Review*, VIII (1968), p. 166. Friar stresses his agreement with this interpretation. "When Kazantzakis says 'Man must save God' he is merely using a hyperbole. What he means is that man must *create* God. God is for K that driving energy, that force, that elan vital in nature that is constantly creating new species, animate and inanimate matter, experimenting, discarding, trying always to purify matter into spirit. Man, thus far, is God's highest spiritual reach. Therefore man must aid God in His struggle toward spirituality by conceiving concepts of truth, beauty, kindness, peace, etc.—concepts which do not exist in Nature itself, although the point is, of course, that man, who has conceived these concepts, is also a product of God or Nature. In this sense is man a Savior of God." Editorial Comment, Athens, March, 1977.

11. Friar, "Preface," to Kazantzakis', *The Saviors of God*, p. 20. Ignazio Silone was one of those contemporaries of Kazantzakis, sensitive and compassionate, attracted to Marxism. Pietro Spina, the central character of Silone's masterpiece, *Bread And Wine*, trans. Harvey Fergusson II, with Afterword by Marc Slonim (rev. ed.; New York: A Signet Classic, The New American Library, 1955), pp. 95–96, joins a socialist youth group in 1921, thereby leaving a church which "was identified with the corrupt, wicked and cruel society which it should have been fighting." Many years later he looks back in dismay. Had not the socialist "community also become a synagogue? . . . Hasn't the truth become for me the party's truth? and justice, party justice? Has not the organization ended up by extinguishing in me all moral values, which are held in contempt as petit bourgeois prejudices, and has not the organization itself become the supreme value? Have I then not fled the opportunism of a decadent church to fall into the Machiavellianism of a sect?"

12. Wilhoite, *Beyond Nihilism*, pp. 91–92. In Sartre's, *The Age of Reason* (New York: Bantam Books, n.d.), pp. 130–32, Brunet, the communist operative in Paris in the 1930s, tells Mathieu, i.e., Sartre: " 'Yes, you need to commit yourself. Don't you feel so yourself? . . . You have gone your

own way. . . . You are the son of a bourgeois, you couldn't come to us straight away, you had to free yourself first. And now it's done, you are free. But what's the use of that same freedom, if not to join us? You have spent thirty-five years cleaning yourself up, and the result is nil. You are an odd sort of creature, you know. . . . You live in a void, you have cut your bourgeois connections, you have no tie with the proletariat, you're adrift, you're an abstraction, a man who is not there. It can't be an amusing sort of life. . . . You renounced everything in order to be free. . . . Take one step further, renounce your own freedom: and everything shall be rendered unto you.' " Failing in this instance to make the commitment, Mathieu becomes an absurd, pathetic figure in contrast to Brunet, of whom Mathieu observes; " 'Now you are very real. . . . You are a man. . . . You have chosen to be a man! A man with powerful, rather knotted muscles, who deals in brief, stern truths, a man erect and self-enclosed, sure of himself, a man of this earth, impervious to the angelical allurements of art, psychology, and politics, a whole man, nothing but a man'. And Mathieu was there, confronting him, irresolute, half his life gone, and still half-raw, assailed by all the vertigoes of non-humanity; and he thought: 'I don't even look like a man . . . if I choose, I must choose your side, for there is no other choice.' "

13. Bien, *Nikos Kazantzakis*, p. 42.

14. What we offer in this and the next section is an "interpretation" of the development of Kazantzakis' political philosophy. Kazantzakis at no time indicated *specific* intent to seek criteria in Hellenism and Christianity to supplement his socialist beliefs. It is obvious, however, that this is in fact what transpired. While non-Greek commentators have duly explored Kazantzakis' Christian themes they have, for the most part, ignored his borrowings from his Greek heritage. Kazantzakis was not a classicist in the sense of ignoring post-Hellenist contributions to Greek culture, yet neither did he reject the ancient lessons. As always, he sought to draw from all available sources. Stanford, *The Ulysses Theme*, p. 237, concurs: "He sees his hero (Odysseus) as the product of over three thousand years of Greek history. In those three millennia many different racial strains have enriched the Greek stock. Some Greeks of the present day would like to prune away all post-classical accretions and recover the pure antique tradition as they imagine it. This policy Kazantzakis rejects. Far better, he thinks, to create a synthesis of all those varied racial elements and to find a way of expressing their variegated richness. His *Odyssey* embodies his conception of this synthesis, and is an expression of this 'hyperhellenic' tradition." Within this tradition Kazantzakis begins where many non-Greek literatists stop, as Friar, "Introduction" to

Kazantzakis' *The Saviors of God*, p. 26, describes: "Like all modern poets who have attempted epical works, whether as concentrated as T. S. Eliot's *The Waste Land* or Hart Crane's *The Bridge*, or as all-inclusive as Ezra Pound's *Cantos* or James Joyce's *Ulysses* or *Finnegans Wake*, Kazantzakis was forced to create his own ideology, since his age gave him none which he could accept as myth, religion, or symbol. He was fortunate to live in the one country in the world where ancient myths are still part of the blood and bone of its people."

15. Bien, *Nikos Kazantzakis*, pp. 34–35. Kazantzakis' rootedness is demonstrated even further through his happy residence, once he was exiled from Greece, in an ancient Greek city, Antibes, on the French Riviera. Mrs. Kazantzakis, in her letter of November 19, 1976, says "the sea, the mountains, the flora, everything reminded us of Greece."

16. Prevelakis, *Nikos Kazantzakis and his Odyssey*, pp. 16, 56.

17. Stanford, *The Ulysses Theme*, p. 235.

18. In *Spain*, p. 46, Kazantzakis beautifully describes Dionysos: "Dionysos had set out from the Indies, so they say, dressed in brightly colored silks, laden with bracelets and rings, his eyes smeared with rouge and his nails dyed cinnabar red. He went on and on in the direction of Greece, and as he approached her clear, graceful shores, he cast off his clothes one by one, threw his bangles into the sea, and stopped dyeing and smearing himself. When at last he reached the Gulf of Eleusis and set foot on the sacred shore, he was stark naked." Needless to say, Kazantzakis owed a great debt to Nietzsche for the fertile Dionysian-Apollonian dialectic.

19. Doulis, *Northwest Review*, VI (Winter 1963), pp. 25–26. Hadgopoulous, "Odysseus' Choice; A Comparison and Contrast of Works by Albert Camus and Nikos Kazantzakis" (unpublished Ph.D. dissertation), pp. 30–31, testifies to her agreement with this interpretation: "His [Kazantzakis'] Dionysos figure is a good key by which to explore this problem of East-West synthesis. Kazantzakis wrote: 'Buddha, Christ, and Dionysos are one—the eternal suffering man'; another time he wrote that Dionysos left Greece and settled in the Orient where he is 'now wearing a kimono and holds cherry blossoms in his hands.' Kazantzakis comments that the white race would have great power if it had a great faith, but 'we either smile idly and eruditely or spin fiercely in a hell of individuality, uprooted, without coherence, without hope.' For Kazantzakis, Western man pits himself against the world around him and imposes his ego upon it, while Oriental man plunges into the world around him and imposes his rhythm with it." Friar, "Introduction" to Kazantzakis' *The Odyssey*, p. xv, says: [Kazantzakis believed] "that

Dionysos as well as Apollo was a god of the Greeks and that the noblest of Greek arts was a synthesis of the two ideals."

20. Rollo May, *Love And Will* (New York: W. W. Norton & Company, Inc., 1969), pp. 187, 28. It is no accident that the most talked about American play of the time, Peter Shaffer's "Equus," is a provocative theatrical exposition of this very theme. With the culture blocking from expression all thought and behavioral aberrations that might be labeled madness, passion, or magic, a young man whose life is dominated by a secret horse worship, the "Equus," inexplicably blinds six horses with a metal spike. (The play loosely follows an actual incident.) His psychiatrist, Dr. Dysert, experiences, through his analysis of the young man, the concrete relationship between psychic repression, apathy, and violence. He comes to realize the great degree to which mythology, gods, magic, and color are banned from his life and others in the name of normality.

21. Ibid., pp. 123, 138, 122, 131.

22. Kazantzakis, quoted in Friar, "Introduction" to Kazantzakis' *The Odyssey*, p. xix.

23. May, *Love And Will*, pp. 142–43.

24. The order is instructive. Enhanced perception is a prerequisite to loving and living the totality. There is a rapidly growing literature critiquing our structured, biased perception. Two efforts are particularly praiseworthy. Robert M. Pirsig, *Zen and the Art of Motorcycle Maintenance* (New York: Bantam Books, 1974), p. 75, believes "we take a handful of sand from the endless landscape of awareness around us and call that handful of sand the world." Life is diminished and sterilized to exactly the degree that this selection is based on purely intellectual, rational grounds to the total exclusion of affective concerns. "Classic and romantic understanding should be united at a basic level. In the past our common universe of reason has been in the process of escaping, rejecting the romantic, irrational world of prehistoric man. It's been necessary since before the time of Socrates to reject the passions, the emotions, in order to free the rational mind for an understanding of nature's order which was as yet unknown. Now it's time to further an understanding of nature's order by reassimilating those passions which were originally fled from. The passions, the emotions, the affective domain of man's consciousness, are a part of nature's order too. The central part." (p. 287) This "noncoalescence between reason and feeling" (p. 162) creates psychic disturbances which are projected into the world: "What's wrong with technology is that it's not connected in any real way with matters of the spirit and of the heart. And so it does blind, ugly things quite by accident and gets hated for that." The solution, as Kazantzakis knew, "isn't that

you abandon rationality but that you expand the nature of rationality so that it's capable of coming up with a solution." (p. 163) The political implications of the several therapies being used to expand our aware- ness, perception, and view of rationality are analyzed in a most lucid fashion by Walt Anderson, *Politics and the New Humanism* (Pacific Palisades, Calif.: Goodyear Publishing Company, Inc., 1973). His basic premise (p. 55) is that "If we can understand unawareness, we can understand political repression."

25. In the Nietzsche section of *Report,* Kazantzakis elaborates on this theme, pp. 319–20. "Although I did not have this consciously in mind at all, the two figures, Christ and AntiChrist, gradually merged. Was it true, then, that these two were not eternal enemies, that Lucifer was not God's adversary? Would evil eventually be able to enter the service of good and collaborate with it? In the course of time, as I studied the work of this prophet opposed to God, I mounted step by step to a foolhardy, mystical unity. The first step of initiation, I said, was this: good and evil are enemies. The second and higher step was: good and evil are fellow workers. The highest step, the highest I was able to reach at present, was: good and evil are identical! On this step I halted, shuddering from a terrible suspicion that flashed across my mind; perhaps this Saint Blas- phemer was prodding me to join him in his blasphemy!" Hesse, who was likewise influenced profoundly by Nietzsche, arrived at much the same conclusion. In *Demian* the young Emil Sinclair explains (p. 96), as he gropes to find his path, " 'uniting of godly and devilish elements' re- sounded within me. Here was something for my thoughts to cling to. This idea was familiar to me from conversations with Demian. During the last period of our friendship he had said that we had been given a god to worship who represented only one arbitrarily separated half of the world (it was the official, sanctioned, luminous world) but that we ought to be able to worship the whole world; this meant that we would either have to have a god who was also a devil or institute a cult of the devil alongside the cult of god."

26. Kazantzakis, letter to Prevelakis, 1950, in H. Kazantzakis, *Nikos Kazantzakis,* p. 549.

27. Blenkinsopp, *Commonweal,* XCIII (February 26, 1971), pp. 516– 17.

28. Hoffman, *The Imagination's New Beginning,* pp. 63–64. In *Report,* p. 250, Kazantzakis expresses this belief: "What does *There Is No God* mean? It means there is no bridle on our instincts, no reward for good or punishment for evil, no virtue, shame, or justice—that we are wolves and she-wolves in heat."

29. Father Yanaros, *The Fratricides,* pp. 249–50, angrily cries out to the Almighty: "This is when we need strength; get up, help me save them! You forget that You're not only the crucified Christ, but the resurrected Christ as well! The world has no need of crucified Christs any longer, it needs fighting Christs! Take a lesson from me. Enough of tears and passions."

30. The schoolteacher in *The Fratricides,* p. 90, appeals from the horror of the times not for humility but, "Oh, proud virtues of man—purity, obstinacy, courage—help us!"

31. Kazantzakis, letter to Borje Knos, 1951, in H. Kazantzakis, *Nikos Kazantzakis,* p. 505.

32. John A. Ryan, "Religion as the Basis of the Postulates of Freedom," in *Freedom,* ed. Ruth Nanda Anshen (New York: Harcourt, Brace and Company, 1940), p. 478.

33. Rev. 22: 17.

34. Chilson, *Thought,* XLVII (Spring 1972), p. 73. Bien, *Nikos Kazantzakis,* p. 19, echoes Chilson's opinion: "The ways of saving god are many, he said. In various ages men as diverse as Jesus, Genghiz Khan, Shakespeare, Lenin, El Greco, Zorba, Buddha, Psycharis (the 'Saint George' who killed the dragon of puristic Greek), Don Quixote, Nietzsche, and Dante, have been saviors of god, each in his own manner. But not all paths are applicable in any given era."

35. In 1940, a year which may well have epitomized the transitional age for Kazantzakis, with the Hitler terrors and with totalitarian communism rearing its ugly head, Tillich—a giant of twentieth-century theology—issued an immensely intriguing tract, "Freedom in the Period of Transformation," in *Freedom,* ed. Anshen, which at least implicitly relates to our discussion. It does so through its emphasis on the fervid necessity of an adequately protected vital sphere of choice in times of crisis. Tillich put forth a brilliant analysis and a rousing defense of freedom that, both logically and theologically, resembles Kazantzakis' concept of saving God through free creative choice. In his analysis (p. 131) Tillich gives the prerequisite of freedom: "freedom exists only if there is a realm of free creativity, a realm within which everyone is able to determine history and to transform human nature through history." The presence of this creative freedom is the core of man's liberty; and by its presence or absence, it is the determinant of whether or not man has freedom. Tillich cites the conditions of creative freedom as being freedom for meaningful creativity, freedom for autonomous creativity, and freedom for self-fulfilling creativity. It may be stretching a point and reading too much into these conditions—for Tillich emphasizes not only

freedom but *being grasped*—but seemingly he has listed as the primary conditions of man's freedom something very akin to Kazantzakis' postulate of free choice. The conditions of freedom—to choose, to will to do what one wished to do, and (p. 133) "to decide about the meaning and purpose of one's creative actions"—are the same criteria as for saving God. A quite clear example of the place which choice occupies in relation to the cause of liberating moral betterment in the world for Tillich and Kazantzakis.

36. Kazantzakis, quoted in Friar, "Introduction" to Kazantzakis' *The Odyssey*, p. xxiii. Kazantzakis evidently first formulated his theory of saving God during a forty-day pilgrimage with Sikelianos in 1914 on Mt. Athos. No women are allowed on the sacred mountain, which is dotted with monasteries. With Aegina, Antibes, Mt. Sinai, Crete, and Knossos, this holy place became one of the world-traveler's favorite places. He always wanted to spend a two-year retreat on Mt. Athos but had to be satisfied with the one visit. In his Paris study in 1939 he kept, among pictures of Saint Francis, Dante, and a copy of a madonna from Mt. Sinai, a copy of a madonna from beloved Mt. Athos. Extracts from Nikos' journal of his first pilgrimage are in H. Kazantzakis, *Nikos Kazantzakis*, pp. 53–57. Kazantzakis also discusses the trip in *Report*, in the section "My Friend The Poet. Mount Athos."

37. Cor. 15: 17, 18.

38. St. Augustine, *The City of God*, p. 205, *Basic Writings of St. Augustine*, Vol. II, ed. with Introduction and Notes by Whitney J. Oates (New York: Random House, 1948), p. 205.

39. Bonhoeffer, *Letters and Papers from Prison*, pp. 178–79, 196–97, and 219–20. Harvey Cox, a prominent contemporary theologian, expounded in *The Secular City* (New York: The MacMillan Co., 1965) similarly on the inherent worth of man and places him almost on a level with God. Like Kazantzakis and Bonhoeffer, Cox views the tragedy of modern Christianity as being the relegation of man to a position inferior to the one to which he is entitled. Cox thinks this is due to a threefold development: (1) following the conversion of Constantine, Christianity was sometimes used to justify oppressive rule; (2) the emergence of pride as the cardinal sin with a resulting emphasis on subordination; (3) the willingness of the classical philosophers to allow the God of the Bible to be blurred into Plato's Idea of the Good or Aristotle's Prime Mover, which, in Cox's view, relegated the creativity and ability of man to a subordinate position. Cox finds an exalted view of man in the Bible, and he feels that in the above processes something essential to Christianity has been lost. He is of the opinion that man works as God's partner in a meaninful

ordering of the world and criticizes biblical scholars (p. 76) who, "claimed by the spell of the Greeks, have overlooked or minimized the astonishing fact that creation is not completed by God in the Bible until after man is formed and begins to work as God's partner in ordering the chaos." The oneness of Cox's view with Kazantzakis' is not merely coincidental. Blenkinsopp, *Commonweal,* XCIII (February 26, 1971), p. 514, tells us that, in the mid-1960s when the theologians discovered Kazantzakis, "quotes, mostly from *Zorba,* appeared with increasing frequency in the works of such trailblazers as John Robinson, Harvey Cox, and Sam Keen."

40. Kazantzakis, letter to E. Samios, 1925, in H. Kazantzakis, *Nikos Kazantzakis,* p. 133.

41. Kazantzakis, conversation with H. Kazantzakis, *ibid.,* p. 520.

42. Rom: 13: 9.

43. See St. Augustine, *The City of God.* This theme permeates the work in it entirety.

44. In addition to *The Secular City,* see Cox's *God's Revolution and Man's Responsibility* (Valley Forge: The Hudson Press, 1965).

45. Decavelles, *Poetry,* XCV (December 1959), p. 177.

46. Augustine, *The City of God,* p. 693.

47. Camus, quoted in T. L. Thorson, "Albert Camus and the Rights of Man," *Ethics,* LXXIV (July 1964), p. 288.

48. George W. Polley, "Reply," *Commonweal,* XCIV (April 23, 1971), p. 175.

49. Blenkinsopp, *Commonweal,* XCIII (February 26, 1971), p. 516.

50. Hadgopoulous, "Odysseus' Choice: A Comparison and Contrast of Works by Albert Camus and Nikos Kazantzakis" (unpublished Ph.D. dissertation), p. 114.

Chapter 5

1. Stanford, *The Ulysses Theme,* p. 210.

2. Twenty years later in the mid-1940s, Kazantzakis again suffered an outbreak of facial skin disease which bothered him periodically until his death a decade later. This was diagnosed as either infant's disease or lymphoma and his illness in the 1920s was most probably the first occurrence of this disease rather than, as he believed, the soul's rejection of fleshly sin.

3. Chilson, *Thought,* XLVII (Spring 1972), pp. 82–83, notes that "women play a major role in the novel. They are a source of temptation, almost symbols of the great temptation, the symbol of bodily embrace

and wifely companionship in God's law, against the harsh way of God alone and the symbol of the Cross. The final temptation of Jesus is to forsake his life of struggle for the life of domesticity. This is the greatest and most enticing threat to the great Cry of the Invisible. . . . God's salvation does not advance through home-making but through setting out from the home, leaving it behind, and facing the unknown and the uncertain."

4. Wilson, *Minnesota Review*, VIII (1968), p. 166.

5. Doulis, *Northwest Review*, VI (Winter 1963), p. 37.

6. Bien, *The Politics of Twentieth Century Novelists,* ed. Panichas, p. 141. Although Bien attributes the rejection by the resistance to fears Kazantzakis was a "German" agent, Mrs. Kazantzakis states emphatically that "the Greek Resistance (in the mountains) rejected Nikos as a suspected agent of the 'English' Intelligence Service." Letter, Geneva, November 29, 1976.

7. Bien, *Antioch Review*, XXV (Spring 1965), p. 154.

8. Albert Camus, *The Fall*, trans. Justin O'Brien (New York: Alfred A. Knopf, 1969), pp. 132–33. Ortega, *The Revolt of the Masses,* believes that through its portrayal of freedom as "a gift box of dainties" liberal democracy has given rise to mass man. This has occurred precisely through the success of its "programme," that being the investiture of men with rights of birth—regardless of social, economic, or political status. In Ortega's elitist view whereas in the nineteenth century men were—though adherent to the natural rights idea—still willing to allow the proper qualitative minority to govern all public matters, in the twentieth century, mass man has come to the fore and not only demanded these rights in name but also in actuality—hence the "accession of the masses to complete social power." (p. 11) The key to the degenerative aspect of this lies in that these "natural rights" were not fought for, not earned, and therefore, are not qualitatively upheld—appreciated. The holders of these rights are not able enough to defend them and therefore do not appreciate the civilization—both historic and modern—which gave rise to their rights.

9. Camus, *The Fall*, p. 135.

10. Bien, *Antioch Review*, XXV (Spring 1965), p. 155.

11. George Scouffas, "Kazantzakis: Odysseus and the 'Cage of Freedom,' " *Accent*, XIX (1959), p. 235.

12. Wilson, *Minnesota Review*, VIII (1968), p. 175. Decavelles, *Poetry,* XCV (December 1959), p. 176, concurs: "This modern epic of 33,333 lines, first published in the original Greek in 1938 in Athens, is undoubtedly the greatest long poem of our time, a colossal achievement in art and substance. It is the mature product of Kazantzakis' deep familiarity with

the best in world literature and thought, of intense living, traveling, and thinking. The creator, himself another Odysseus, came to know 'the cities and minds of many people,' and made them his own in a passionate record of wide experience which he has given meaning and value. Its hero, Odysseus, is Homeric only so long as he does not conflict with Kazantzakis' own self. It is not without significance that the old Adventurer was re-created once more in his own native land, and in his own tongue. Odysseus has never ceased to be the supreme and lasting embodiment of Greece, its spirit of an unfailing faith in life and freedom, of enrichment and rebirth through ever-new experience. Yet the range in which Odysseus shapes and fulfills his destiny in this new poem is far wider than when he gave us his old, Homeric report. Three thousand years of further physical and spiritual exploration have passed since then."

13. Kazantzakis once wrote to Prevelakis (*Nikos Kazantzakis and His Odyssey*, p. 63): "My Odyssey continues the enormous epic of the white race—the epic of Homer. It closes a circle left open for so many centuries. And it closes it when the state of the world is astonishingly like it was in the twelfth century B.C., shortly before the descent of the Dorians and the creation—after a middle age—of a new civilization."

14. Kazantzakis, cited by Friar, "Introduction" to Kazantzakis' *The Odyssey*, p. xi. Compare Kazantzakis' sentiment above, which was essentially his goal in life, with Thoreau's purpose in life, as stated in *Walden* (*The Portable Thoreau*, p. 343): "I went to the woods because I wished to live deliberately to confront only the essential facts of life, and see if I could learn what it had to teach, and not when I came to die, discover that I had not lived. I did not wish to live what was not life, living is so dear; nor did I wish to practise resignation, unless it was quite necessary. I wanted to live deep and suck out the marrow of life, to live so sturdily and Spartan-like as to put to rout all that was not life, to cut a broad swath and shave close, to drive life into a corner, and reduce it to its lowest terms." Although Thoreau's and Kazantzakis' lives and prose differed substantially, the oneness of the goal in life of the parochial New Englander immersed in the study of nature and who ventured very little from his beloved Concord woods, and the cosmopolitan world-traveler whose flights of brilliance took him far beyond the reality of the world of things is, at the very least, startlingly similar.

15. C. N. Stavrou, "Some Notes on Nikos Kazantzakis," *Colorado Quarterly*, XIII (Winter 1964), pp. 324–25.

16. Bien, *Antioch Review*, XXV (Spring 1965), p. 155.

17. Stavrou, *Southwest Review*, LVII (Winter 1972), pp. 58–59, elabo-

rates in some detail on the parallels between *The Odyssey* and Nietzsche's *Thus Spake Zarathustra:* "In the two works we discern many similar ideas: scorn for herd morality together with a compassionate concern for man's destiny; worship of creativity and of man as sole creator; redefinition of nihilism as that which militates against life; celebration of conflict as a spur to higher and higher forms of life.

"Nietzsche and Kazantzakis preferred vehement paroxysms of Promethean defiance to passive babblings of hopeless apathy. They adjured man to retrieve from programmed electronics a portion of his instinctual spontaneity. They besought man to find life's good and meaning. . . . They demand that man master his panic impulse for oblivion sought through an escape out of life or a frenetic submersion in life. . . .

"Nietzsche and Kazantzakis envisioned as their ideal a society which would be the very opposite of that in which anonymity is the most prized virtue, numerical strength the decisive factor, and majority opinion the ' divine oracle. . . . Both endeavor to aid man who, more often than not, refuses to cooperate. Both are attracted to a hermit existence amid mountains and forests, although both disclaim the label of ascetic. Both are given to dreams, visions, and prognostication. Both see death as the last act in the interlude called life and conceive of it in terms of a sea voyage. Both soliloquize interminably, discourse garrulously, and harangue formidably. Both implore men to attain to self-mastery, even to the conquest of hope and pity. Both castigate those who, through benighted mores, self-distrust, constitutional impotency, or reliance on superterrestrial Edens, are afraid of life and hence condemn it."

18. Wilson, *Minnesota Review,* VIII (1968), p. 177.

19. Ibid., p. 161.

20. Stanford, *The Ulysses Theme,* p. 236.

21. Prevelakis, *Nikos Kazantzakis and his Odyssey,* footnote 110, p. 179.

22. Scouffas, *Accent,* XIX (1959), p. 246. Prevelakis also points out this insistence on freedom. Whereas before the city was destroyed Odysseus had achieved freedom from public opinion, social confinement, and necessity, after Book XVI (*Nikos Kazantzakis and his Odyssey,* p. 106) "Odysseus rebels against God, as if God had broken his promise. The world suddenly seems absurd to him: 'No master-god exists, nor virtue, no just laws, no punishment in Hades, no reward in Heaven' (XVI, pp. 1241–42). Odysseus calls this *void* 'complete freedom.'

"The world is deserted, absurd, unreal. This is the moment for the free Odysseus to fashion a world of his own and to 'play'—to fashion and dissolve it: to play the part of God."

Stanford, *The Ulysses Theme,* p. 236, also notes this obsessive demand for freedom: after the city is destroyed Odysseus' "Chief task is to discipline himself in the way of true liberty. But, significantly, from beginning to end he is the Lonely One.

"The Lonely One: here is the nemesis of absolute freedom. Kazantzakis does not flinch from its terrors (although he lessens them a little for his hero at the last by introducing the negro boy, i.e., Jesus, in the death scene). Absolute freedom means absolute separation from one's fellow-men; and each degree of freedom must be achieved by giving up some element in social life. . . . Kazantzakis sends his hero, when he has freed himself in turn from the Ego, the Race, and the World, to a much more desolate place—to the wastes of polar ice. . . . The Odysseus of Kazantzakis has pursued personal liberty to the zero-point of the earth."

23. Stanford, *The Ulysses Theme,* p. 246.

24. Joseph Flay, "The Erotic Stoicism of Nikos Kazantzakis," *Journal of Modern Literature,* II (November 1971), pp. 294–95.

25. Friar, "Introduction" to Kazantzakis' *The Saviors of God,* pp. 20–21.

26. Kazantzakis, cited by Friar, "Introduction" to Kazantzakis' *The Odyssey,* p. xxi.

27. "Man must," says Stavrou in *Southwest Review,* LVII (Winter 1972), p. 58, "assume the entire onus of responsibility and freedom; he must heft his Sisyphean rock and trudge up the hill, braced by the knowledge that human struggle can only end in provisional victories which will ceaselessly be called into question. Having posited life's patent absurdity and fortuity, man must then embrace them as the destiny he neither can nor wish to propitiate."

28. Flay, *Journal of Modern Literature,* II (November 1971), p. 301.

29. On this point see above, pp. 70, 146, 156–63.

30. Sheldon S. Wolin, *Politics and Vision: Continuity and Innovation in Western Political Thought* (Boston: Little, Brown & Co., 1960), p. 17.

31. George Lichtheim, *The Concept of Ideology and Other Essays* (New York: Random House, Inc., 1967), p. 57.

32. Wolin, *Politics and Vision,* p. 434.

33. Bertrand Russell, cited by Lionel Rubinoff, *The Pornography of Power* (New York: Ballantine Books, 1967), p. 95.

34. James Baldwin, *The Fire Next Time* (New York: Dial Press, 1963), p. 24.

35. Camus, quoted in Thorson, *Ethics,* LXXIV (July 1964), p. 288.

36. Walker Percy, *The Moviegoer* (New York: Alfred A. Knopf, 1961), p. 193.

37. Friedrich Hölderlin, *Hyperion,* trans. Willard R. Trask with

Foreword by Alexander Gode-von Aesch (New York: The New American Library, A Signet Classic 1959), p. 36.

38. Percy, *The Moviegoer*, p. 228.

39. Kazantzakis' appeal to the young, for whom in a large measure he wrote, is recognized by a number of observers:

Blenkinsopp, *Commonweal*, XCIII (February 26, 1971), p. 514: "It no longer occasions surprise on American campuses to hear students, especially theological students, speak of prayer as reporting (to whom is not always clear), or of being saved from salvation or going beyond hope and fear. The Ecumenical Institute of Chicago has even modeled its curriculum on insights traceable to *The Saviors of God, Report To Greco,* and yes, *Zorba.* With the dionysian theologians now in the saddle and riding hard, it is safe to predict that his influence will continue to be felt. And this might appear to call for an explanation since Kazantzakis, who never visited the United States, speaks out of an experience and in an idiom quite foreign even to a generation of Americans nourished on Marcuse, Brown, Watts, and the rest."

Wilson, *Minnesota Review,* VIII (1968), p. 179: "I have spent a great deal of time lecturing at American universities in recent years, and I have discovered that Kazantzakis is a cult with a certain type of highly intelligent student. Almost without exception, someone asks me: 'Do you know the work of Kazantzakis?' There is good reason for this, and it is the direct outcome of Kazantzakis' peculiar greatness."

Chilson, *Thought,* XLVII (Spring 1972), p. 69: "In the last few years, Nikos Kazantzakis has remained one of the most popular authors, particularly among young college students."

40. Hughes, *Consciousness and Society*, pp. 364–65.

41. A. Den Doolard, "Preface" to Kazantzakis' *Freedom or Death*, p. v.

Bibliography
Published works of Nikos Kazantzakis

Books

Kazantzakis, Nikos. *The Greek Passion*. Translated by Jonathan Griffin. New York: Simon & Schuster, Inc., 1953.

————. *Zorba the Greek*. Translated by Carl Wildman with Introduction by Ian Scott-Kilvert. London: The Modern European Library, John Lehmann, 1953.

————. *Freedom or Death*. Translated by Jonathan Griffin with Preface by A. Den Doolard. New York: Simon & Schuster, Inc., 1955.

————. *The Odyssey: A Modern Sequel*. Translated with Introduction, Synopsis, and Notes by Kimon Friar. New York: Simon & Schuster, Inc., 1958.

————. *The Last Temptation of Christ*. Translated with a Note on the Author and his Use of Language by P. A. Bien. New York: Simon & Schuster, Inc., 1960.

————. *The Saviors of God: Spiritual Exercises*. Translated with Introduction by Kimon Friar. New York: Simon & Schuster, Inc., 1960.

————. *Saint Francis*. Translated by P. A. Bien. New York: Simon & Schuster, Inc., 1962.

————. *Japan-China*. Translated by George C. Pappageotes with Epilogue by Helen Kazantzakis. New York: Simon & Schuster, Inc., 1963.

————. *Spain*. Translated by Amy Mims. New York: Simon & Schuster, Inc., 1963.

————. *The Fratricides*. Translated by Athena Gianakas Dallas. New York: Simon & Schuster, Inc., 1964.

————. *Toda Raba*. Translated by Amy Mims with Afterword by Helen Kazantzakis. New York: Simon & Schuster, Inc., 1965.

————. *England*. New York: Simon & Schuster, Inc., 1965.

————. *Report To Greco*. Translated by P. A. Bien with Introduction by Helen Kazantzakis. New York: Simon & Schuster, Inc., 1965.

————. *Journeying Travels in Italy, Egypt, Sinai, Jerusalem and Cyprus*. Translated by Themi and Theodora Vasils. New York: Little, Brown & Co., 1975.

Articles

————. "The Immortal Free Spirit of Man," *Life and Letters*, L (September 1946), 123–26.

Secondary Sources
Books

Anderson, Walt. *Politics and the New Humanism*. Pacific Palisades, Calif.: Goodyear Publishing Company, Inc., 1973.

Aron, Raymond. *Main Currents In Sociological Thought*. Translated by Richard Howard and Helen Weaver. Vol. I. *Karl Marx*. New York: Basic Books, Inc., 1965.

Baldwin, James. *The Fire Next Time*. New York: W. W. Norton & Company, Inc., 1952.

Barrett, William. *Irrational Man: A Study In Existential Philosophy*. Garden City, N.Y.: Doubleday & Co., Inc., 1958.

Bien, Peter. *Nikos Kazantzakis*. New York: Columbia University Press, 1972.

Bonhoeffer, Dietrich. *The Cost of Discipleship*. Translated by R. H. Fuller with Foreword by G.K.A. Bell and A Memoir by G. Leibholz. New York: The MacMillan Co., 1949 (revised).

————. *Letters and Papers from Prison*. Translated by R. H. Fuller. Edited by Eberhard Bethge. New York: The MacMillan Co., 1953.

Brumbaugh, Robert S. and Stallknecht, Newton P. *The Spirit of Western Philosophy*. New York: David McKay Co., Inc., 1964.

Camus, Albert. *The Rebel*. Translated by Anthony Bower. New York: Alfred A. Knopf, 1957.

————. *The Fall*. Translated by Justin O'Brien. New York: Alfred A. Knopf, 1969.

Cox, Harvey. *God's Revolution and Man's Responsibility*. Valley Forge, Pennsylvania: The Judson Press, 1965.

————. *The Secular City*. New York: The MacMillan Co., 1965.

Dewey, John. *Liberalism and Social Action*. New York: G. P. Putnam's Sons, 1935.

Dupre, Louis K. *The Philosophical Foundations of Marxism*. New York: Harcourt, Brace, & World, Inc., 1966.

Eliot, T. S. *Notes Toward the Definition of Culture*. London: Faber & Faber Ltd., 1948.

Good News for Modern Man: The New Testament in Today's English Version. New York: American Bible Society, 1966.

Hesse, Hermann. *Demian*. Translated by M. Roloff and M. Lebeck. New York: Harper & Row, Publishers, 1965.

Hölderlin, Friedrich. *Hyperion*. Translated by Willard R. Trask with Foreword by Alexander Gode-von Aesch. New York: A Signet Classic, The New American Library, 1959.

Hughes, Stuart. *Consciousness and Society: The Reorientation of European Social Thought, 1890–1930.* New York: Alfred A. Knopf, 1958.

Kazantzakis, Helen. *Nikos Kazantzakis: A Biography Based on His Letters.* Translated by Amy Mims. New York: Simon & Schuster, Inc., 1968.

———. *Nikos Kazantzakis.* Simon & Schuster, Inc., 1970.

Lichtheim, George. *The Concept of Ideology and Other Essays.* New York: Random House, 1967.

Mannheim, Karl. *Ideology and Utopia: An Introduction to the Sociology of Knowledge.* Translated by Louis Wirth and Edward Shils. New York: A Harvest Book, Harcourt, Brace, & World, Inc., 1936.

Marcuse, Herbert. *One-Dimensional Man: Studies in the Ideology of Advanced Industrial Society.* London: Routledge & Kegan Paul, Ltd., 1964.

Marx, Karl. *Economic and Philosophic Manuscripts of 1844.* Translated by Martin Milligan. Moscow: Foreign Language Publishing House, 1959.

May, Rollo. *Love and Will.* New York: W. W. Norton & Co., Inc., 1969.

Nietzsche, Friedrich. *The Portable Nietzsche.* Selected and Translated with Introduction and Notes by Walter Kaufmann. New York: The Viking Press, 1954.

———. *The Will To Power.* Translated with Commentary by Walter Kaufmann and R. J. Hollingdale. New York: Vintage Books, A Division of Random House, 1968.

Ortega y Gasset. *The Revolt of the Masses.* Translator anon. New York: W.W. Norton & Co., Inc., 1932.

Percy, Walker. *The Moviegoer.* New York: Alfred A. Knopf, 1961.

Pirsig, Robert M. *Zen and the Art of Motorcycle Maintenance.* New York: Bantam Books, 1974.

Plato. *The Republic.* Translated by B. Jowett. New York: Vintage Books, A Division of Random House, n.d.

Prevelakis, Pandelis. *Nikos Kazantzakis and his Odyssey.* Translated by Philip Sherrard with Preface by Kimon Friar. New York: Simon & Schuster, Inc., 1961.

Rubinoff, Lionel. *The Pornography of Power.* New York: Ballantine Books, Inc., 1967.

Sartre, Jean-Paul. *The Age of Reason.* New York: Bantam Books, n.d.

Silone, Ignazio. *Bread and Wine.* Translated by Harvey Fergusson II with Afterword by Marc Slonim. New York: A Signet Classic, The New American Library, 1955 (revised).

Spinoza, Benedict de. *Ethics.* Translated by William Hale White. Edited with Introduction by James Gutmann. New York: The Hafner Library of Classics No. XI, Hafner Publishing Co., 1949.

St. Augustine. *Basic Writings of St. Augustine.* Edited by Whitney J. Oates. Vol. II. *The City of God.* New York: Random House, 1948.

Stanford, William B. *The Ulysses Theme: A Study in the Adaptability of a Traditional Hero.* New York: Barnes & Noble, Inc., 1964.

Thoreau, Henry David. *The Portable Thoreau.* Edited by Carl Bode. New York: The Viking Press, 1965.

Tucker, Robert. *Philosophy and Myth in Karl Marx.* Cambridge: Cambridge University Press, 1961.

Wallbank, J. Walter, *et al. Civilization: Past and Present.* 6th ed. Glenview, Ill.: Scott, Foresman, & Co., 1969.

Wilhoite, Fred. *Beyond Nihilism: Albert Camus's Contribution to Political Thought.* Baton Rouge, La.: Louisiana State University Press, 1968.

Wilson, Colin. *The Strength to Dream.* Boston: Houghton Mifflin Co., 1962.

Wolin, Seldon S. *Politics and Vision: Continuity and Innovation in Western Political Thought.* Boston: Little, Brown & Co., 1960.

Articles

Aldridge, A. Owen. "The Modern Spirit: Kazantzakis and Some of His Contemporaries," *Journal of Modern Literature,* II (November 1971), 303–13.

Bien, Peter. "Kazantzakis' Nietzschianism," *Journal of Modern Literature,* II (November 1971), 245–66.

———. "*Zorba the Greek,* Nietzsche, and the Perennial Greek Predicament," *Antioch Review,* XXV (Spring 1965), 147–63.

———. "Nikos Kazantzakis," *The Politics of Twentieth-Century Novelists.* Edited by George A. Panichas. Hawthorn Books, Inc., 1971. 137–60.

Blenkinsopp, Joseph. "My Entire Soul Is A Cry," *Commonweal,* XCIII (February 26, 1971), 514–18. Reply by George A. Polley, XCIV (April 23, 1971), 155, 175.

Bloch, Adele. "The Dual Masks of Nikos Kazantzakis," *Journal of Modern Literature,* II (November 1971), 189–98.

Chilson, Richard W. "The Christ of Nikos Kazantzakis," *Thought: A Review of Culture and Ideas,* XLVII (Spring 1972), 69–89.

Cox, Louis O. "A Romantic Failure," *Poetry,* XCV (December 1959), 179–81.

de Caro, F.A. "Kazantzakis, Folklore, and the Politics of Reaction," *Journal of Popular Culture,* VIII (Spring 1975), 792–804.

Decavelles, Adonis. "The Torrent and the Sun," *Poetry*, XCV (December 1959), 175–178.

Doulis, Tom. "Kazantzakis and the Meaning of Suffering," *Northwest Review*, VI (Winter 1963), 33–57.

Durant, Will and Ariel. "Nikos Kazantzakis," *Interpretations of Life: A Survey of Contemporary Literature*. New York: Simon & Schuster, Inc., 1970. 269–98.

Eliot, Alexander. "The Widening Gyre," *Book Week*, II (August 8, 1965), 1.

Flay, Joseph C. "The Erotic Stoicism of Nikos Kazantzakis," *Journal of Modern Literature*, II (November 1971), 293–302.

Friar, K. "Nikos Kazantzakis in the United States," *Literary Review*, XVIII (Summer 1975), 381–97.

Friedman, Maurice. "The Modern Vitalist: Bergson and Kazantzakis," *To Deny Our Nothingness: Contemporary Images of Man*. New York: Delacorte Press, 1967. 63–79.

Gill, J.H. "Conflict and Resolution: Some Kazantzakian Themes," *Encounter*, XXXVI (Summer 1974), 204–21.

Hoffman, Frederick J. "The Friends of God: Dostoevsky and Kazantzakis," *The Imagination's New Beginning: Theology and Modern Literature*. South Bend, Ind.: University of Notre Dame Press, 1967. 49–72.

Kazantzakis, H. "Kazantzakis and Freedom," *Encounter*, XXXVI (Spring 1975), 123–32.

Kazin, A. "Thoreau and American Power," *Atlantic Monthly*, CCXXXLLL (May 1970), 61–9.

Kierkegaard, Soren A. "The Aesthetic, The Ethical, and The Religious," *Kierkegaard*. Presented by W.H. Auden. Edited with Introduction by Alfred O. Mendel. The Living Thoughts Library. New York: David McKay Co., Inc., 1952. 56–115.

Levitt, Morton P. "The Cretan Glance: The World and Art of Nikos Kazantzakis," *Journal of Modern Literature*, II (November 1971), 163–88.

Osborn, R.E. "Modern Man's Search for Salvation—Nikos Kazantzakis and his Odyssey," *Encounter*, XXXV (Spring 1974), 121–31.

Poulakidas, Andreas K. "Kazantzakis' *Zorba the Greek* and Nietzsche's *Thus Spake Zarathustra*," *Philological Quarterly*, XLIX (April 1970), 234–44.

————. "Kazantzakis and Bergson: Metaphysic Aestheticians," *Journal of Modern Literature*, II (November 1971), 267–83.

──────. "Kazantzakis' Spiritual Exercises and Buddhism," *Comparative Literature*, XXVII (Summer 1975), 208–17.

Ryan, John A. "Religion as the Basis of the Postulates of Freedom," *Freedom*. Edited by Ruth Nanda Anshen. New York: Harcourt, Brace, & World, Inc., 1940. 475–84.

Savvas, Minas. "Kazantzakis and Marxism," *Journal of Modern Literature*, II (November 1971), 284–92.

Scouffas, George. "Kazantzakis: Odysseus and the 'Cage of Freedom,' " *Accent*, XIX (1959), 234–46.

Stavrou, C.N. "Some Notes on Nikos Kazantzakis," *Colorado Quarterly*, XII (Winter 1964), 317–34.

──────. "The Limits of the Possible: Nikos Kazantzakis' Arduous Odyssey," *Southwest Review*, LVII (Winter 1972), 54–65.

Thorson, T.L. "Albert Camus and the Rights of Man," *Ethics*, LXXIV (July 1964), 287–96.

Tillich, Paul. "Freedom in the Period of Transformation," *Freedom*. Edited by Ruth Nanda Anshen. Harcourt, Brace, & World, Inc., 1940. 123–44.

Wilhoite, F. "Albert Camus's Politics of Rebellion," *Western Political Quarterly*, XIV (June 1961), 408–19.

Wilson, Colin. "The Greatness of Nikos Kazantzakis," *Minnesota Review*, VIII (1968), 159–80.

Unpublished Material

Eubanks, Cecil L. and Lea, James F. "Nikos Kazantzakis: The Politics of Salvation." Unpublished article.

Hadgopoulos, Saralyn P. "Odysseus' Choice: A Comparison and Contrast of Works by Albert Camus and Nikos Kazantzakis." Unpublished Ph.D. dissertation, Emory University, 1965.

King, Thomas L. "Kazantzakis' Prometheus Trilogy: The Ideas and their Dramatic Rendering." Unpublished Ph.D. dissertation, Indiana University, 1970.

Lea, James F. "The Politics of H.D. Thoreau." Unpublished Master's thesis, Louisiana State University, 1971.

Poulakidas, Andreas K. "The Novels of Kazantzakis and Their Existential Sources." Unpublished Ph.D. dissertation, Indiana University, 1967.

Acknowledgments

My debts are many; therefore, I acknowledge only the most important. To Dr. Cecil L. Eubanks, who directed the dissertation with which this study began, is owed more than can be repaid. Beginning with my initial graduate studies and continuing to the present he has combined the roles of teacher, scholar, and friend, to provide vital, compassionate intellectual stimulation. Further, he has been unsparing of time and energy in both substantive criticism of the ideas expressed within and editorial suggestions as to the manner of their presentation.

Thanks are due to Dr. James J. Bolner, who gave a most helpful reading of the text at its inception. I should also like to extend my appreciation to Professor Rene De Visme Williamson, whose courses in the history of political philosophy enhanced greatly whatever merit this exercise may have.

This book benefited greatly from the perceptive comments of three anonymous and kind individuals who consented to read the manuscript for The University of Alabama Press. Their stimulating critiques aided in the effort to transform a predictably awkward graduate school style into a more readable one. Also, it is indeed encouraging to find a major academic press, such as that of The University of Alabama, willing to take a chance on a virgin author, knowing full well the dubious nature of the project as a financial proposition. Editors like Sarah Teal Demellier and James Travis, who are committed to publishing provocative works and are sympathetic with the impatience and frustrations of authors, are truly owed a debt of thanks by writers such as myself.

Through a most interesting and felicitous series of occurrences, it has been my happy lot to have the two most prominent authorities on Kazantzakis read this book in manuscript form. I refer, of course, to Mrs. Kazantzakis and Kimon Friar. Both were overly kind in their many helpful comments. These enabled me to correct numerous factual errors and to refine various interpretations. If this were not enough good fortune, I am also realizing a fond dream in embarking, as this goes to press in late 1977, on a tour of Greece, Crete, and Cyprus, to lecture on Kazantzakis for the United States Information Agency. Kazantzakis would surely have appreciated the mysterious coordination of circumstances leading me inexorably to his homeland on the twentieth anniversary of his death.

I am grateful to Livingston State University and the United States Office of Education for financial support during the initial stages of this endeavor. The University of Southern Mississippi was very helpful in providing the typists, facilities, and materials necessary to compose the much revised final copy of the manuscript.

The greatest debt is owed to my wife, Cynthia, and my sons, Christopher and Joshua, who experienced far too many nights without my presence, over several years, as I labored on this manuscript.

As is customary and correct, I wish to absolve all those mentioned from blame for any flaws, errors, and misinterpretations, for these would be my own contributions.

Finally, for permission to quote from copyrighted materials I wish to thank the following: Simon & Schuster, Inc. for permission to quote from *The Odyssey: A Modern Sequel* by Nikos Kazantzakis, translated by Kimon Friar, copyright © 1958 by Simon & Schuster, Inc., reprinted by permission of Simon & Schuster, a Division of Gulf & Western Corporation; Simon & Schuster, Inc. for permission to quote from *The Last Temptation of Christ* by Nikos Kazantzakis, copyright © 1960 by Simon & Schuster, Inc., reprinted by permission of Simon & Schuster, a Division of Gulf & Western Corporation; Simon & Schuster, Inc. for permission to quote from *Fratricides* by Nikos Kazantzakis, copyright © 1964 by Simon & Schuster, Inc., reprinted by permission of Simon & Schuster, a Division of Gulf & Western Corporation; Simon & Schuster, Inc. for permission to quote from *Report to Greco* by Nikos Kazantzakis, copyright © 1965 by Simon & Schuster, Inc., reprinted by permission of Simon & Schuster, a Division of Gulf & Western Corporation; Simon & Schuster, Inc. for permission to quote from *Nikos Kazantzakis: A Biography Based on His Letters* by Helen N. Kazantzakis, copyright © 1968 by Simon & Schuster, Inc., reprinted by permission of Simon & Schuster, a Division of Gulf & Western Corporation; Simon & Schuster, Inc. for permission to quote from *Spain* by Nikos Kazantzakis, copyright © 1963 by Simon & Schuster, Inc., reprinted by permission of Simon & Schuster, a Division of Gulf & Western Corporation; Simon & Schuster, Inc. for permission to quote from *Nikos Kazantzakis and His Odyssey* by Pandelis Prevelakis, copyright © 1961 by Simon & Schuster, Inc., reprinted by permission of Simon & Schuster, a Division of Gulf & Western Corporation; Simon & Schuster, Inc. for permission to quote from *England* by Nikos Kazantzakis, copyright © 1965 by Simon & Schuster, Inc., reprinted by permission of Simon & Schuster, a Division of Gulf & Western Corporation; Simon & Schuster, Inc. for permission to quote from *The Greek Passion* by Nikos Kazantzakis, copyright © 1953 by Simon & Schuster, Inc., reprinted by permission of Simon & Schuster, a Division of Gulf & Western Corporation; Simon & Schuster, Inc. for permission to quote from *Japan-China* by Nikos Kazantzakis, copyright © 1963 by Simon & Schuster, Inc., reprinted by permission of Simon & Schuster, a Division of Gulf & Western Corporation; Simon & Schuster, Inc. for permission to quote from *Freedom or Death* by Nikos Kazantzakis, copyright © 1955 by Simon & Schuster, Inc., reprinted by permission of Simon & Schuster, a Division of Gulf & Western Corporation; Simon & Schuster, Inc. for permission to quote from *Saint Francis* by Nikos Kazantzakis, copyright © 1962 by Simon & Schuster, Inc., reprinted by permission of Simon & Schuster, a Division of Gulf & Western Corporation; Simon & Schuster, Inc. for permission to quote from *Saviors of God* by Nikos Kazantzakis, copyright © 1960 by Simon & Schuster, Inc., reprinted by permission of Simon & Schuster, a Division of Gulf & Western Corporation; Simon & Schuster, Inc. for permission to quote from *Toda Raba* by Nikos Kazantzakis, copyright © 1965 by Simon & Schuster, Inc., reprinted by permission of Simon & Schuster, a Division of Gulf & Western Corporation; Colin Wilson for permission to quote from his essay, "The Greatness of Nikos Kazantzakis," copyright © 1968 by Colin Wilson; and The Modern Poetry Association for permission to quote from Andonis Decavalles's "The Torrent and the Sun," which first appeared in *Poetry*, copyright © 1959 by The Modern Poetry Association, and which is reprinted by permission of the editor of *Poetry*.

Index